Computer Science Workbench

Editor: Tosiyasu L. Kunii

Computer Science Workbench

N. Magnenat Thalmann, D. Thalmann: Image Synthesis. Theory and Practice. XV, 400 pp., 223 figs., including 80 in color. 1987

B. A. Barsky: Computer Graphics and Geometric Modeling Using Beta-splines. IX, 156 pp., 85 figs., including 31 in color. 1987

H. Kitagawa, T. L. Kunii: The Unnormalized Relational Data Model. For Office Form Processor Design. XIII, 164 pp., 78 figs. 1989

N. Magnenat Thalmann, D. Thalmann: Computer Animation. Theory and Practice. Second Revised Edition. XIII, 245 pp., 156 figs., including 73 in color. 1990

N. Magnenat Thalmann, D. Thalmann: Synthetic Actors in Computer-Generated 3D Films. X, 129 pp., 133 figs., including 83 in color. 1990

K. Fujimura: Motion Planning in Dynamic Environments. XIII, 178 pp., 85 figs. 1991

Kikuo Fujimura

Motion Planning in Dynamic Environments

With 85 Figures

Springer-Verlag Tokyo Berlin Heidelberg New York
London Paris Hong Kong Barcelona

PROF. DR. KIKUO FUJIMURA
Department of Computer and Information Science
The Ohio State University
2036 Neil Avenue Mall
Columbus, OH 43210, USA

Series Editor:
PROF. DR. TOSIYASU L. KUNII
Department of Information Science
Faculty of Science
The University of Tokyo
7-3-1 Hongo, Bunkyo-ku
Tokyo, 113 Japan

ISBN-13:978-4-431-68167-0   e-ISBN-13:978-4-431-68165-6
DOI: 10.1007/978-4-431-68165-6

© Springer-Verlag Tokyo 1991
Softcover reprint of the hardcover 1st edition 1991

Series Preface

Computer Science Workbench is a monograph series which will provide you with an in-depth working knowledge of current developments in computer technology. Every volume in this series will deal with a topic of importance in computer science and elaborate on how you yourself can build systems related to the main theme. You will be able to develop a variety of systems, including computer software tools, computer graphics, computer animation, database management systems, and computer-aided design and manufacturing systems. Computer Science Workbench represents an important new contribution in the field of practical computer technology.

TOSIYASU L. KUNII

To my parents
Kenjiro and Nori Fujimura

Preface

Motion planning is an area in robotics that has received much attention recently. Much of the past research focuses on static environments — various methods have been developed and their characteristics have been well investigated. Although it is essential for autonomous intelligent robots to be able to navigate within dynamic worlds, the problem of motion planning in dynamic domains is relatively little understood compared with static problems.

This research monograph is the first book dedicated to algorithmic and computational aspects of motion planning in dynamic environments. Chapter 1 is an introduction. Chapter 2 contains a brief survey of motion planning problems and preliminaries. In Chaps. 3 through 5, various properties of time-minimal motions are derived and proved which are of fundamental importance in the study of motion planning among dynamic obstacles. Chapter 6 is independent of the previous three chapters and treats the problem from a different perspective. Chapter 7 contains an investigation of a challenging problem on distributed mobile agents.

Research on the subject of this monograph has just begun and there are many important issues which remain to be investigated. It is my hope that the research contained in this monograph will serve as a basis for further studies and motivate more research on related subjects.

July 1991

Kikuo Fujimura

Acknowledgements

I am grateful to all the people who helped me in writing this volume at various stages. Special thanks go to Dr. François G. Pin of the Oak Ridge National Laboratory who supported and encouraged the work. Drs. Reinhold C. Mann, Fred C. Maienschein, and Robert C. Ward have provided an excellent research environment at the Oak Ridge National Laboratory, where completion of this volume was possible.

Some chapters of the monograph are based on my PhD thesis written at the University of Maryland. I would like to express my sincere thanks to Professor Hanan Samet, my thesis advisor, for his support and understanding in my work at the University of Maryland. I greatly benefited from his detailed comments which helped me clarify my ideas and present the materials in a suitable way. Without his help, my thesis could not have been completed. It has been truly a privilege to work with him.

I am deeply indebted to Professor Azriel Rosenfeld who proofread my thesis carefully. He gave me technical as well as stylistic suggestions on nearly all paragraphs of earlier drafts of my thesis. Professor Gary Knott made keen observations on my formulations of motion planning problems. Discussions with Professor David M. Mount were extremely helpful for putting the problems in a proper perspective. Professors James H. Duncan and Larry S. Davis also gave me helpful comments.

I received insightful comments from Professors Mickael Dillencourt and Kenichi Kanatani. They affected the way I presented the materials in various ways. Drs. Vladimir Protopopescu, Philip F. Spelt, and Michael A. Unseren gave me valuable comments on various parts of this monograph. Dr. Gerard de Saussure read earlier drafts carefully and gave me many suggestions for improvement. Professor Joseph S. B. Mitchell provided me with some references. Karen Harber helped

me in T_EX formatting. I discussed motion planning problems
with the following colleagues at the University of Maryland: John
Aloimonos, Anup Basu, John Canning, Jean-Yves Herve, and
Rajeev Sharma.

Professor Tosiyasu L. Kunii of the University of Tokyo
extended to me the opportunity to write this research monograph.
I would like to thank him for his invaluable advice and for being
always supportive of my research in the past.

At the University of Maryland, the research was supported
by the National Science Foundation under Grant IRI-88-02457.
At the Oak Ridge National Laboratory, the work is supported
in part by an appointment to the U.S. Department of Energy
Postgraduate Research Program administered by Oak Ridge
Associated Universities and in part by the Office of Engineering
Research Program, Basic Energy Sciences, of the U.S. Department
of Energy, under contract No. DE-AC05-84OR21400 with Martin
Marietta Energy Systems, Inc.   The grants are gratefully
acknowledged.

Table of Contents

Chapter 1
Introduction

1.1 Dynamic Environments

Planning is a part of everybody's activities in daily life. We need to plan our actions from the moment we get up in the morning. We plan what to do for the day, what to eat for lunch, whom to speak to, how to get to the party in time in the evening, etc. When we wish to go somewhere, we need to plan our route to get there. For example, suppose we are in a supermarket and wish to buy some vegetables. Usually, we cannot just move straight to the vegetable section from the entrance of the supermarket because we would probably run into something, e.g., a shelf, a person, or a wall. We realize that it is necessary to plan a proper motion, i.e., path, to reach our goal. This process is usually called *route planning*. In robotics where the process is automated, the terms *path planning* or *motion planning* are used to refer to this type of computational process of moving an object from one place to another in the presence of obstacles. This monograph focuses on computational aspects of motion planning in dynamic domains, i.e., how to plan a motion, when the environment is changing over time.

The capability of motion planning in dynamic domains is important for autonomous robots. We would like a robot to perform assigned tasks by itself without the need to specify every action that is to be taken by the robot. To realize such an autonomous robot, it is necessary to synthesize many techniques including some elements from artificial intelligence. Typically, the robot needs to obtain information from the outside world using tactile, visual or auditory sensors; it needs to design an appropriate plan to execute a given task as well as handle unexpected events that arrive either from the outside world or from the robot itself and it needs to learn from experience to improve on its performance.

Planning future actions is one of the fundamental components for such an intelligent mobile robot to carry out its tasks. The motion planning problem is that of finding a motion for a mobile robot that must move from a given start position to a given destination position (the target position to be reached) in an environment that contains a pre-defined set of obstacles so that the robot does not collide with any of the obstacles. An obstacle can be a solid object that the robot can not physically pass through, a slippery area where the robot wants to go around, a dangerous area on the ground on which the robot cannot function well for some reason, an area that needs to be avoided because other robots are at work, etc. Solving this problem is crucial for many tasks such as navigation and factory automation. Generally, obstacles may not always be static. We call an object static when it is stationary in the environment, i.e., fixed permanently at a location, while a dynamic object can move, change its shape and size, and even disappear and reappear over time.

A relevant issue is whether or not the obstacles are known ahead of planning. When all information regarding the obstacles, i.e., sizes, locations, motions, etc., of the obstacles, is completely known a priori, the obstacles are said to be *completely known*, or the obstacles are in a *known environment*. On the other hand, the environment is *partially known*, when complete information about the obstacles is not available at the time of planning. In this case, the robot (planning agent) needs to determine its motion based on incomplete information about its environment. The planning agent is to make an appropriate decision when it finds new information about the environment. Such an ability is required when the robot's mission is to complete a map of the environment by exploring the area or to explore a certain area to report if any changes (e.g., new objects) are found in the area. In a partially known environment, the planning agent will have to handle an event such as unexpectedly encountering some moving objects on its way. In such a case, an original plan may no longer be executable in the new situation. This happens, for example, when the new obstacle is on the initially planned path. The robot must abandon some part of its initial plan and revise the motion as new information about the environment becomes available. Such a process is usually called reactive planning.

We have characterized the environment as either static or dynamic, and completely known or partially known. In terms of this classification, the environment can be categorized into four groups (Fig. 1.1), i.e., (i) completely known static environment, (ii) partially known static environment, (iii) completely known dynamic environment, and (iv) partially known dynamic environment. Much of the prior work on motion planning is concerned with case (i) completely known static environments — the environment that

	Static obstacles	Dynamic obstacles
Known	Case i	Case iii
Partially known	Case ii	Case iv

Fig. 1.1. Classification of the obstacles

contains only stationary obstacles whose locations and sizes are precisely known ahead of time. Realistically, however, the environment may be only partially known or dynamic, i.e., it can change over time. It should be clear that a robot that can deal with such dynamic obstacles will be capable of performing a much larger and more complex class of tasks. This monograph concerns planning motion in dynamic environments. We start our investigation by studying completely known dynamic environments, i.e., case (iii), and then extend our approach to partially known dynamic environments, i.e., case (iv).

As an example of motion planning involving dynamic obstacles, consider a factory floor, where a number of carts are moving simultaneously from one place to another. Suppose that a new cart needs to be moved to a desired position. It is necessary to plan a collision-free motion for the cart. In such a case, the motions of the other carts may be completely under control (i.e., known) prior to the departure of the new cart, so techniques from case (iii) in the above classification may be used to find a solution. The cart may be required to arrive at the destination point during some specified time interval. In such a case, it is important to plan the motion so as not to be late for the specified time. Another example of a dynamic environment is an airport where an unmanned cart moves among taxiing airplanes, carrying their cargoes from one place to another. Airplanes that land and take off may be modeled as appearing and disappearing obstacles.

The ability to handle dynamic obstacles is indispensable for the navigation of any realistic robot. Consider a vehicle navigating along a specified route. The robot's sensor may suddenly perceive a moving object crossing its path. In such a case, it should be able to generate and execute a movement to safely avoid the object, e.g., by decelerating to let the object pass by, or by accelerating to dodge the object. In this case, although the size of the problem in terms of distance, time, and the number of obstacles involved may be smaller than that of the previous example, prompt judgement is a key to successfully handling the situation. Also, in a computer-aided manufacturing environment, a robot arm may be required to reach a moving object on a conveyor belt, while avoiding moving obstacles. As can be seen from these examples, the ability to deal with dynamic obstacles will significantly increase the potential capabilities and the range of applications of intelligent robots.

From a technical point of view, the presence of dynamic obstacles gives rise to new aspects of the motion planning problem. For example, when moving obstacles are involved, the shortest distance path is not always the minimum time path. Therefore, more work is required to generate the optimal path with respect to both the travel time and the distance traveled. In addition, if our goal is to find an economical path, that is, a path that requires the consumption of a minimum amount of energy, then we must also pay attention to the speed and acceleration of the mobile robot. Also, safety (clearance from moving obstacles) is an important issue when dealing with moving obstacles. However, a safe path tends to be inefficient in terms of path length. We need to generate a path without losing much efficiency.

Thus, the problem of motion planning in dynamic domains is in many ways different from, and usually more complex than, that of motion planning in static domains. In this monograph, we will discuss some fundamental issues relating to the avoidance of dynamic obstacles, and present basic solutions to the problem.

1.2 Statement of the problem

We consider a two or three-dimensional environment that contains static and dynamic obstacles. In static motion planning problems, a path is specified as a subset in the plane, such that the path does not intersect any of the stationary obstacles. The term "trajectory" is usually used to contain velocity and acceleration information along a path. Usually, a path is first determined in space, and then a refinement of the path follows, taking into account dynamic considerations, such as velocity and acceleration. In a dynamic environment, a collision-free path for a particular time period may not be collision-free for another time period. Therefore, a path must also be specified as a function of time from the beginning. In the following chapters, we use the term "motion" to mean a path with timing information, while the term "path" is used to specify a curve in space without timing information.

In a dynamic environment, it is natural to impose constraints on a motion such as bounds on its speed or acceleration. In other words, the dynamic motion planning problem can be formulated as follows:

Given an initial position S and a final position G of a robot, and a set of moving and stationary obstacles $O_i(t)$, find a continuous function $\Gamma(t)$ of time $[t_s, t_e]$, such that $\Gamma(t_s) = S$, $\Gamma(t_e) = G$, and $\Gamma(t) \cap O_i(t) = \phi$ for t in $[t_s, t_e]$.

Usually, the function $\Gamma(t)$ must satisfy a constraint with respect to a given speed bound. The function Γ may also be subject to additional constraints such as an acceleration bound, a curvature constraint, non-holonomic constraints, etc. At times, it is possible that no such function exists, i.e., no collision-free path exists for a given set of obstacles and a pair of initial and final positions. This can happen, for example, when some of the obstacles move faster than the robot, or the robot is trapped (or crushed) between two moving obstacles.

In this monograph, we are particularly interested in minimizing the travel time of the robot, since the time factor plays a crucial role in dynamic environments. Suppose that a robot is located inside a room with a door, and the robot is to reach a point outside the room (Fig. 1.2a). Suppose that there are a number of moving and stationary obstacles inside the room and the door is open for a certain time period after which it is closed. When the door closes, the interior of the room and the outside of the room are no longer connected. The robot must reach the door before the door closes. The arrangement of the obstacles inside the room may be contrived in such a way that the robot can move to the door in time only when it makes a certain smart motion. In other words, the robot should try to waste as little time as possible inside the room. Figure 1.2b shows a more critical situation for the mobile robot where it is about to be crushed between obstacles. Here, it is a matter of paramount importance that the robot move to a safe area before a crush happens. As can be seen from the above examples, time-minimality of robot's motion is one of the primary concerns in dynamic environments. Although time-minimality is also one of the desired criteria for a path in a static environment, such a critical situation as in Fig. 1.2b will never arise when the environment does not change over time.

In this book, each chapter deals with some restricted cases of the aforementioned motion planning problem in dynamic domains. For example, Chap. 2 and Chap. 3 are primarily concerned with the case in which the robot can move faster than any of the obstacles. This constraint is lifted in a later chapter. Solutions in some chapters require the robot to be omnidirectional, i.e., the platform is assumed to be able to change the direction of motion arbitrarily. Mobile robots with omnidirectional wheels can closely follow the path generated by the methods in these chapters.

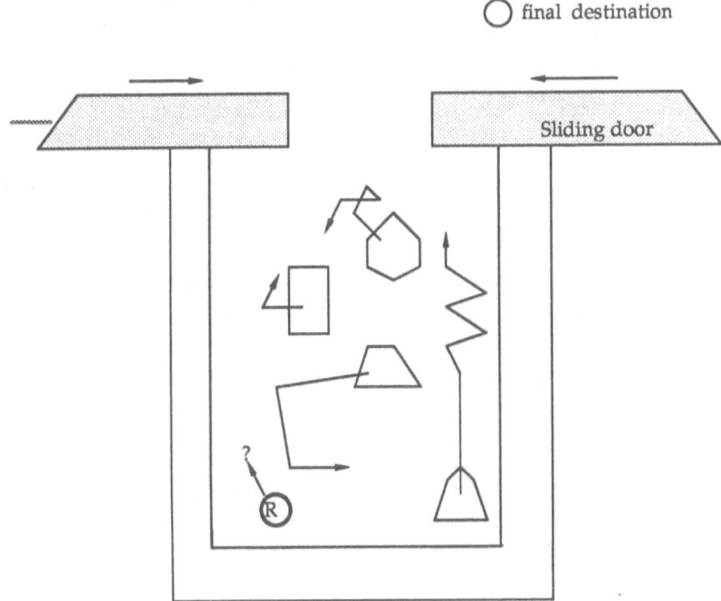

(a) The robot needs to move outside the room before the door closes.

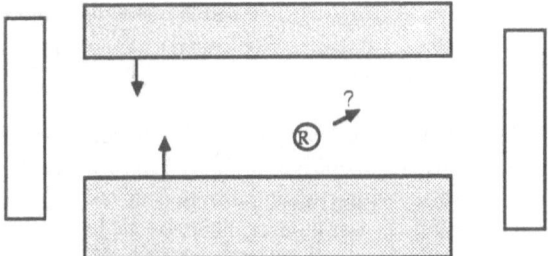

(b) The case that the robot may not survive.

Fig. 1.2 Time-varying environments

The robot can be a point or a polygon. A polygonal robot is allowed to make a motion in which its edges or vertices touch some of the edges or vertices of the obstacles. In a realistic environment, such a motion would cause friction between the obstacles and the robot. We do not discuss the issue of effects caused by friction and assume that it is possible to move the robot even when the robot's edges occasionally touch some of the obstacles. However, we do discuss the issue of how to plan a motion that maintains some given minimum clearance around the obstacles. We mainly consider an environment in which the robot is under perfect control without any motion error and the obstacles move along their trajectories exactly as defined without any delay or positioning error in their motions. However, we breifly discuss the issue of how to extend our approach to the case where there is some uncertainty in the motions of the obstacles due to some error in the measurement of the sensors.

1.3 Scope of the monograph

The rest of the monograph is organized as follows. Chapter 2 contains a survey of some approaches to the problem. After describing some basic concepts in motion planning in Chap. 2, we start our investigation in motion planning in an environment containing dynamic obstacles of various forms. We attack the problem by first solving simpler cases of the problem, and then moving to more complex cases.

In Chap. 3, we give an answer to the following basic form of the dynamic motion planning problem. Each obstacle is a convex polygon that moves in a fixed direction at a constant speed without colliding with each other. The robot is a point that can move faster than any of the obstacles. The point robot is subject only to a speed bound. The point to be reached (referred to as the destination point) also moves along a known trajectory. The concept of 'accessibility' from a point to a moving object is introduced, and is used to define a graph called the accessibility graph on a set of moving obstacles. We prove that the graph exhibits an important property: a time-minimal motion is given as a sequence of edges in the graph. We also give a procedure *PlanMotion* to generate a time-minimal motion using the accessibility graph, and analyze the execution time of procedure *PlanMotion*. It takes $O(n^2 \log n)$ time to generate a time-minimal motion, where n is the total number of vertices of the obstacles.[1]

In Chap. 4, we show that a number of dynamic motion planning problems can be solved by extending the approach proposed in Chap. 3. For example, when the obstacles are all convex, the asymptotic computation time is reduced to $O(nk \log k)$, where k is the number of convex polygons in the environment. Most importantly, we consider the case in which the obstacles have piecewise linear motions. Motion of an obstacle consists of a number of consecutive segments, during each of which its speed and direction of motion remain constant. An obstacle's speed may change in different segments. It is shown that it takes $O(n^2 \log(nm))$ time to generate a time-minimal motion, where n

---

[1] The time complexity of a function $g(n)$ is said to be $O(f(n))$ if there exist positive constants n_0 and C such that $g(n) \leq C \cdot f(n)$ for all $n \geq n_0$.

is the total number of vertices in the obstacles and m is the average number of turns taken by an obstacle.

Next, we consider the case where the obstacles may rotate in the environment. A heuristic making use of the concept of accessibility is shown to generate a motion in the presence of rotating obstacles. We also consider the case where obstacles are allowed to overlap (i.e., two obstacles are allowed to merge or split) each other. This enables us to solve an important case of dynamic motion planning — namely, generating a time-minimal collision-free motion for a polygonal robot that can be translated without rotation. Motion planning is considered in a configuration space. A fundamental difficulty of the problem is that configuration space obstacles may change their connectivity relationships over time. We still assume that the robot is subject to a speed bound. It takes $O(n^4 \log n)$ time to produce a motion in such an environment in the worst case.

In Chap. 5, the accessibility approach is generalized to solve two formulations in motion planning in dynamic domains. First, we consider motion planning in the presence of appearing and disappearing obstacles in two dimensions. The obstacles are present in the plane for certain pre-determined time intervals. This is to model a situation for mobile robots in the plane where some of the obstacles are picked up by, say a crane and moved to other locations in the same environment. Aircraft (e.g., helicopters) that land and take off in a scheduled manner may be modeled as appearing and disappearing objects. We also show how the concept of appearing and disappearing obstacles may be used to handle obstacles moving at very high speeds.

Second, we attack the problem of motion planning among moving polyhedral obstacles in three dimensions. We assume that the obstacles are not colliding each other and the robot is a free-flying point that can move faster than any of the moving obstacles. This basic formulation has many potential applications. For example, a spacecraft or a submarine that must maneuver itself among other moving objects in three dimensions may find such a capability useful.

In Chap. 6, we study motion planning with constraints on the motion: a motion is subject to an acceleration bound and a curvature bound as well as a speed bound. This problem (sometimes referred to as the kinodynamic motion planning problem) is known to be hard even for the case that all obstacles are stationary — no polynomial time algorithm is known that generates a path that satisfies curvature constraints along the path. Our approach is to use discretized control points in space-time. A motion is then defined by a sequence of control points. We make use of a hierarchical data structure to encode space-time to facilitate the search process. Although computation time is still at least exponential in the input size, our experimental results demonstrate that our approach is effective when an environment contains only a few moving obstacles.

In Chap. 7, we discuss the case that involves more than one mobile robot in the environment. In such a case, it is necessary to coordinate the motions of multiple robots. This is another area where efficient solutions are being sought. We assume that each planning agent (i.e., mobile robot) decides its own motion based on local information about each agent. When a new object is detected, the agents need to act appropriately to handle the situation. We investigate the case that two heterogeneous mobile agents (agents with different capacities) interact in the same environment. Finally in Chap. 8, we summarize the monograph and discuss some potential future problems.

Chapter 2
Background

There has been a wealth of research on path planning in an environment that contains a set of stationary obstacles. This chapter begins with a brief overview of some of the basic approaches to dealing with stationary obstacles. Especially, the concepts of "visibility" and "space decomposition" play fundamental roles in path planning in two dimensions. These concepts also form the basis of our approaches to solving motion planning problems in dynamic domains in the following chapters. The concept of visibility is important as it is used to generate a shortest path between given start and destination points in a two-dimensional environment cluttered with polygonal obstacles. The idea of space decomposition has led to a number of fast methods to generate reasonably good paths in an environment with stationary obstacles.

In this chapter, we also review previous approaches to the problem of motion planning in dynamic domains. Some authors have shown from a computational theoretical point of view that the problem of motion planning in the presence of moving obstacles is inherently harder than the case where the obstacles are stationary. They show that even for a simple case in two dimensions, the problem falls into the category called NP-hard. This means that the problem belongs to the class of problems to which no polynomial time algorithm is known to date. (See (Garey and Johnson 1979) for introduction on theory of computation.) However, there are a variety of approaches at solving the problem. Some authors make use of heuristics, while others attempt to solve some subclasses of the problem in polynomial time.

When dealing with dynamic domains, an issue arises regarding how to represent time information when the environment changes. A powerful concept is space-time in which an additional dimension represents time. A dynamic object in a n-dimensional space $(n = 1, 2, 3)$ is represented as a stationary object in space-time of $(n+1)$-dimensions. For example, a moving object in two dimensions can be viewed as a cylindrical object in a three-dimensional space where the third dimension represents time. However, the problem of finding a path in a three-dimensional space-time is not the same as that of finding a path in a three-dimensional space cluttered with stationary polyhedra. It is often the case that only some portion of space-time is reachable from a given start point (a point in space-time is a pair of a location and a time) due to a speed bound imposed on the robot. To identify the portion that can be reached from a start point in space-time, the idea of reachable region is often used. A reachable region represents the set of points that can be reached from a given start point in space-time while observing a given speed bound (and other constraints, if any). If the destination point is contained in the reachable region, then there exists a motion from the start point to the destination point. Otherwise, it is not possible to reach the destination point even when the destination point is always located outside any of the space-time obstacles. The idea of space-time as well as other methods are further discussed in Section 2.2.

2.1 Stationary Obstacles

Motion planning problems in static domains are usually solved in the following two steps. First, a graph is defined to represent a geometric structure of the environment. Next, graph search is performed to find a connected component between the node containing the start point and the node containing the destination point. The meaning of geometric structure embodied in the graph varies from one approach to another. For example, a node of the graph in a particular approach can represent a convex safe region (i.e., an area that is not occupied by any of the obstacles), while an edge of the graph can represent adjacency relationship between safe regions. A connected component in the graph in such formulations represents a series of safe regions that are adjacent to each other, from which a collision-free path is obtained.

Note that the graph may not be actually constructed in the first step. It is often a better strategy not to build the entire graph, especially when the number of nodes in the graph is potentially very large. In such a case, the graph is just defined on the environment and the second step incrementally constructs the graph starting from the start node, while searching for a path. Construction of the graph terminates as soon as the node containing the destination point is found.

When the number of nodes in the graph is relatively small, Dijkstra's shortest path algorithm is often used to find a path after the graph has been constructed. Dijkstra's algorithm runs in $O(n^2)$ time for a graph with n nodes (Aho *et al* 1974). When the number of nodes in the graph is large, search methods that make use of heuristics such as A* (Nilsson 1980) are often used to accelerate the search process.

2.1.1 Configuration spaces

We first review the concept of a configuration space, which has been used for motion planning among stationary obstacles (Udupa 1977; Lozano-Pérez and Wesley 1979; Ilari and Torras 1990; Bajaj and Kim 1990). The configuration space is a transformation from the physical space in which the robot is of finite-size (e.g., a polygon) into another space in which the robot is treated as a point. Intuitively, the configuration space is obtained by shrinking the robot to a point, while growing the obstacles by the size of the robot. Formally, the configuration space is described as follows. The position and orientation of a rigid object, say A, in the plane can be specified by a 3-tuple (x, y, θ) in a three-dimensional space, called the *configuration space* of the object, and denoted by $Cspace_A$. Here (x, y) represents the position of a *reference point* of A in the plane, and θ represents the angle made by a *reference axis* of A relative to the x-axis. When the orientation of A is fixed, its configuration space is two-dimensional, because the pair (x, y) is sufficient to specify the location of A.

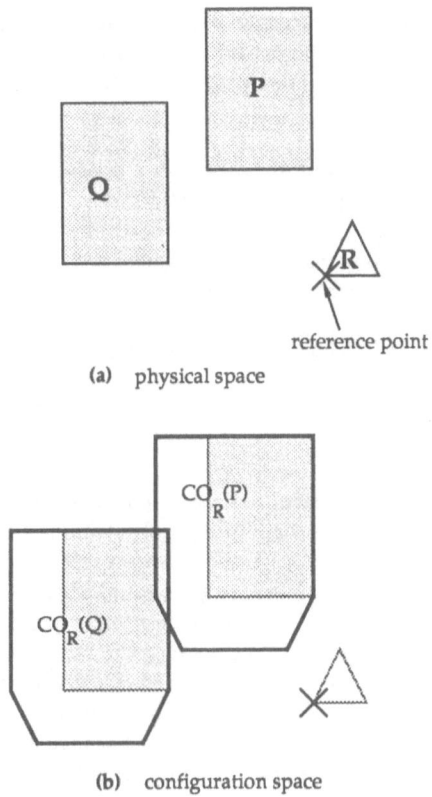

(a)   physical space

(b)   configuration space

Fig. 2.1. Physical space and its configuration space

In $Cspace_A$, some points correspond to placements of A in which A overlaps other objects in physical space. Such points are called *illegal*, while all other points are called *legal*. More specifically, the set of points in $Cspace_A$ that correspond to the placements of A where A overlaps with object B in physical space is called a *Cspace obstacle for A due to B* and denoted by $CO_A(B)$. The problem of motion planning for A in physical space is transformed into the problem of finding a path for the point in the configuration space such that every point on the path is legal.

Figure 2.1 illustrates the concept of configuration space. In Fig. 2.1a, P and Q are fixed objects in physical space, and R is the robot. We assume that the orientation of R in physical space is fixed. Figure 2.1b represents R's configuration space. The two objects delineated by thick lines are $CO_R(P)$ and $CO_R(Q)$ with respect to the reference point on R shown in Fig. 2.1a.

When the orientation of A is fixed, $Cspace_A$ is two-dimensional. When both A and B are convex polygons, $CO_A(B)$ is a convex polygon and the shape is given by taking the convex hull of $vert(B) - vert((A)_0)$. Here $vert(X)$ is the set of vertices of the polygon X; $X - Y = \{x - y | x$ in X and y in $Y\}$; and $(X)_0$ is the polygon X in its initial configuration, where its reference vertex is at the origin. See (Lozano-Pérez 1983; Whitesides 1985) for detailed algorithms for construction of configuration spaces. For an n-sided polygon A and an m-sided polygon B, $CO_A(B)$ is at most $(n+m)$-sided (Kedem and Sharir 1985).

As a result of the expansion, configuration space obstacles may overlap. In a time-varying environment, it is possible that two configuration space obstacles that do not overlap in their initial positions do overlap for a certain period of time, then cease to overlap and move away from each other. This happens even when the physical obstacles do not overlap at all. This motion of two overlapping obstacles can act as a gate-opening for a point-robot in configuration space when the robot needs to pass between the two obstacles. This issue is further discussed in Section 4.6.

2.1.2 Shortest path problems

The problem of finding a path of minimal total length in two and three dimensions has attracted much attention. The visibility graph (Nilsson 1969; Lozano-Pérez and Wesley 1979; Ghosh and Mount 1987) has been an important combinatorial structure in planning shortest paths among stationary polygonal obstacles in the plane, as well as in acquiring information about the environment while exploring it in two dimensions (Oommen *et al* 1987). In shortest path problems, the robot that follows the path is usually assumed to be of negligible size. Vertices of the visibility graph are vertices of the obstacles plus given start and goal points. A line segment connecting two vertices is an edge of the graph when the line segment does not pass through the interior of any of the obstacles. Figure 2.2 is an example of a visibility graph. The three shaded polygons represent obstacles. Points S and G are the start and goal points, respectively. An important property of the visibility graph is that a shortest path from the start point to the goal point is given as a finite sequence of edges of the graph. A sequence of

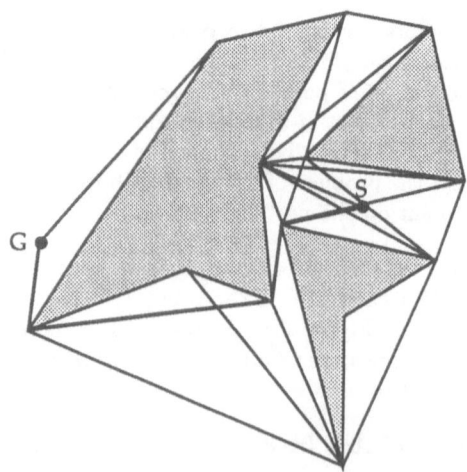

Fig. 2.2. A visibility graph

thick line segments in Fig. 2.2 represents a shortest path from S to G. Besides shortest path computations, the concept of visibility has also been a subject of much study in computer graphics (Pavlidis 1982) and computer vision (Ballard and Brown 1982) as well as in computational geometry (O'Rourke 1987; Preparata and Shamos 1985). In shortest path computations making use of the visibility graph, it is necessary to determine which obstacle vertices are visible from a given point. It takes $O(n \log n)$ time to determine visible vertices from a given point in the plane by an angular sweep about the given point, where n represents the total number of vertices in the polygons. This technique is used later and is fully explained in Section 3.5. By applying this process at all vertices in the input polygons, the entire visibility graph can be constructed in $O(n^2 \log n)$ time. However, by making use of the duality principle between a line and a point in geometry (Chazelle and Guibas 1985; Asano *et al* 1986; Welzl 1985), construction of the visibility graph for a given polygonal environment can be achieved in $O(n^2)$ time.

Recently, a number of authors have shown that some speedup is possible. For an environment containing m stationary polygonal obstacles with a total of n vertices, Reif and Storer (1985) have shown an algorithm that runs in $O(nm + n \log n)$ time. Ghosh and Mount (1987) have demonstrated an algorithm to construct the visibility graph in $O(E + n^2)$ time, where E is the numbers of edges in the visibility graph. Kapoor and Maheshwari (1988) have observed that a shortest path can be computed in $O(E_S + n^2)$ time, where E_S is the number of edges in the visibility graph that are tangents at both endpoints. Here the quantities E and E_S are bounded by n^2 and m^2, respectively. Mitchell (1990a) proposes yet another method that runs in $O(kn \log^2 n)$ time, where k is a parameter bounded by n. This method runs asymptotically faster than other methods when k is much smaller than n. Recently, Mitchell (1990b) has obtained an optimal algorithm for finding a shortest path in the plane in $O(n \log n)$ time.

For some special cases, faster computation of shortest paths is possible. For example, the case that the obstacles are line segments that are parallel to each other has been solved by Lee and Preparata (1984) in $O(n \log n)$ time, which is optimal. When all obstacles are convex, some speedup is possible (Rohnert 1986). Also, the problem of shortest path planning inside triangulated simple polygons is studied in (Guibas *et al* 1987). A shortest path in a three-dimensional space containing polyhedral obstacles is known to be a polygonal path that bends at some internal points on obstacle edges as well as at nonconvex vertices of the obstacles (Sharir and Schorr 1986). See Section 5.2 for more detailed discussions.

A related problem called the weighted region problem has been investigated by a few authors (Mitchell and Papadimitriou 1990; Mobasseri 1990; Rowe and Richbourg 1990). The plane is subdivided into regions of different weights which represent costs per unit distance in the corresponding regions. The problem is to find a least cost path between given start and destination points. The conventional shortest path problem is a special case of the weighted region problem in which a point on the plane is assigned a weight of ∞ if it is inside an obstacle, and 1, otherwise. In designing the algorithm, the above authors make use of a well-known fact that a least cost path locally obeys Snell's Law of Refraction from optics.

Kanayama and DeHaan (1988) consider cost functions based on the clearance from the obstacles. They define a cost per unit along the path by $w^{-1/k}$, where w is the clearance from the obstacles in the environment and k is a positive integer called the safety index. The total cost of the path, which is obtained by integrating the above cost over the entire path, i.e., $\int w^{-1/k} ds$, is to be minimized. This minimization problem is solved by using the calculus of variations. In the above formulation, a small k results in a path which is safer but longer. Kanayama (1989) also considers the use of cost functions of the form $w^{1/k}$ along the path. In contrast with the path obtained in the previous case, the path obtained by using this cost function prefers to pass close to the obstacles. See (Suh and Shin 1988) for an alternative approach to path planning using cost functions.

2.1.3 General problems

We have so far considered the case that the robot translates without rotation (i.e., robot with two degrees of freedom). The more general problem of moving a system of rigid bodies by means of translation and rotation in the presence of stationary obstacles is at times referred to as the "Piano-Movers' Problem" (Schwartz, Sharir, and Hopcroft 1987). In contrast with shortest path problems, any collision-free path is acceptable as a solution to the Piano-Movers' problem. Reif (1979) shows that the problem is PSPACE-hard when the number of degrees of freedom is encoded in the input specification. Canny (1988b) shows that the problem is actually in PSPACE, thus establishing that the problem is PSPACE-complete.

Some authors have shown that it is possible to compute a motion in polynomial time when the number of degrees of freedom is a fixed number. Especially, Schwartz and Sharir (1987, Chap. 2) have demonstrated that the Piano Movers' problem is solvable in doubly-exponential time in terms of input specification. They formulate the problem in terms of semi-algebraic sets and then apply a cell decomposition of n-dimensional Euclidean space called the "cylindrical algebraic decomposition" (Collins 1975). Canny (1988a) has improved the complexity of the problem to singly-exponential time by making use of techniques called multivariate resultants and stratification. See (Yap 1987; Sharir 1989) for surveys of exact algorithms for motion planning.

The above mentioned algebraic method is very powerful and general; it can solve any motion planning problem with an arbitrary number of degrees of freedom as long as the environment is defined by semi-algebraic sets. However, the method involves several steps (e.g., quantifier elimination, cell decomposition, connectivity analysis) each of which requires much work to actually implement. When the degree of freedom is a small fixed number, less powerful but more suitable alternative approaches have been proposed (Guibas, Sharir, and Sifrony 1989). These approaches include use of heuristics and approximating methods (Brooks 1983; Brooks and Lozano-Pérez 1985; Rueb and Wong 1987; Donald 1987). In doing so, many make use of some form of space decomposition methods such as quadtrees.

Many authors report on motion planning based on the idea of recursive subdivision of space such as quadtrees (Kambhampati and Davis 1986; Fryxell 1987; Noborio, Naniwa, and Arimoto 1990; Zhu and Latombe 1991). Figure 2.3 contains an example of regular decomposition of space. The idea is to keep subdividing space into subspaces of equal size recursively until each subspace is either completely occupied by some obstacle, or completely outside of any of the obstacles, or the pre-specified resolution limit is reached. As a result, the obstacles as well as free space are represented as a collection of blocks of various sizes. A hierarchical data structure called the region quadtree (Samet 1990a) is often used to store these blocks. After the decomposition, a collision-free path is obtained as a sequence of blocks that are adjacent to each other. The method is particularly attractive when the environment is given in the form of a two-dimensional array whose pixels indicate whether or not corresponding locations in the environment are occupied by obstacles. This form of input is typically obtained by taking an image of the environment from above by a camera fixed at the ceiling of the environment. When the environment is given as a two-dimensional binary image, the visibility graph approach has a disadvantage; due to digitization, there can be many corners in the image, which make it time-consuming to construct the visibility graph. Yet, much of the details in geometry may not affect the choice of the path. In other words, the effort of constructing the visibility graph may not be very relevant to finding of a path.

The idea of using the quadtree representation for motion planning is to ignore such details that have little to do with generation of the path. First, the input binary image (typically obtained as an array of size 512 by 512) is converted to the quadtree representation. (See (Shaffer and Samet 1987) for a fast conversion method from a binary array to a quadtree.) Now the environment is represented as a collection of blocks of various sizes. In this way, large blocks representing free space are quickly identified, resulting in a fast computation of a path. Then, some heuristic search method such as A* is used to search for a path together with the representation. Although the path obtained in this representation is usually not shortest in terms of Euclidean distance, Noborio *et al* (1990) report experimental results indicating that path planning based on the quadtree representation takes a less amount of computation time to generate a path than the method using the visibility graph when input data is given as a binary image.

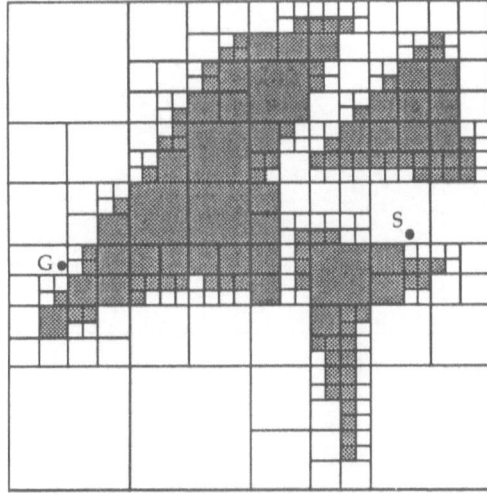

Fig. 2.3. Quadtree decomposition of space

Figure 2.4 contains a variant of the quadtree representation called the PM-quadtree (Samet and Webber 1985). The idea is to subdivide space into subspaces recursively until the contents of each subspace become simple enough (e.g., each subspace contains only one vertex of an input polygon or each subspace is intersected by only one edge of an input polygon). This representation can store polygonal shapes exactly (rather than approximation) with less storage than the region quadtree representation. Such a representation is attractive to store a large amount of polygonal shapes as required in geographical information systems.

The idea of hierarchical decomposition naturally extends to three dimensions. Three-dimensional binary images can be represented by using a regular decomposition by means of the x, y, z-axes, which results in an octal tree called the octree representation (Meagher 1982). The octree representation has been used to detect collision between two three-dimensional objects and planning a path among stationary obstacles in three dimensions (Herman 1986; Faverjon 1984; Wong and Fu 1986). A variety of hierarchical decomposition schemes and their applications are discussed in detail in (Samet 1990a; Samet 1990b). Relevant data structures such as pyramids are often used in image analysis. For more details, see a collection of papers in (Rosenfeld 1983).

The Voronoi diagram and its variants are also used for planning a path among stationary obstacles (Ó'Dúnlaing and Yap 1985; Takahashi and Shilling 1989). The Voronoi diagram is a planar network of line segments and parabolic curves, which are the set of points equidistant from at least two obstacles. Figure 2.5 contains an example of a Voronoi diagram. In contrast with the path in the visibility graph along which the robot passes through vertices of the obstacles, the path generated by the Voronoi diagram is much safer as it keeps the robot as far as possible from the obstacles. There

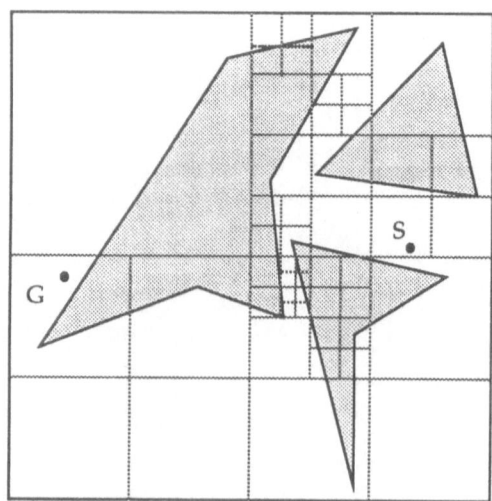

Fig. 2.4. PM-quadtree decomposition of space

are approaches that make use of artificial potential fields (Khatib 1986; Koditsheck 1989; Hague *et al* 1990; Barraquand and Latombe 1990) to plan a safe trajectory for the robot. The idea is to apply artificial force to the mobile robot so that it is repelled by the obstacles while being attracted to the destination point. This approach can be applied to sensor-based local planning of robot motion as well as to map-based global planning. The two major problems of this approach are that the robot may get trapped in local minima and that the robot's path may oscillate in certain situations. Tilove (1990) and Koren and Borenstein (1991) discuss these issues in depth. Whitesides (1985) surveys a variety of methods including space decomposition approaches.

2.2 Dynamic Obstacles

This section overviews a number of studies on motion planning in time-varying environments. Some researchers analyze the general form of the problem from a theoretical point of view. Some of their results indicate that planning a motion among moving obstacles is intrinsically harder than planning a motion among stationary obstacles. Most of the problems dealing with stationary obstacles in the plane are solvable in polynomial time, while even some basic problems in two dimensions dealing with moving obstacles do not seem to be solvable in polynomial time. Nevertheless, there are a number of algorithms that have been proposed to solve dynamic motion planning problems. Many of these algorithms work in limited domains and produce a motion in polynomial time. We overview a number of such approaches and discuss their efficiency and limitations.

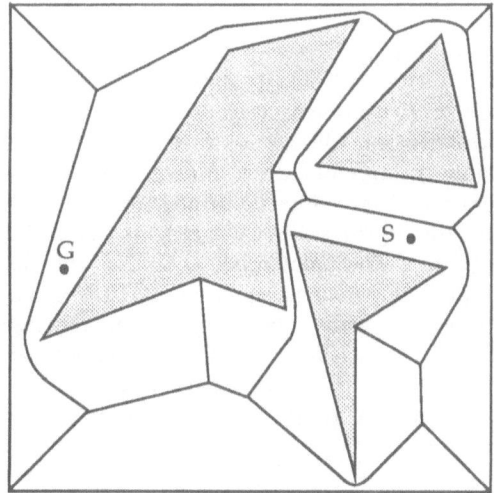

Fig. 2.5. A Voronoi diagram

2.2.1 Hardness results

Reif and Sharir (1985) show that the problem of planning motions of a three-dimensional rigid body in an environment containing stationary and moving obstacles is PSPACE-hard when the moving object's velocity is bounded, and NP-hard without such a bound.

Canny and Reif (1987) show the following lower bound on the problem: motion planning for a point in the plane with bounded velocity is NP-hard, even when the moving obstacles are convex polygons moving with constant linear velocities without rotation. The problem is shown to be in PSPACE (Canny 1988b). The hardness of the general problem of avoiding dynamic obstacles in two-dimensions has also been investigated by Sutner and Maass (1988). They have used a time-dependent graph to formulate the problem and proved that the path existence problem for time-dependent graphs is PSPACE-complete.

There is a similar but different category of problems that are usually called *coordinated motion problems.* They involve planning coordinated motions for multiple robots. This problem is dynamic in the sense that the planner must consider the motions of several robots at the same time. Hopcroft, Schwartz and Sharir (1984) consider the problem of coordinating multiple robots. They show that the two-dimensional problem of coordinating the motions of an arbitrary number of rectangles in a rectangular region is PSPACE-hard. Spirakis and Yap (1984) show that coordinating many disks is NP-hard in the strong sense. However, for some special cases, there exist polynomial time algorithms. Yap (1984), for example, presents an algorithm which runs in $O(n^2)$ time for two discs and in $O(n^3)$ time for three disks, where n is the number of walls. Section 7.1 has more references on a related subject.

2.2.2 Space-time formulations

Despite hardness results of the problem, various methods have been proposed to attack motion planning amidst dynamic obstacles. Sutner and Maass (1988) have shown that the problem of avoiding dynamic obstacles in one dimension is tractable by applying a plane-sweep technique to space-time polygonal obstacles. Figure 2.5 contains an example of a two-dimensional space-time diagram in which time-dependent obstacles are represented as polygons. The point robot as well as the obstacles exist in an one-dimensional space (i.e., a line), which is represented by the vertical axis in the diagram. The horizontal axis represents time. In this diagram, rectangle A represents a line segment in the line that exists only for a certain interval of time $[t_1, t_2]$. Objects B and C represent a line segment in space whose length varies as a function of time. Object D represents a line segment that moves at a constant speed in a fixed direction in the line.

Given a start point in space-time (a pair of a location and a time), the set of points in space-time that can be reached from the start point is called a reachable region. When the point robot is subject only to a speed bound, the robot can only reach a region bounded by two rays emanating from the start point in space-time (i.e., a cone in space-time whose vertex is at the start point). However, due to dynamic obstacles in space-time, the reachable region is a part of the cone as illustrated in Fig. 2.6. The shaded area in Fig. 2.6 represents the set of points in space-time that are reachable from S. For a two-dimensional space-time, the reachable region can be efficiently computed in $O((n + s) \log n)$ time where n is the total number of vertices in the polygonal obstacles and s is the number of intersections between obstacle edges.

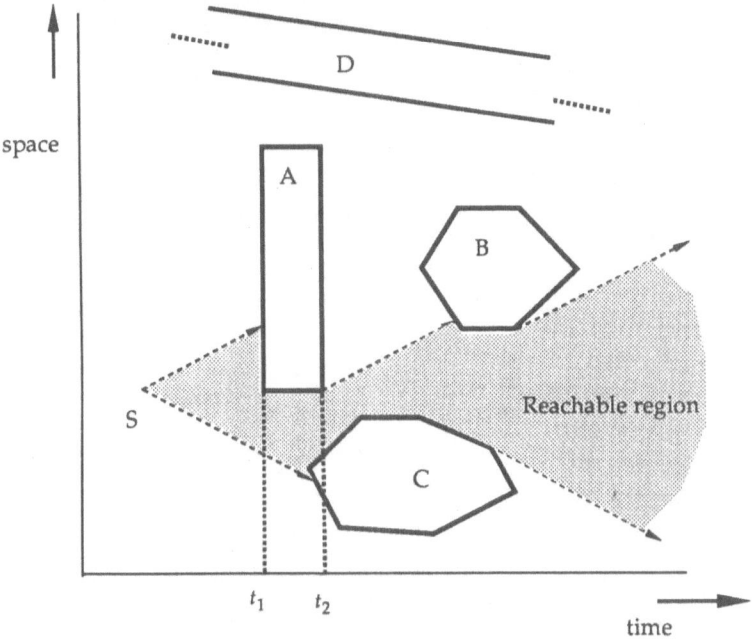

Fig. 2.6. Space-time diagram for one-dimensional dynamic objects

After the reachable region has been identified, a time-minimal motion to any point can be easily computed. This process bears some resemblance to the problem of compliant motion planning problem by using backprojections (Donald 1988). Likewise, dynamic objects in two dimensions can be represented as three-dimensional objects in space-time and reachable regions can be similarly defined as a volume in three dimensions. However, construction of the reachable region in a three-dimensional space-time is substantially more complicated than the case of two-dimensional space-time. Sutner and Maase (1988) have shown that it takes $O(n^7)$ to construct the reachable region for a single polyhedral dynamic object in space-time of three dimensions. In view of this result, dealing with more than a single polyhedral object in three-dimensional space-time seems non-trivial.

Ó'Dúnlaing (1987) discusses a similar problem with an acceleration bound. He considers the problem of moving a particle (a point robot) placed on a line from one location on the line to another location without colliding with two particles that are moving at both ends. The motions of the two obstacle particles are defined by piecewise parabolic functions. He shows that the problem is solvable in $O(n^2)$ time, where n is the number of pieces that define the two obstacles.

Kant and Zucker (1986) have applied the idea of avoiding one-dimensional dynamic obstacles to the problem of avoiding obstacles moving in the plane. They divide the problem into two sub-problems: the Path Planning Problem among stationary obstacles (PPP) and the Velocity Planning Problem along a fixed path (VPP). In the first part (PPP), they plan a path among stationary obstacles while ignoring all the moving obstacles. In the example of Fig. 2.7a, path SABCG is collision-free with respect to stationary obstacles in the scene.

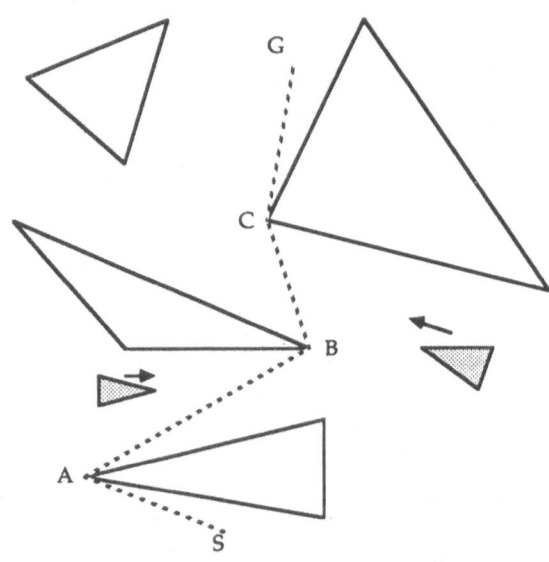

(a) Plan a path among stationary obstacles, while ignoring moving obstacles.

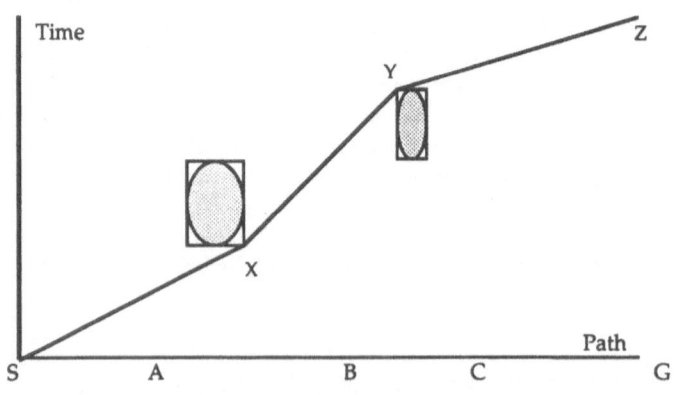

(b) Plan a motion in space-time

Fig. 2.7. Path-time decomposition

In the second part (VPP), moving obstacles are mapped in space-time, where the horizontal axis represents the path specified in the first part. Shaded areas in Fig. 2.7b represent regions through which the robot may not pass when following the path computed in the first part. The positions of these regions influence the choice of the speed. The shapes of these regions may be complicated. Therefore, they are approximated by enclosing rectangles to facilitate the second part. A space-time path that satisfies the maximum speed constraint is adopted as a final solution. A graph search method instead of plane-sweep may be used to find a feasible path. The point-robot makes a series of vertex-to-vertex transitions, as illustrated in Fig. 2.7b. Here a vertex means a vertex of a space-time polygon. A space-time path SXYZ determines speed profile along path SABCG.

As Kant and Zucker point out, there are cases in which this approach fails to produce a motion even when there exists a motion. This happens, for example, when a part of a moving obstacle is always coincident with the path determined in the first stage. This is because the path is fixed in the second stage; thus the robot is not allowed to circumnavigate moving obstacles. Also, since the path is fixed in the first stage, their method cannot easily incorporate a moving destination point.

A number of studies have been made based on path-velocity decomposition. Lee and Lee (1987) use a similar idea of path-velocity decomposition to plan motions of two robots. Tournassoud (1988) solves a one-dimensional moving obstacle avoidance problem by using a visibility graph similar to the graph used in (Kant and Zucker 1986). Griswold and Eem (1990) takes uncertainty of the moving obstacles into account while using the same principle for path planning. Pan and Luo (1990) also apply the idea of path-velocity decomposition to deal with moving obstacles in two dimensions. They use the idea of traversability vectors to determine if a given motion segment is free of collision with moving obstacles. Kyriakopoulos and Saridis (1991) has extended the idea to deal with unexpected moving obstacles.

Erdmann and Lozano-Pérez (1987) represent the motions of moving obstacles using a set of slices which embody space-time. The slices represent configuration spaces at particular times. The times are those at which some moving obstacle changes its velocity. A motion consists of a series of straight motion segments each of which starts at a vertex of an obstacle in one slice and terminates at a vertex of an obstacle in the next slice. Between two vertices, the moving obstacle moves in a straight line with a constant speed. As a result, along the final path, a point robot changes its velocity only at some of the vertices of the obstacles when some obstacle's velocity changes. Their approach is complete when the topology of free space does not change (i.e., the obstacles do not merge or split) and runs in time $O(rn^3)$, where n is the total number of edges in the environment and r is the number of slices constructed. When the obstacles do not change their velocities at all, the robot is to move at a constant speed from start to end. For the problem of coordinating multiple moving objects as is done by Erdmann and Lozano-Pérez, this does not seem to cause a problem since all obstacles will eventually come to stop. It is possible to incorporate the case of a moving destination in the space-time approach. See Section 4.4 for more discussions.

Reif and Sharir (1985) show that the problem of deciding whether a motion exists in the presence of obstacles moving with fixed velocities without rotation in the plane is solvable in polynomial time in the number of vertices and exponential time in the total number of obstacles in the environment. They use the property that whenever there is a path in space-time, there is a polygonal path that bends only at edges of space-time obstacles. For each vertex of the obstacles, they keep track of all time intervals in which the vertex is reachable.

Shih, Lee, and Gruver (1990) represent free space in space-time by a collection of polytopes. Linear programming is used to identify non-empty polytopes defined by the boundaries of space-time obstacles. Then, a graph is constructed to represent adjacency relationship between the non-empty polytopes. Finally, graph search is performed to generate a piecewise linear motion in free space. Their method has advantages over other approaches; it can be generalized to higher dimensions as well as handle overlaps of moving obstacles in a uniform manner. Warren (1990) also uses space-time to represent moving obstacles. He uses artificial potential fields in space-time to search for a motion.

2.2.3 Divide-and-conquer strategy

Suzuki and Arimoto (1990) consider using the divide-and-conquer paradigm for motion planning in the presence of time-varying obstacles in two dimensions. First, they encode time-varying obstacles in space-time using the grid representation. Then, a subgoal is selected in space-time such that the subgoal is reachable from the start point and that the destination point is reachable from the subgoal. Thus, the original problem is decomposed into two subproblems of smaller size. Each subproblem is further decomposed into two subproblems in a similar manner. This process is repeated until each subproblem becomes simple enough so that a solution is easily found. A final solution is obtained by concatenating the solutions for all subproblems.

Lamadrid (1986) has also adopted a recursive strategy for avoidance of moving obstacles in two dimensions. The point robot is assumed to move at a constant speed, while the obstacle motions are defined by quadratic functions of time. First, a straight line motion from the start point to the destination point is considered. This motion is checked to see if the robot collides with any of the moving obstacles while moving along the path. If no collision is detected, the path is accepted. Otherwise, an appropriate subgoal is selected based on some criteria. Then, the same procedure is applied recursively with the subgoal as a new destination point to determine a motion to the subgoal.

2.2.4 Collision avoidance with moving obstacles

At times, the motions of moving obstacles are not known precisely ahead of time. Even worse, the robot may encounter moving obstacles unexpectedly while in motion. In such a case, it is important to be able to act quickly so as to avoid imminent collision. Optimization of the motion is of secondary consideration in such a situation. Here, reactive behavior is more important than long-term planning of robot motion.

This reactive approach leads to an alternative strategy to dealing with moving obstacles, i.e., to keep avoiding obstacles near at hand, hoping that the robot eventually reaches its destination point. The robot avoids obstacles based on a certain set of predetermined rules. One such rule could be "if an obstacle is approaching from the left and there is no obstacle to the right, move toward the right." The motion of the robot is determined by a collection of such heuristic rules with respect to the location of the destination point and locations of nearby obstacles relative to the robot.

Maeda and Takegaki (1988) report such a reactive obstacle avoidance scheme based on production rules encoded in fuzzy logic. In their simulation, relative speeds of moving obstacles are represented by fuzzy numbers. These numbers, together with distances to the obstacles, indicate how dangerous the obstacles are and then used to determine the direction of motion of the robot. They use 112 rules to achieve flexible obstacle avoidance. They assume that the robot encounters one moving obstacle at a time and that the motion of the robot is controlled only by steering angles. Koyama *et al* (1991) also consider dynamic obstacle avoidance using fuzzy production rules in the presence multiple obstacles moving at different speeds. Takeuchi (1988) reports on autonomous mobile robot navigation among stationary obstacles by using fuzzy control.

Some other approaches to handling moving obstacles include the following. Tournassoud (1986) considers a local collision avoidance problem using separating hyperplanes. Kehtarnavaz and Li (1988) consider a collision-free navigation scheme in the presence of moving obstacles with unknown trajectories. They use an autoregressive model to predict the future positions of the obstacles. Kehtarnavaz and Griswold (1990) use a collision zone for a high collision likelihood space for obstacle avoidance. Yagi, Kawato and Tsuji (1991) has used a conic mirror which enables an omnidirectional view around the mobile robot for moving obstacle avoidance. Basu (1990) has introduced a probability model for avoidance of moving obstacles.

Parker (1988) represents an obstacle by a circle. A tangent point is a point on the circle at which the robot and the obstacle meet tangentially. The point robot moves in the direction of the tangent point at a constant speed. The A* algorithm is used to search for a motion to the goal point. See Section 4.2 for more details. Wilfong (1988) has studied motion planning in the presence of movable obstacles.

2.2.5 Collision detection among moving objects

There is another related but different category of problems usually called collision detection. This is to answer the question of the form: "Is there a collision between two moving objects?" Although the answer to this problem may not provide a direct solution to collision avoidance problems, it can serve as a useful component of collision avoidance problems as it can report a potential collision between, say a mobile robot and its surroundings.

Cameron (1985) discusses three approaches for collision detection for moving objects. The first one is to perform static collision detection repetitively over some period of time. The major difficulty in this approach is to choose appropriate time-steps; if time-steps are large, collision may not be detected even when it occurs. If they are small, then much computation time is wasted. The second approach is to perform collision detection in space-time. The idea of space-time was discussed earlier.

Although this method is complete, it may require complex computation to process four-dimensional space-time. The third approach is to represent moving objects by their sweeping volumes.

Samet and Tamminen (1985) describe a way to add the time dimension to a CSG tree. By converting a CSG tree to the bintree representation, dynamic collision detection can be efficiently performed. The problem of collision detection is also discussed by Esterling and van Rosendale (1983). They divide the time dimension as well as the other dimensions recursively to quickly locate the collision point between two moving objects. This idea is further developed by Cameron (1990) who reports a collision detection method based on four-dimensional space-time. He extends a CSG representation into four dimensions and adopts a divide-and-conquer strategy to locate collision between moving objects.

Other authors who have studied collision detection include (Canny 1986; Liu, Noborio, and Arimoto 1989b; Ottman and Wood 1984). A related problem of determining the minimum distance between two objects in three dimensions is studied by (Gilbert and Hong 1989; Lin and Canny 1991).

2.3 Summary

Our survey on motion planning in dynamic domains shows that the main problem in one dimension has been efficiently solved, while the problem in higher dimensions is still a subject of active investigation. A number of methods have been proposed to attack the problem. Although these methods are successful in some domains, the motions generated by these methods are not time-minimal in general. None of these approaches address the issue of time-minimal motions except for a particularly simple one-dimensional case.

Yet another formulation for motion planning in dynamic domains would be to use a time-varying graph. Suppose that a network of roads is represented as a graph. When a moving obstacle is coincident with some arc of the network, the arc becomes temporarily "not passable". This means that the connectivity in the graph changes with time. This can be represented by assigning a time-varying weight to each arc of the network. Hence, path planning is reduced to the problem of finding a least weight path in such a time-varying graph. The problem of finding a least weight path in a time-dependent graph, although for different applications, is studied in (Orda and Rom 1990). The formulation making use of time-varying graphs does not seem to have been applied to the area of motion planning in dynamic domains.

Planning in dynamic domains has also been discussed from an artificial intelligence perspective (Vere 1983; Slack and Miller 1987; Schoppers 1987; Sanborn and Hendler 1988). For mobile robot applications, Georgeff, Lansky and Schoppers (1987) describe a system for reasoning and planning in dynamic environments. McDermott and Davis (1984) discuss how a mobile robot could use a cognitive map to navigate through an uncertain area by using a vision system.

Robot motion planning is usually described under the generic category of *task planning* in textbooks on robotics (Brady *et al* 1982; Fu *et al* 1987). A collection of papers edited by Schwartz, Hopcroft, and Sharir (1987) treat the Piano-Movers' problem and related topics in depth. A recent book by Latombe (1991) contains detailed discussions on various aspects on robot motion planning.

Chapter 3
Time-Minimal Motion: Basics

3.1 Introduction

We have seen in Chap. 2 that the visibility graph plays an important role in planning shortest paths among stationary obstacles in a two-dimensional world. In this chapter, we study the concept of *accessibility* (Fujimura and Samet 1988), which is a generalization of the concept of visibility. Making use of accessibility, we define a graph called the *accessibility graph* to represent moving objects for the purpose of planning the motion of a robot. The robot is assumed to be a point that moves in a two-dimensional world in which polygonal obstacles, as well as the destination point, are in motion. The accessibility graph is shown to be a generalization of the visibility graph in the sense that paths to the destination point are found as sequences of edges of the graph. In fact, when all the obstacles have zero velocity, the accessibility graph becomes the visibility graph of these polygonal obstacles. More importantly, if the robot is able to move faster than any of the obstacles, then the graph exhibits a property: a time-minimal motion is represented as a sequence of edges of the accessibility graph. In this chapter, we describe an algorithm for generating a time-minimal motion, prove its time-minimality, and analyze its execution time. The utility of the concept of accessibility is further demonstrated in Chap. 4 and Chap. 5 by solving a number of motion planning problems in dynamic domains.

In this chapter, we study the case that the robot can move faster than any of the obstacles. This condition is the key that makes our problem tractable. Given a velocity (i.e., a speed and a direction in which to proceed), a robot can travel a certain distance before it meets with some obstacle (or it may never meet any obstacles). Let us call such a meeting point, if any, the collision point with respect to the velocity. The set of collision points around the start point, with respect to a certain speed, can be decomposed into subsets which we call *collision fronts.* They consist of a number of curves or line segments. Having computed collision fronts at the start point, the robot moves to an endpoint of one of the collision fronts, say E. At E, the robot is coincident with one of the vertices of the obstacles. Next, we compute another collision front with E as a start point. Now, the robot moves from E to one of the endpoints of the collision fronts that are generated about E. We repeat this process until we reach the destination point.

In a stationary environment, a path is specified as a subset in the plane and the term "trajectory" is usually used to refer to velocity and acceleration information along a path. In a dynamic environment, a collision-free path for a particular time period may not be collision-free for another time period. Therefore, a path must also be specified as a function of time. In this chapter, we use the term "motion" to mean a path with timing information, while the term "path" is used to specify a curve in space without timing information. Throughout this chapter, a goal point in motion is called a "destination point", and the term "point robot" is used to refer to a point to be moved from the start point to the destination point. Note that we use the term "velocity" to include both the speed and direction of a motion, while we use the term "speed" to mean the magnitude of a motion.

3.2 Accessibility graphs

Throughout this section, O, G and R are used to denote the start point, the destination point and the point robot, respectively. First, we define the motions of the obstacles, the point robot, and the destination point.

Motion of an Obstacle: An obstacle is a convex polygon that moves in a fixed direction at a constant speed. We call such a straight motion a *movement*. To simplify the explanation, we treat the line segments (edges) that constitute polygons as the basic units of our discussion. A *movement* is defined by a tuple (L, d_L, v_L) that represents the motion of line segment L in direction d_L at speed v_L. We will consider an environment that contains a finite set of movements, $M = \{M_1, M_2, \ldots, M_n\}$, where each M_i represents a movement as defined above. Note that M corresponds to the motions of all the edges in the environment, not just those in one polygon. Hence, if a polygon P_i consists of l_i edges (thus vertices), we have $n = l_1 + l_2 + \ldots + l_k$ where k is the number of polygons in the environment.

Motion of a Point Robot: After leaving the start point at the start time, R can have any motion as long as its speed does not exceed a given maximum speed and as long as R does not pass through the interiors of obstacles. We assume that the maximum speed of R is greater than that of any of the obstacles, and is also greater than that of the destination point. (The latter condition can be relaxed. See Section 4.4 for more details.)

Motion of a Destination Point: The motion of the destination point consists of a finite series of steps. Within a step, the destination point moves in a constant direction at a constant speed. We assume that the number of steps is bounded. (This condition can be relaxed. See Section 4.4 for more details.)

Now, let us define the concepts of meeting point, accessibility, collision front, accessible vertex set, and accessibility graph.

Meeting Point: Consider a possibly-moving point V (V is either the destination point or a point on a polygonal obstacle). Let R be a point initially located at O at time t_0. Suppose that R starts moving at time t_0 at a speed v. After R starts moving, it moves in a fixed direction. We say that V and R meet if there exists a location X through which both V and R pass at the same time t, where $t > t_0$. The location X is called an *meeting point* of V with respect to v and O. The time t is called the *meeting time* of X

with respect to V and is denoted by $t(X)$. When R moves faster than V, the meeting point of V is uniquely determined. When the speed of R is slower than that of V, it is possible that R is never able to meet V (see Section 4.3 for more details). The meeting point of a possibly-moving point V varies for different values of the speed and the initial location of R.

Accessibility: Consider a set of obstacle movements $M = \{M_1, M_2, \ldots, M_n\}$ and G, the destination point. Let R be a point robot located initially at O at time t_0. Suppose that R starts moving at time t_0 at a speed v. After R starts moving, it moves in a fixed direction. A point V (V is either the destination point or a point on a polygonal obstacle) is said to be *accessible* from O (with respect to t_0 and v), if R meets V without prior interception by any other movement. The meeting point and meeting time are called the *accessible point* and *accessible time* of V, respectively. Note that if a stationary point V (V is either a stationary destination point or a point on a stationary obstacle) is accessible, then its accessible point is V itself.

Collision Front: Consider an environment that contains one movement, say (L, d_L, v_L). Let V_a and V_b be the two endpoints of L, and let P_a and P_b be accessible points corresponding to V_a and V_b, with respect to R's initial location O, start time t_0, and speed v. The set of accessible points corresponding to all points in L forms a segment. As will be shown later in Section 3.4, this segment takes the form of either a straight line segment or a conic section. We will call this segment a *collision front* of L (with respect to O, t_0, and v). Figure 3.1 contains an example of a collision front. It can be shown that P_a and P_b are the two endpoints of the collision front. For an environment that contains more than one movement, there can be more than one collision front, each of which corresponds to some movement. In this case, however, it is possible that only a part of a collision front is accessible. Notice that if two moving obstacles (e.g. edges) do not collide, then the corresponding collision fronts do not intersect. The characterization of the collision front is as follows. Suppose that R departs O at time t_0 and keeps moving at a constant speed v along a ray, say l, emanating from O. The

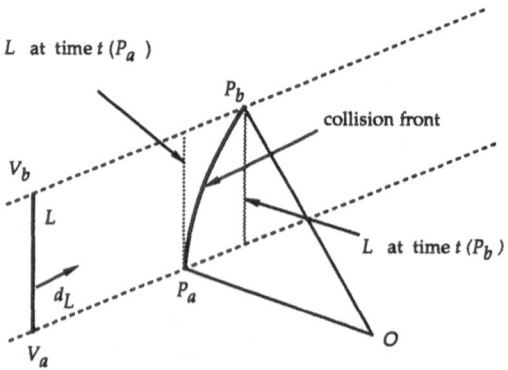

Fig. 3.1. A collision front

point robot R does not meet any of the obstacles in motion if and only if l does not intersect any of the collision fronts. The collision front of a stationary edge L is L itself or consists of subsets of L.

Accessible Vertex Set: Let VS be the set consisting of the destination point and the vertices of the polygonal obstacles in motion M, and let O, t_0, v be as in the definition of accessibility. The set of accessible points corresponding to elements of VS with respect to O, t_0, v is called the *accessible vertex set* and denoted as $AVS(M, O, t_0, v)$. Since some vertices in VS may not be accessible from O, the size of AVS is at most $|VS|$.

Accessibility Graph: Let O be the start point (i.e., the point at which point robot R is initially found), t_0 be the start time, v be the start speed and G be the destination point. With each accessible point X corresponding to a point V, we also associate a time value (i.e., timestamp), say $t(X)$, to denote X's accessible time with respect to V. We define a directed graph called the *accessibility graph*, or $AG(M, O, G, t_0, v)$, by the following construction:

1. Insert O in the vertex set of AG, and set its default accessible time to t_0.

2. For every newly added vertex U in the set of vertices in AG, consider the accessible vertex set with U as the initial point, i.e., $AVS(M,\ U,\ t(U),\ v)$. Insert the elements of this AVS in the vertex set of AG, and the edges from U to these points in the edge set of AG.

The graph is a (directed) tree rooted at O. (In degenerate cases, the graph might not be a tree but only a DAG, e.g., when there are two shortest paths to a vertex.) Note that for a given set of M, O, and G, AG varies for different values of t_0 and v. This graph is infinite according to our definition. However, we can make it finite by adopting the rule that when a vertex of an input polygon is used more than once to define vertices of AG, then the instance with the youngest accessible time is the one that is retained. Under this rule, the number of vertices in AG does not exceed $|VS|$. Also note that the vertices of AG are the accessible points and not the original points on the obstacles.

Example. Figures 3.2a and 3.2b demonstrate how to construct an accessibility graph. Points S and G are the starting and destination points, respectively. Triangle ABC and rectangle DEFH are obstacles moving in the indicated directions. First, S is inserted in the vertex set of the accessibility graph (step (1)). Vertices B, C, and F are accessible from S at P, Q, and U, respectively, but E is not accessible because obstacle ABC is in the way. Therefore, $AVS(M, S, t(S), v) = \{P, Q, U\}$. Points P, Q, and U are inserted in the vertex set of the accessibility graph. Accordingly, SP, SQ, and SU are inserted in the edge set of the accessibility graph (step (2)). Next, let us take Q as a newly added vertex in step (2) of the construction (Fig. 3.2b). Vertices A, B, E and F of the obstacles are accessible at locations X, Y, V, and W, respectively, i.e., $AVS(M, Q, t(Q), v) = \{X, Y, V, W\}$. Thus, X, Y, V, and W are inserted in the vertex set of the graph, and QX, QY, QV, and QW are inserted in the edge set of the graph. This process is applied to other vertices such as P, U, etc.

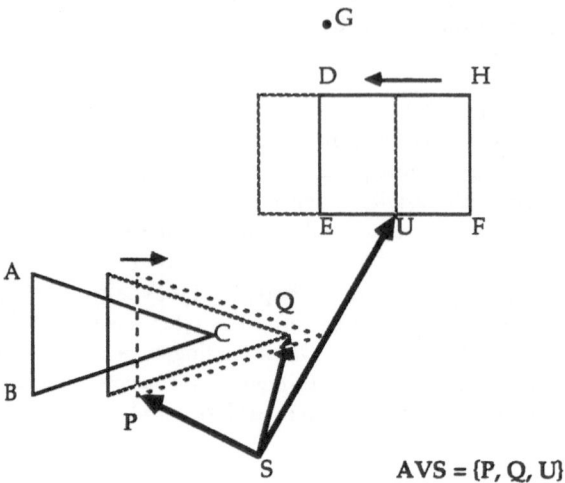

(a) Insert the start point in the vertex set of AG.

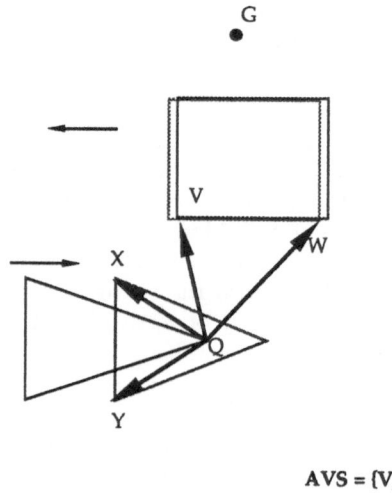

AVS = {V, W, X, Y}

(b) The AVS as Q as the start point.

Fig. 3.2. Construction of an accessibility graph

Note that in the finite version of the accessibility graph, points Y and W (Fig. 3.2b) will not appear in the graph since P and U (the accessible points of B and F from S, respectively, as can be seen in Fig. 3.2a) have younger accessible times when they are reached from S.

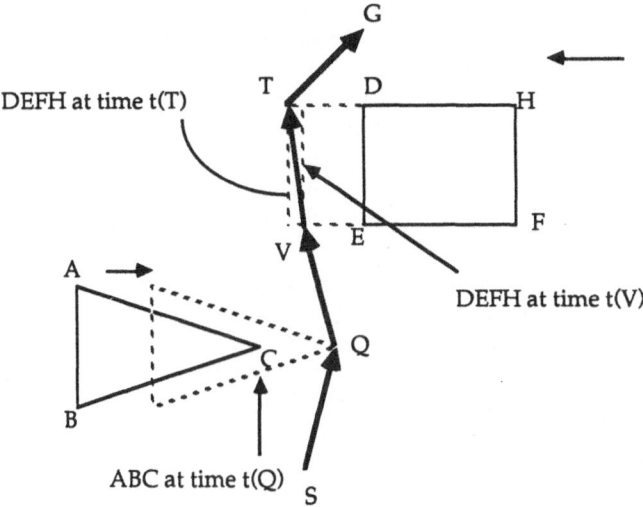

DEFH at time t(T)

DEFH at time t(V)

ABC at time t(Q)

(c) The result of applying procedure *PlanMotion* to (a).

Fig. 3.2.

The accessibility graph is related to the visibility graph in the following manner. Consider a stationary set of movements M whose elements do not overlap. Construct the (infinite) accessibility graph for M, and make all directed edges in AG undirected and remove the timestamps at all the vertices. The resulting graph is the visibility graph for M. Since we will need only the finite part of the accessibility graph in the subsequent sections, we retain its finite formulation.

3.3 Planning and Motion

In this section, we first describe a procedure that finds a motion to the destination point using AG as defined in the previous section. Next, we prove that the motion found by the procedure is time-minimal. In this process, we use a priority queue of vertices where the accessible time of each vertex serves as the vertex's priority.

Procedure *PlanMotion*:

1. Insert the starting vertex O into the queue.

2. Remove a vertex, say V, from the queue whose associated accessible time is the youngest.

3. If vertex V in step (2) is the destination point G, then report the motion and exit; otherwise, insert all the vertices that are adjacent to V in AG into the queue, and repeat steps (2) and (3).

Step (3) needs some care. An element of AVS is inserted into the queue when the corresponding vertex has not been seen before or it has a younger accessible time than the one (for the same corresponding vertex) that is already in the queue in which case the old element is deleted. When a new element has an older accessible time than the one for the same vertex that is already in the queue, the new element is not added. As a result, the size of the queue never exceeds the sum of the total number of vertices of the input polygons plus the destination point. By constructing the graph in this way, we obtain the finite version of the accessibility graph defined in Section 3.2.

Example.   Figure 3.2c is an example of planning a motion using procedure *PlanMotion*. Points S and G are the start and destination points, respectively. Triangle ABC is an obstacle moving towards the right, and rectangle DEFH is an obstacle moving towards the left. Points Q, V, and T are the accessible points of C from S, of E from Q, and of D from V, respectively. The dashed objects show the locations of the corresponding obstacles at the indicated times. Note that while the robot is moving between V and T, it is coincident with some point on edge DE of obstacle DEFH. The sequence of line segments (SQ, QV, VT, TG) constitutes the final motion.

We claim that procedure *PlanMotion* yields a fastest motion to reach the destination point of all motions whose speed is less than or equal to v.   When there is more than one time-minimal motion to the same destination point, procedure *PlanMotion* gives one of them as a solution. In the above example, this means that no other motions can reach the destination point G at an earlier time than SQVTG under the condition that the point robot cannot move faster than its maximum speed. This claim is proved in the next section.

3.4 Time-Minimal Motion Theorem

In this section, we prove that the motion obtained by procedure *PlanMotion* is time-minimal. Before presenting a formal proof, we give the intuitive idea behind our proof using a simple example. Figure 3.3a is a scene that contains one line segment L moving in the indicated direction. Let U and V be the two endpoints of L. Let O and G be the start and destination points, respectively, for the point robot R. The motion of L is such that if R moves straight towards G with its given maximum speed v, then R will meet an interior point of L. Let C denote this meeting point. Let A and B be the accessible points of U and V, respectively. According to procedure *PlanMotion*, the fastest motion to G must be either OAG and OBG.

A natural question to ask is: "Would not it be faster if the point robot moves straight towards G until it hits L at C, waits for L to pass by, and then continues to move on the straight line to G?"

We now show that this is not the case. Let α be the motion described above (Fig. 3.3b). Let β be motion OAG. We propose an alternative motion β' defined as follows. Motion β' is identical to β from O to A. From A, its motion is identical with the endpoint of L, (i.e., U) until U reaches C. After C, the rest of motion β' is identical to motion α. Obviously, β' arrives at G exactly at the same time as α. On the other hand, motion β

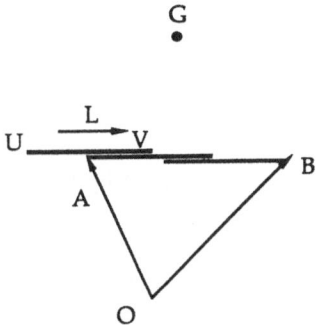

(a)   Line segment L is moving towards the right.

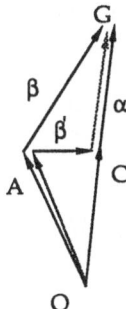

(b) Some example motions.

Fig. 3.3. Illustration of the time-minimality of *PlanMotion*

arrives at G earlier than β', since β moves straight from A to G. Therefore, motion β arrives at G before motion α.

The above example illustrates why the motion given by procedure *PlanMotion* is faster than other motions. Of course, it is more complex to prove the claim for the general case in which there is more than one moving line segment.

In the rest of this section, let $v_{\max}$ denote R's maximum speed, and let O and G be the start and destination points, respectively. We divide the motions from O to G into two groups, i.e.,

Group 1 - motions that begin with a segment that is traversed at speed $v_{\max}$ in a constant direction through a point in $AVS(M, O, t_0, v_{\max})$, say P. The motion from P is arbitrary but must eventually reach G.

Group 2 - the other motions.

It is assumed that speeds along motions in both groups do not exceed $v_{\max}$. In the rest of this chapter, we assume the following two conditions.

(A1) The maximum speed of the point robot $v_{\max}$ is greater than the speed of any of the obstacles,

(A2) The obstacles never collide with each other nor do they collide with the destination point.

Proposition 1. Given a set of movements M and a destination point G, suppose that point R and vertex V, the common endpoint of edges UV and VW of the same polygonal obstacle, are at location X at time t_1. Let M_i and M_j be the movements of edges UV and VW, respectively, and let M_k be the movement corresponding to the motion of the new edge UW. If there exists a motion starting from X at time t_1 and terminating at G at time t_2 ($> t_1$) in $M - \{M_i, M_j\} + \{M_k\}$ (i.e., an environment formed by removing the triangle UVW from the polygonal obstacle, but leaving edge UW), then there exists a motion in M, starting from X at time t_1 and terminating at G at time t_2.

Proof: Let α be a motion from X to G in $M - \{M_i, M_j\} + \{M_k\}$. There are two cases depending on whether or not α collides with movement M_i (or M_j) in M.

(Case 1): *Motion α does not collide with movement M_i or M_j in M.*

By construction, α does not collide with $M - \{M_i, M_j\}$. When α does not collide with M_i or M_j, it is collision-free in M. The case that the robot passes through the triangle interior while avoiding the triangle edges can be taken care of by applying the argument of Case 2.

(Case 2): *Motion α collides with movement M_i (or M_j) in M.*

Without loss of generality, let L denote the movement (i.e., M_i or M_j) with which α collides last. We construct an alternative motion β such that β is collision-free in M in the following manner. Let Y be the location of the occurrence of the last collision of α with L (see Fig. 3.4). Starting at time t_1, define β as the straight-line motion followed by R from X to Y with a constant speed such that β reaches Y exactly at the same time as α reaches Y for the last time. This means that until reaching Y, R is always coincident with some point on L. The length of this motion is shorter than the corresponding segment of α, since the shortest distance between two points is a straight line. After Y, R follows the remaining part of motion α. The point R reaches G at the same time regardless of whether motion α or β is used. Along β, R moves at a speed slower than $v_{\max}$ from X to Y. To see this, consider two motions from X to Y, namely

α and β, both starting and arriving at the same time. Since β is shorter than α, the speed of R between X and Y must be less than $v_{\max}$.◊

As a special case of this proposition, we consider a case in which an obstacle is just a single edge. We have the following proposition; its proof is similar to the proof of Proposition 1.

Proposition 1′. Assume the same environment as in Proposition 1 except that UV, with movement M_i, is a single edge obstacle. Suppose that at time t_1, point R and vertex V are at location X. If there exists a motion starting from X at time t_1 and terminating at G at time t_2 in $M - \{M_i\}$, then there exists a motion in M starting from X at time t_1 and terminating at G at time t_2.

Proposition 2. Let σ_1 be a motion of a point robot, say R_1, consisting of two linear movements. Let the first movement be from O to A at a constant speed v_1 along a line-segment OA and the second movement be from A to infinity at a constant speed v_2. Let $v_1 < v_{\max}$ and $v_2 < v_{\max}$. For any point P on σ_1, there exists a motion of a point robot, say R_2, from O to P such that R_2 leaves O at the same time as R_1, R_2 moves along a straight line OP at a speed v' ($v' < v_{\max}$), and R_2 arrives at P either before R_1 or at the same time.

Proof: Choose $v' = \max\{v_1, v_2\}$. This proposition holds by applying the triangle inequality to OAP (Fig. 3.5).◊

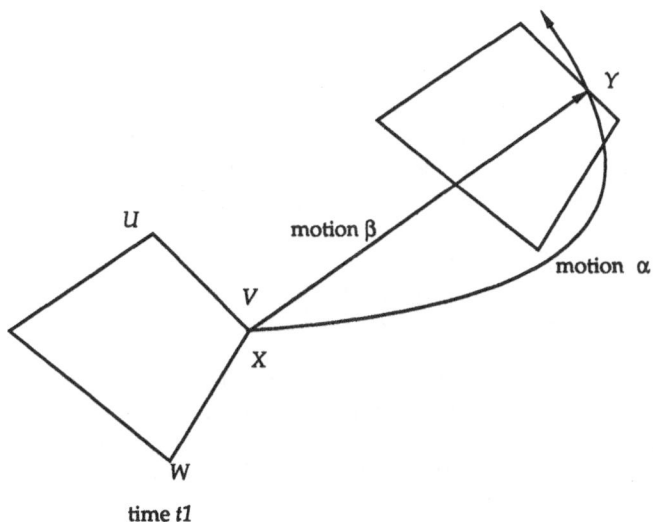

time *t1*

Fig. 3.4. Illustration of Proposition 1

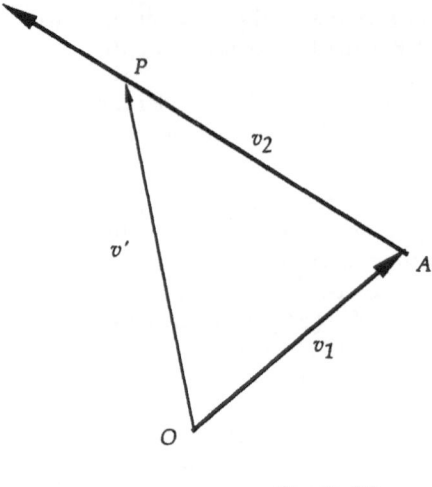

$$v_1 , v_2 < v_{max}$$

Fig. 3.5. Illustration of Proposition 2

The following proposition is essential in our proof of the Time-Minimal Motion theorem. In the case where all obstacles are stationary, a shortest path is known to be a sequence of edges in the visibility graph. This means that a shortest path bends only at vertices of the polygon. If a polygonal path bends at a point that is not a vertex in the visibility graph, we can show that a short-cut is possible by a path through a vertex in the visibility graph. Proposition 3 is a generalization of this claim to the accessibility graph.

Proposition 3. Suppose that G is not accessible from O. Let π_2 be a collision-free motion from O to G. Let π_2 be in Group 2. There exists a collision-free motion from O to G in Group 1, say π_1, that is identical to π_2 starting at some point J. The speed along some portion of π_1 before J is less than v_{max}.

Proof: In the first part of the proof, let us assume that there is only one collision front about O for $v = v_{max}$. Let V_1 and V_2 denote the two endpoints of the collision front. Let v_o denote the maximum speed of the obstacles in the scene.

The outline of the proof is as follows: as candidates for π_1 in Proposition 3, we construct two motions, τ_1 and τ_2, that start with segments OV_1 and OV_2, respectively, each moving at speed v_{max}. Next, each of them moves at a speed that is infinitestimally less than v_{max} (i.e. $v_{max} - \epsilon$ for a small ϵ; the value of ϵ remains to be determined) and heads for the earliest point J on π_2 that they can reach.

In the following, we show that it is possible to choose one of τ_1 or τ_2 as π_1. To carry out the proof, we classify the collision front into three types: *receding obstacle*, *proceeding obstacle*, and *degenerate obstacle*, as defined below. To see this classification, consider a point robot that moves straight from O to a point in the collision front V_1V_2 at speed v_{max}, and let the point robot stand still at that spot for a brief moment, while the obstacle continues moving.

Type 1 (receding obstacle): The point robot will not collide with the obstacle.

Type 2 (proceeding obstacle): The point robot will collide with the obstacle.

Type 3 (degenerate case): Until the point robot stops moving, it is always collinear with the obstacle.

Figures 3.6a, 3.6b, and 3.6c contain examples of a receding obstacle, a proceeding obstacle, and a degenerate obstacle, respectively. The type can be determined by the relation between the initial location of the obstacle (line segment) and O. Let l be the line in motion that is the extension of the obstacle. When l intersects O after it starts moving, l is a proceeding obstacle (type 2). When it does not, it is a receding obstacle (type 1). When O is on l, it is of type 3.

Case 1: Receding obstacle:

Proof: We consider two auxiliary motions, σ_1 and σ_2, starting from V_1 at time $t(V_1)$ and from V_2 at time $t(V_2)$, respectively (see Fig. 3.7a). Motions σ_1 and σ_2 move at constant speeds v_{c1} and v_{c2}, respectively, where $v_{ci} < v_{max}$ $(i=1,2)$, and they are always coincident with some point in L. Let W be the point at which σ_1 and σ_2 meet. Choose v_{ci} so that the ray OW crosses the collision front. (This serves to make the following exposition slightly clearer.) Let l_1 and l_2 be the two rays emanating from V_1 and V_2 that are extensions of rays OV_1 and OV_2, respectively. An open-ended serial chain of line segments l_1, V_1W, WV_2, and l_2 partitions the plane into two regions. Let A be the region that contains O and let B be its complement.

First we show that if there are not any moving obstacles besides L, then one of τ_1 or τ_2 will reach π_2 in region A. There are two cases depending on whether or not π_2 crosses the border of the two regions. In the first case, we assume that π_2 crosses the border of the two regions and let Z be the first point at which such a crossing occurs. We show that either τ_1 or τ_2 can reach π_2 before π_2 enters region B (i.e., J occurs at or before Z along π_2).

Suppose that Z lies on WV_1 or WV_2 (see Fig. 3.7a). Let Y be the point at which π_2 crosses the collision front V_1V_2. Motion π_2 goes through Y at the same time as or after L has gone through Y, because Y is an accessible point and π_2 is a Group 2 motion. Since it is impossible for π_2 to penetrate L between Y and Z, π_2 also goes through Z at the same time as or after L has gone through Z. Now, recall that segment V_1W (or V_2W) is a trajectory for a point robot whose motion is always coincident with some point in L. Therefore, the point robot goes through Z at the same time as or earlier than π_2 goes through Z. This implies that ϵ can be chosen so that one of τ_1 or τ_2 will reach π_2 in region A. For the case that Z lies on l_1 (or l_2 as in Fig. 3.7b), it should be clear that by choosing ϵ to be sufficiently small, τ_1 (or τ_2) with a speed $v_{\max} - \epsilon$ will reach π_2 in region A.

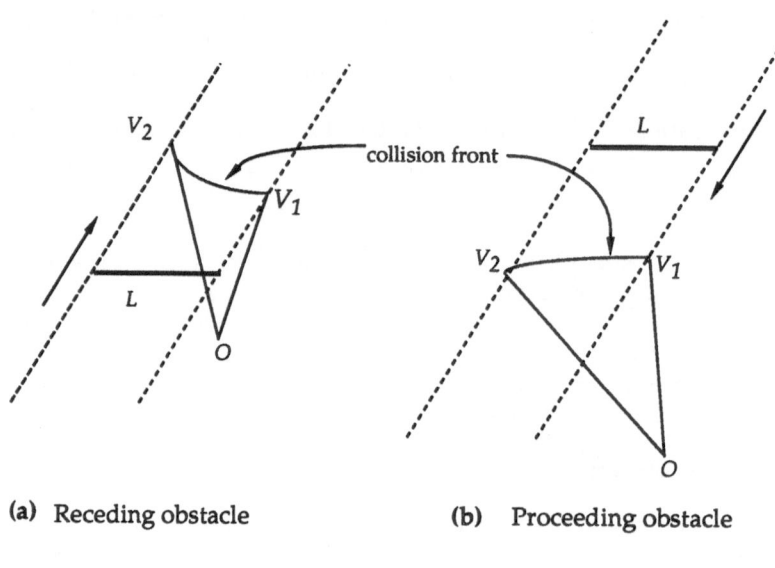

(a) Receding obstacle   **(b)**   Proceeding obstacle

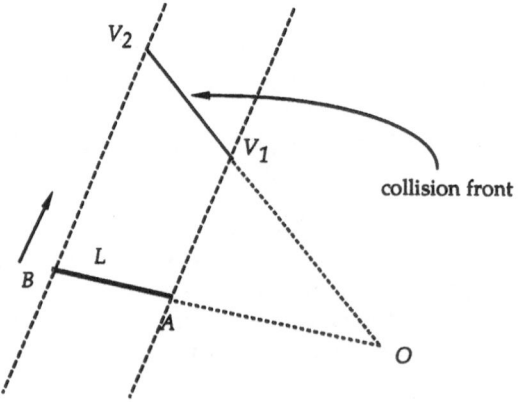

(c)   Degenerate obstacle

Fig. 3.6. Three types of obstacles

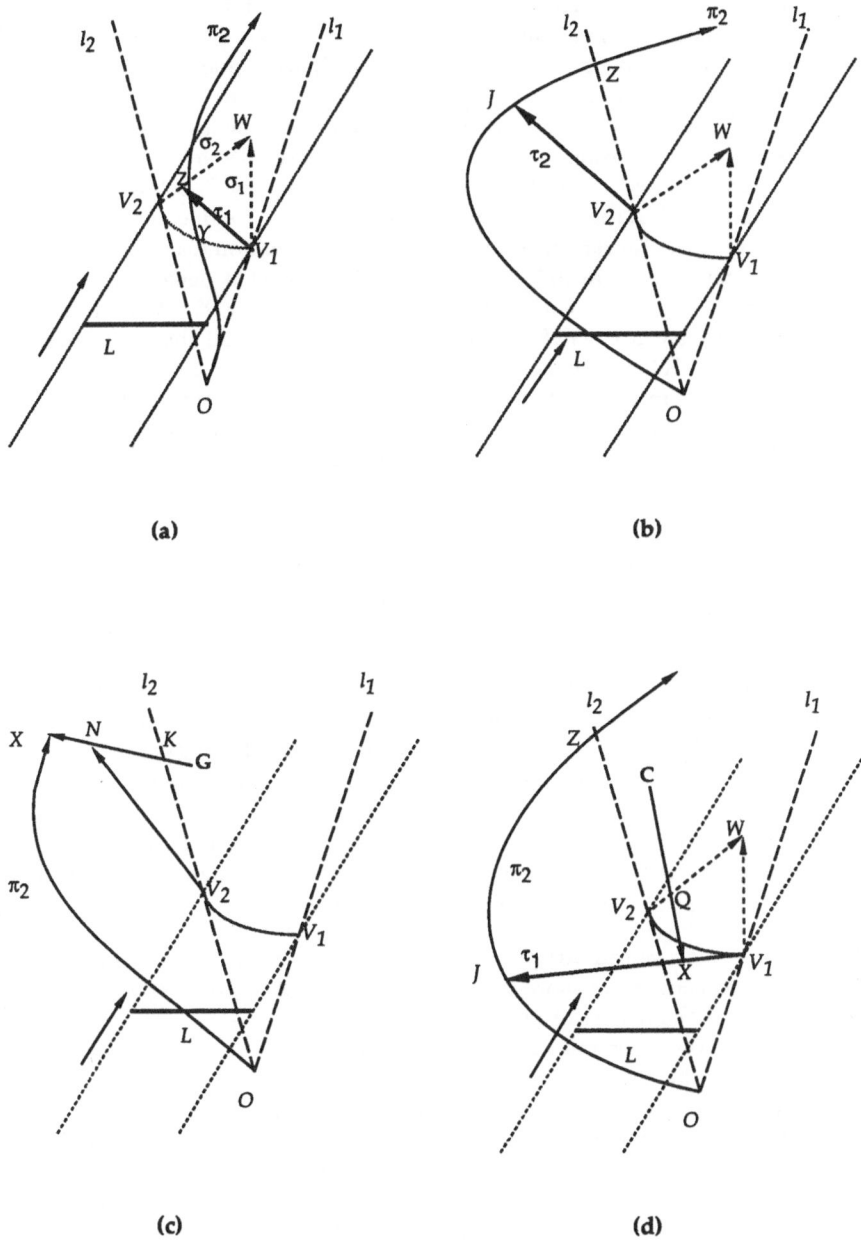

Fig. 3.7. A proceeding obstacle for the proof of Proposition 3

In the second case, we assume that π_2 does not cross the border of the two regions. If π_2 reaches the destination point without crossing the border, then either π_1 (one of

τ_1 or τ_2) can reach the destination point before π_2 does, or π_1 can reach π_2 before π_2 reaches the destination point. This can be shown as follows. (The following proof does not require that the robot move faster than the destination point.) Let K be the point at which G crosses the border (Fig. 3.7c). Let K lie on l_2 as in Fig. 3.7c (proofs for the case that K lies on the other part of the border is analogous). Let X be the point at which π_2 meets G. Consider a point robot that departs V_2 at time $t(V_2)$ and moves straight to X at speed $v_{\max} - \epsilon$. If the point robot arrives at X before π_2, then we are done since it implies that there is a motion from V_2 at $v_{\max} - \epsilon$ that reaches π_2 before π_2 reaches X. Otherwise, we can show that there exists a location (say N) between K and X at which π_1 can meet G as follows. Consider a motion that departs V_2 at time $t(V_2)$ with a speed $v_{\max} - \epsilon$. This motion is directed towards K or X. When this motion is aimed towards K, it can reach K before G reaches K. (Recall that G is assumed not accessible from O.) When this motion is directed towards X, it reaches X only after G has reached X. This means that there exists a point, say N, between K and X having the property that if the motion is directed towards N, then it will reach N just as G passes N. We choose this motion as τ_2 (a candidate for π_1).

Now, we must show that one of τ_1 or τ_2 is indeed collision-free, even when there are other obstacles present besides L.

At this point, let us describe how we choose a speed along τ_1 or τ_2 (i.e., the choice of $v_{\max} - \epsilon$). Consider all obstacles that exit from region B into region A that possibly intercept τ_1 or τ_2. Since $V_1 V_2$ is the only collision front in the scene, the motions of the obstacles must cross l_1, l_2, $V_1 W$, or $V_2 W$ at some point. Moreover, the crossing times have the following characteristic. Let Q be the last crossing point between regions A and B. When Q lies on l_1 (or l_2), the crossing time must be strictly later than the time at which a point that moves along l_1 (or l_2) at $v_{\max}$ departing O at time t_0 would reach Q. Otherwise, it contradicts our assumption that there is only one collision front. When Q lies on $V_1 W$ (or $V_2 W$), the crossing time must be strictly later than the time at which motion σ_1 (or σ_2) passes Q, since the obstacles cannot collide (in this case, this would have required the obstacle to collide with L).

This implies that we can always construct a motion[1] from V_1 (or V_2) at a speed less than $v_{\max}$ that reaches any of those obstacles when it crosses l_1 or $V_1 W$ (l_2 or $V_2 W$). Let v_d be the speed of the fastest of all such motions. Let $v_{\max} - \epsilon = \max\{v_o, v_{c1}, v_{c2}, v_d\}$. Recall that v_o is the maximum speed of the obstacles in the scene. Then applying Proposition 2 (letting the appropriate one of V_1 and V_2 correspond to O, and letting Q correspond to A), τ_1 will not collide with any obstacle crossing l_1 or $V_1 W$, and τ_2 will not collide with any obstacle crossing l_2 or $V_2 W$. For π_1 of Proposition 3, choose the one of τ_1 or τ_2 that reaches π_2 earlier. We prove that motion π_1, chosen as such, is collision-free. Without loss of generality, let τ_1 be chosen as π_1. By construction, τ_1 does not collide with any obstacle that crosses l_1 or $V_1 W$. Now, suppose that τ_1 collides with an obstacle crossing l_2 or $V_2 W$. Figure 3.7d shows such a scene, where V_1 and V_2 are the accessible points of P_1 and P_2, respectively. Let C be an obstacle that intercepts motion τ_1 at X. Let Q be a point at which C crosses $V_2 W$. Note that the time at which C passes Q must be strictly later than the time at which motion σ_2 passes Q. Applying Proposition 2 to $V_2 Q X$ (letting V_2 and Q correspond to O and A, respectively) as well

---

[1] This motion itself may or may not be collision-free. However, it does not affect our proof.

as to V_2XJ (letting V_2 and X correspond to O and A, respectively), it can be shown that there is a motion that will reach J before τ_1. This implies that τ_2 can reach π_2 earlier than τ_1. This contradicts the choice of π_1. (The same argument works if Q is on l_2.)

Case 2: Proceeding obstacle:

Proof: The proof for this case is analogous to the proof for receding obstacles. This time, the plane is divided into two regions by l_1, l_2, and the collision front. Let A be the region that contains O and let B be its complement. Let Y be the first point at which π_2 crosses the border. We consider only the case that Y lies on the collision front. The other cases (i.e., the case that Y lies on either l_1 or l_2 and the case that π_2 reaches the destination point without crossing the border) are proved in the same manner as the corresponding parts of the proof for receding obstacles.

We consider motions σ_1 and σ_2 at a speed v_c, where $v_o < v_c < v_{\max}$. Let W be the point at which σ_1 and σ_2 meet. It should be clear that π_2 must cross either V_1W or V_2W (as in Fig. 3.8a) before π_2 reaches Y. Note that when the trajectory of L contains O (Fig. 3.8b), it is impossible for π_2 to reach the destination point without placing itself outside L's trajectory (even just momentarily), since π_2 cannot penetrate L.

Let Z be the point at which π_2 crosses V_1W or V_2W for the last time before π_2 passes Y. Note that portion ZY of π_2 is entirely inside the trajectory swept by L, and that π_2 passes Y after L has passed it. Motion π_2 must pass Z only after L has passed Z, since π_2 cannot penetrate L. This means that π_2 passes Z later than the time at which σ_1 or σ_2 pass Z. For the same reason as in the case of receding obstacles, τ_1 departing from V_1 or τ_2 departing from V_2 can reach π_2 before π_2 reaches Z. As π_1, pick one of τ_1 or τ_2 that reaches π_2 earlier. Motion π_1 is shown to be collision-free as in the case of a receding obstacle.

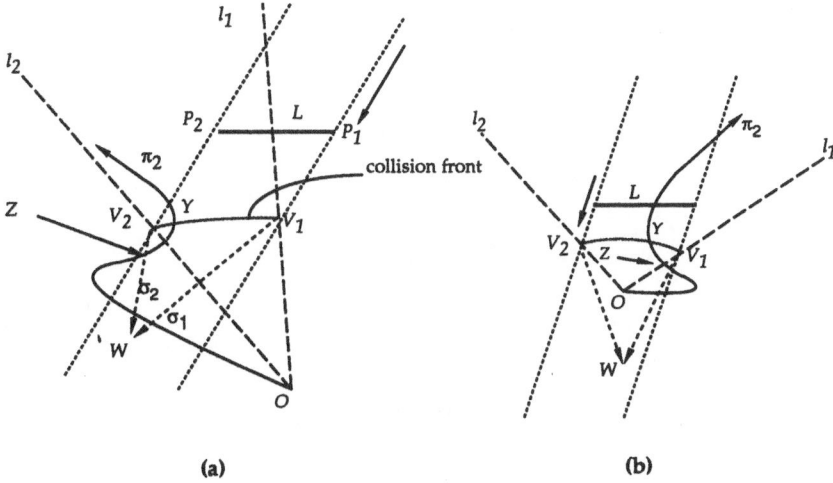

(a)   (b)

Fig. 3.8. A proceeding obstacle for the proof of Proposition 3

Case 3: Receding and proceeding obstacle: (This is a degenerate case.)

Proof: In this case, the collision front is collinear with O. The destination point G must be on the extension of the collision front (otherwise, G is accessible from O). For a sufficiently small ϵ, it is clear that τ_1 or τ_2 will reach π_2 before π_2 reaches G.

Next, we consider the case that there is more than one collision front generated at O. If there are n collision fronts, then there are at most n regions designated as B. Let us use B_i to denote such a region behind collision front CF_i (Fig. 3.9). There are at most $2n$ choices for motion π_1—two for each collision front. For each of the collision fronts, CF_i, there is a range of speed values $[v_{max} - \epsilon_i, v_{max})$ such that the corresponding motion π_{1i} joins motion π_2 at point J_i. Pick a value of the speed v_ϵ such that v_ϵ is in each of $[v_{max} - \epsilon_i, v_{max})$. Choose a motion π_{1i} such that J_i is reached at the earliest time of all J's. Now we must show that this motion is collision-free. Suppose that it is not. In this case, the obstacle intercepting π_{1i} must come from some B_j region $(j \neq i)$. Then, it can be shown that a motion π_{1j} (a candidate for π_1 departing from an endpoint of CF_j) will join motion π_2 at an earlier time by applying Proposition 2 twice. In Fig. 3.9, let Z be a point at which C crosses the boundary between A and B_j, let V_j be an endpoint of collision front CF_j. Applying Proposition 2 on $V_j Z X$ and $V_j X J_i$, we can construct a motion that reaches J_i before π_{1i}. This means that π_{1j} can reach π_2 earlier than π_{1i} (i.e., J_j occurs before J_i along π_2), which contradicts the choice of π_1. $\diamond$

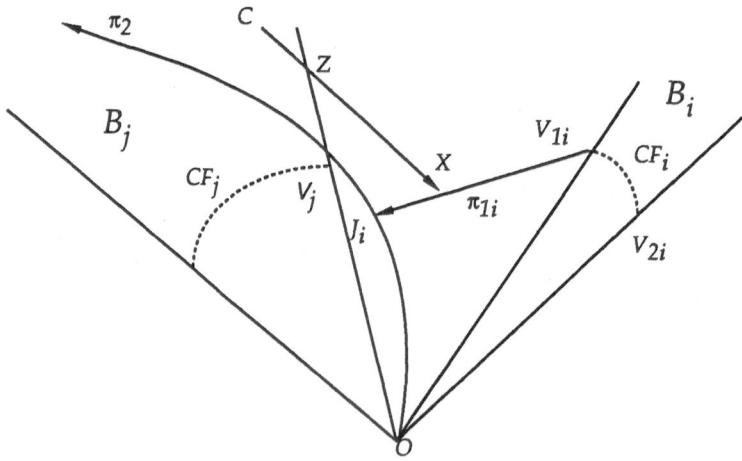

Fig. 3.9. Multiple collision fronts

Theorem (Time-Minimal Motion): A time-minimal motion is given as a sequence of edges of $AG(M, O, G, t_0, v_{\max})$.

As a result of this theorem, point robot R moves at the maximum speed along a time-minimal motion. In other words, if a motion contains some portion during which R moves at a slower speed, then that motion is not time-minimal. We prove the theorem by induction on n, the total number of movements in the given environment.

Proof: (Base Step): In the base case (i.e., $n = 0$) G is accessible from O, the start point, since there are no obstacles (stationary or moving) in the scene. Recall that we treat stationary obstacles as obstacles with zero velocity. Thus, G's accessible point, X, is in $AVS(M, O, t_0, v_{\max})$, and the procedure terminates with motion OX along which R moves at $v_{\max}$. Now we show that this motion OX is time-minimal. Suppose that it is not. Let γ be a time-minimal motion and Y be the point at which R reaches G. Motion γ can be extended to point X such that R is always coincident with G from Y to X. Now, there are two motions from O to X, i.e., OX and γ plus its extension, both of which reach X at the same time. This is a contradiction since R moves at $v_{\max}$ along straight line OX.

(Inductive step): Next, we consider an environment that contains n movements. We assume that the theorem holds for an environment with $n - 1$ movements. If G is accessible from O, then the theorem obviously holds as in the case of $n = 0$. Therefore, assume that G is not accessible from O. The theorem follows from the following two properties proved below. Let V be a point in $AVS(M, O, t_0, v_{\max})$.

Property 1: A time-minimal motion from V to G in M consists of a sequence of edges in $AG(M, V, G, t(V), v_{\max})$.

Property 2: For any motion in Group 2, a better motion in Group 1 exists. Thus a motion in Group 2 is never time-minimal.

(Proof of Property 1): Let V be the accessible point (from O) of a vertex in movement M_i. Note that at time $t(V)$, R is on a vertex of some polygon. Suppose that L_i and L_j are the two edges that are incident on the vertex. We remove L_i and L_j from the polygon and introduce a new edge L_k that connects the two endpoints of L_i and L_j that are not incident at the vertex. This results in a polygon that has one less edge than before. By the induction hypothesis, a time-minimal motion γ exists from V to G in $M - \{M_i, M_j\} + \{M_k\}$, consisting of the edges of $AG(M - \{M_i, M_j\} + \{M_k\}, V, G, t(V), v_{\max})$, where M_i, M_j, and M_k are the movements of L_i, L_j, and L_k, respectively. We show that this motion γ is also collision-free in M. In other words, γ does not collide with M_i or M_j.

Assume that γ collides with M_i. Since R is located at V, we can use Proposition 1 to construct a motion γ' in M that terminates at G at the same time as γ in $M - \{M_i, M_j\} + \{M_k\}$. In case M_i is a single edge, then Proposition 1' is applied and $M - \{M_i\}$ is used in place of $M - \{M_i, M_j\} + \{M_k\}$ in the following argument. Motion γ' must be one of the time-minimal motions from V to G in $M - \{M_i, M_j\} + \{M_k\}$, as it terminates at G at the same time as γ. However, γ' contains a path segment along which R moves at a slower speed than $v_{\max}$ (as noted in the proof of Proposition 1). Therefore, by the induction hypothesis, γ' cannot be a time-minimal motion from V to G in $M - \{M_i, M_j\} + \{M_k\}$. Since γ and γ' terminate at G at the same time, γ is also not a time-minimal motion, which is a contradiction (recall our initial assumption was that γ is time-minimal). Thus, motion γ does not collide with M_i and is a collision-free time-minimal motion from V to G in M as well. This can be seen by noting that if a collision-free motion is time-minimal in $M - \{M_i, M_j\} + \{M_k\}$, then it is also time-minimal in M.

Let π be a motion from V to G in M that contains a segment during which R moves at a speed less than $v_{\max}$. We now show that π will terminate at G at a time later than γ. By the induction hypothesis, in $M - \{M_i, M_j\} + \{M_k\}$, π terminates at G later than γ. Since γ is also a motion in M, as we showed above, π terminates at G later than γ in M, and thus π is not time-minimal in M. Thus our first property has been proved.

(Proof of Property 2): Assume that there exists a motion α in Group 2. We show that there exists a motion in Group 1 that reaches G earlier than α. Let β be a motion from O to G constructed in the following manner. After leaving O at time t_0, β moves to one of the vertices in $AVS(M, O, t_0, v_{\max})$ (let us call this vertex V) at speed $v_{\max}$, and then turns to rejoin motion α at a speed v less than $v_{\max}$. Proposition 3 assures that this rendezvous is possible. After rejoining α, the remaining parts of motion β are identical to motion α, and β terminates at G at the same time as α. On the other hand, in every time-minimal motion γ from V to G in M, every motion segment has speed $v_{\max}$, as described in the first property. Since β has a motion segment along which R moves at a slower speed than $v_{\max}$, β is not time-minimal from V to G and β terminates at G later than γ. This implies that we can construct a motion in M that terminates at G earlier than α by concatenating motions β and γ at V. Thus our second property has been proved.

From the first property, we have that the time-minimal motion from V to G consists of edges in $AG(M, V, G, t(V), v_{\max})$, which is a subgraph of $AG(M, O, G, t_0, v_{\max})$. From the second property, a time-minimal motion from O to G must contain edge OV (for some V); this is an edge of $AG(M, O, G, t_0, v_{\max})$. Thus the time-minimal motion is a sequence of edges of $AG(M, O, G, t_0, v_{\max})$.$\Diamond$

3.5 Analysis

We now analyze the time required to generate a collision-free motion using the algorithm described in Section 3.3. First, we show that the shape of the collision front for a single moving segment is either a part of a conic section. Without loss of generality, we consider a line segment L lying parallel to the y-axis. Let (x_0, y_0) be the location of one of L's endpoints at the start time, l be the length of L, v_L be the speed of L, $v_{\max}$ be the speed of the robot, and θ be the angle formed by the direction of the movement and the x-axis (Fig. 3.10). Suppose that a point P at (x_0, Y) in L is accessible from the origin $O(0,0)$ at point A at (x, y). We set the start time t_0 at the origin to be 0. Coordinates x and y must satisfy

$$t(A) = \frac{\sqrt{x^2 + y^2}}{v_{\max}} = \frac{\sqrt{(x - x_0)^2 + (y - Y)^2}}{v_L} \tag{3.1}$$

$$y = (x - x_0)\tan\theta + Y \tag{3.2}$$

$$y_0 \le Y \le y_0 + l \tag{3.3}$$

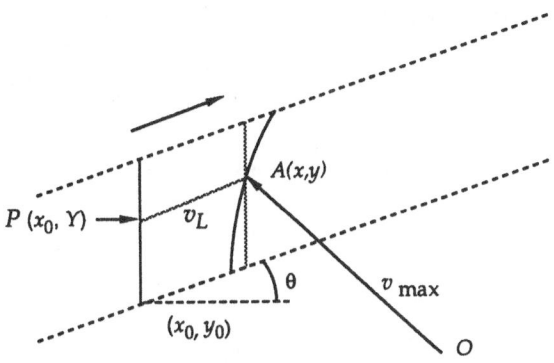

Fig. 3.10. A movement

The points (x, y) that satisfy (3.1) and (3.2) form the collision front. These equations define a quadratic relationship - i.e., the collision front lies either on a parabola, hyperbola, or ellipse. The curve is a hyperbola when $v_{\max} > v_L\cos\theta$, parabola when $v_{\max} = v_L\cos\theta$, and ellipse when $v_{\max} < v_L\cos\theta$, respectively. The curve degenerates to a line segment when the direction of motion is parallel to L or when the initial position of L is collinear with the origin. Also, we can show that the origin is on the same side of the collision front as one of the foci of the curve. Generally, the two endpoints of a collision front (accessible points) can be computed by setting Y to y_0 and $y_0 + l$ in equations (3.1) and (3.2).

Having computed two endpoints of the collision front of a single movement, we must now compute all the endpoints of the collision fronts (AVS) when the robot is at a given start point with a given speed v. For a set of polygonal obstacles with n vertices, there are n candidate points. However, some points may not be accessible from the start point since some other movement may intercept the accessibility of that point. We now show that it takes $O(n\log n)$ time to compute AVS. The set of accessible points is determined by using a similar technique to that used to compute the visibility of a given set of line segments. This is also known as a plane-sweep algorithm (Preparata and Shamos 1985). This is a two-step process. The first pass sorts all the vertices, say in a clockwise direction with respect to O. This sorting process takes $O(n\log n)$ time. The second pass rotates a line about O. It halts each time the line intersects a vertex, and checks whether or not the collision front associated with the vertex is accessible from O. This process can be achieved in $O(\log n)$ time by using a 2-3 tree (Aho, Hopcroft, and Ullman 1974) to maintain the active collision fronts based on their distances from O. In this way, the closest collision front is marked as accessible from O. Since it takes at most $O(n\log n)$ time to build the initial 2-3 tree and $O(\log n)$ time for each update at a vertex, the determination of accessibility of n candidate points takes $O(n \log n)$ time. Therefore, given a start point and a set of candidate points, it takes $O(n \log n)$ time to compute accessible vertices from the start point. Alternately, since no two collision fronts intersect, we can use the approach of Asano *et al* (1986) to find the accessible points in $O(n)$ time after the sorting pass. This gives no asymptotic speedup, but it does avoid the use of 2-3 trees.

At this point, note that as a result of our theorem, a motion that meets with the same vertex of an obstacle more than once is not time-minimal. As there are n vertices in the environment, an *AVS* needs to be generated at most n times before a time-minimal motion reaches the destination point. This observation leads to an asymptotic computation time of $O(n^2 \log n)$ to compute a motion using procedure *PlanMotion*.

Proposition 4. It takes $O(n^2 \log n)$ time to compute a time-minimal motion using procedure *PlanMotion*.

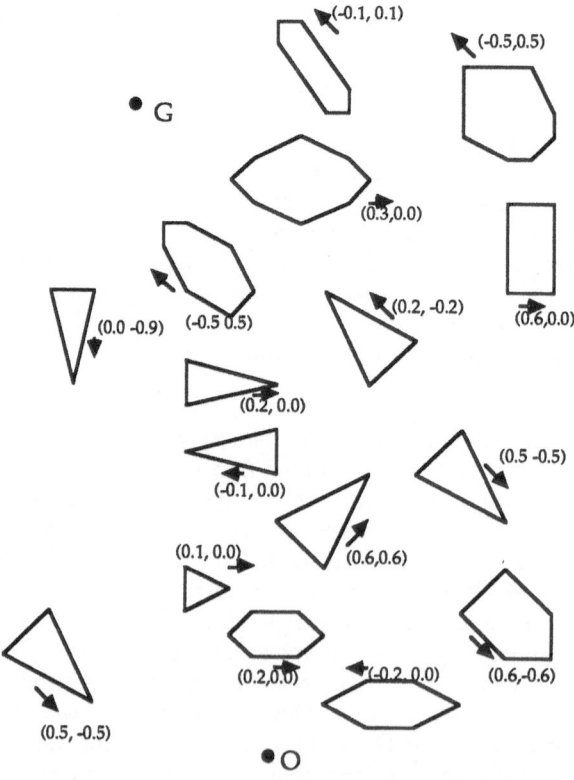

Fig. 3.11. A scene containing 16 moving obstacles ($v_{\max}=1.0$)

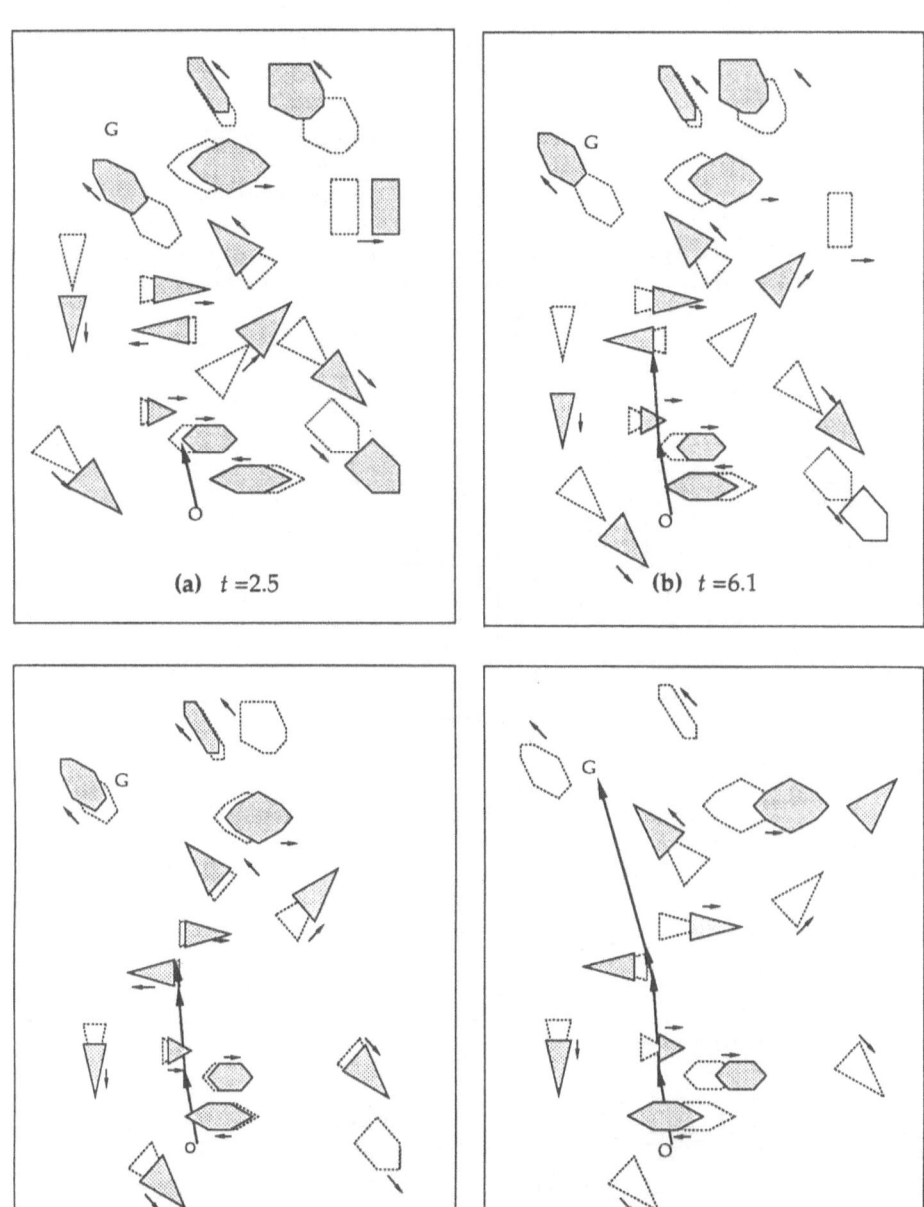

Fig. 3.12. A time-minimal motion

Example. Figure 3.11 shows a scene that contains 16 moving obstacles with a total of 78 vertices. Points O and G are the start and destination points, respectively. Each polygonal obstacle moves in the direction indicated by the arrow near the obstacle at a velocity given in parentheses. In Figs. 3.12a-d, the thick arrows show the motion generated by our algorithm. Hatched obstacles indicate the locations of the obstacles when the point robot is at the end of the thick arrow, and dotted obstacles show the locations of the obstacles from the previous figure. For an environment containing this number of obstacles, it takes about 0.85 seconds to compute a motion using a VAX 11/785. Figure 3.13 contains a maze-like environment where a total of 31 obstacles are moving either towards the right or towards the left. The time-minimal motion generated by *PlanMotion* is shown in Fig. 3.13 a–f.

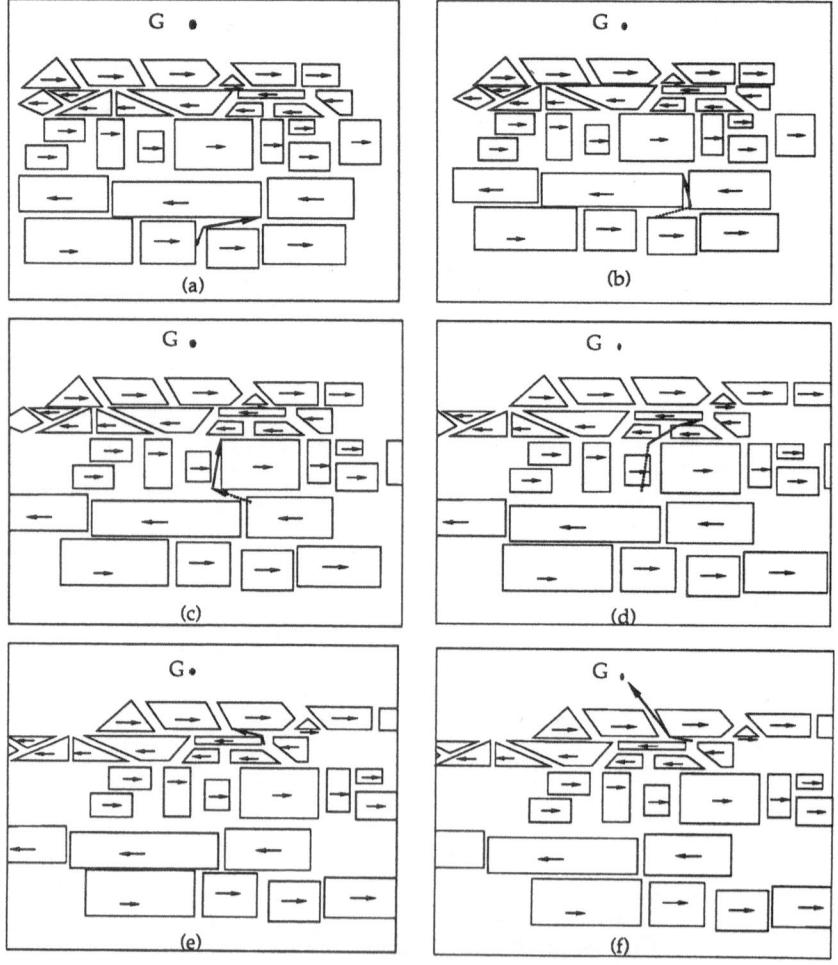

Fig. 3.13. Moving through a time-varying maze

For an environment such as Fig. 3.13 where obstacles' motions are all horizontal, a network of roads could be constructed to embody its structure (Fig. 3.14). In Fig. 3.14, horizontal lines represent corridors between rows of obstacles and vertical and sloped "ladders" represent passages between the corridors. Locations of ladders are time-varying as the obstacles move, while horizontal corridors are fixed. A time-varying graph can be defined such that a vertex of the graph is an intersection of a corridor and a ladder and that an edge exists between two vertices on the same ladder or corridor. A path to the destination point can be searched in the graph in a manner similar to graph search using the accessibility graph. In the time-varying graph, accessibility to a vertex of the graph (rather than a vertex of a polygon) can be used to find a path. Search in this time-varying graph would take less time than search in the accessibility graph as the size of the time-varying graph is smaller than that of the accessibility graph and would generate a similar result. However, it is less straightforward to define such a time-varying graph on a scene such as Fig. 3.12.

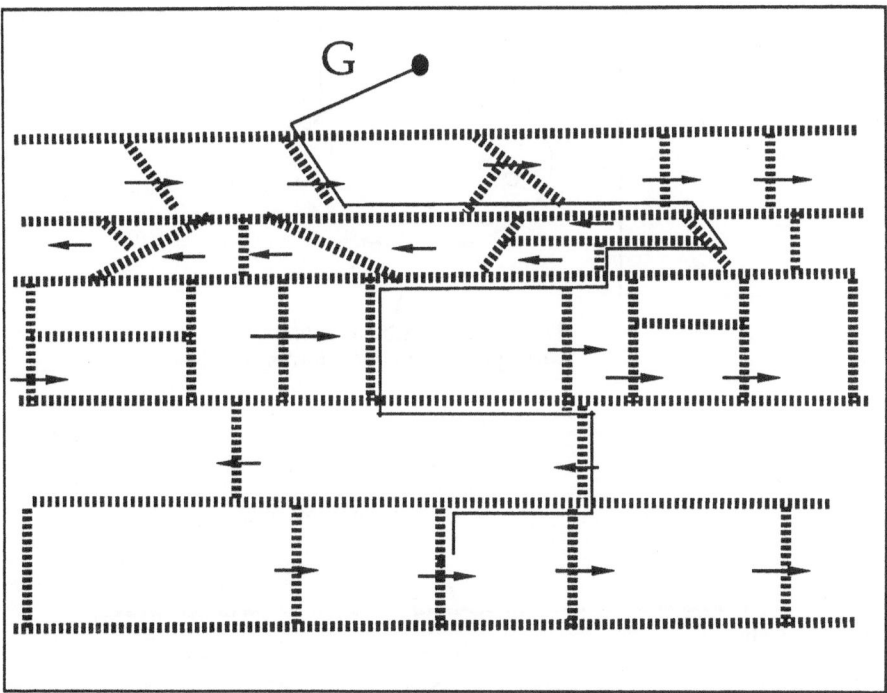

Fig. 3.14. A time-varying graph representing a network of roads
The polygonal arc indicates the same path class as the path in Fig. 3.13.

3.6 Discussions

The property of time-minimality is useful since it provides an exact answer to a decision problem: "Is there a motion to reach the destination point by a given deadline t_{final}?" Also, it is possible to answer the question: "What is the latest starting time for the robot to make a given deadline?" We can consider the environment that has the given deadline as the starting time, the given start point as the destination point, and the same set of obstacles with the reversed moving directions. The arrival time at the destination point (i.e., the original start point) gives the answer. Another related question is: "What is the slowest speed for the robot to depart the start point at a given start time and arrives at the destination point exactly at the given arrival time?" A simple bisection search with respect to speed will be able to find a speed that is arbitrarily close to the desirable slowest speed.

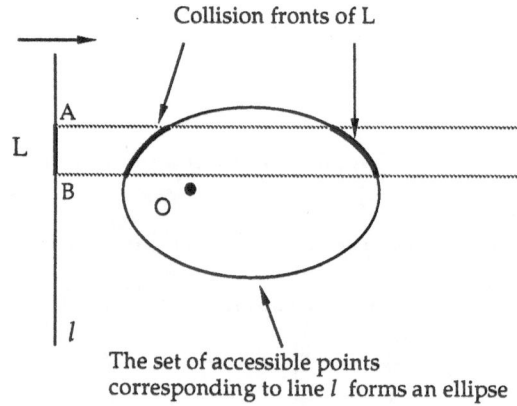

(a) An ellipse

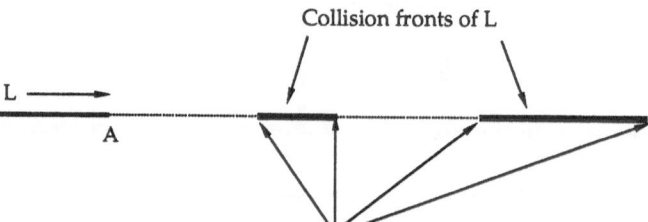

(b) A degenerate case

Fig. 3.15. A fast-moving obstacle

For a point robot to always terminate successfully at the destination point, it is essential that the robot can move faster than any of the obstacles. If some of the obstacles move faster than the robot, procedure *PlanMotion* may not generate a motion. In fact, such a motion may not even exist. This is possible when the robot is right next to an obstacle that is moving toward the robot at a speed much faster than the robot itself. Of course, there are cases where procedure *PlanMotion* can successfully generate a collision-free motion even when the environment contains obstacles that move faster than the robot. When a line segment moves faster than the robot, the line segment gives rise to zero, one, or two collision fronts. This can be seen by observing that the set of accessible points of fast-moving line is in general (a portion of) an ellipse (Fig. 3.15a) or a line in degenerated cases (Fig. 3.15b). (As discussed in Section 4.3, for the destination point, we adopt the one with the younger accessible time as the accessible point.) In such cases, however, the resulting motion that passes through endpoints of collision fronts may not be time-minimal. Nevertheless, we have a few claims for these cases.

Let us call a vertex V of a moving polygon a *critical vertex* with respect to O (a start point of R) and a start time t_0 of R if the following condition is met: R would hit the moving polygon if R were to move in the same direction at a speed infinitesimally smaller than v_{max}. For example, vertex A in Fig. 3.15 is a critical vertex. For the case of slowly-moving obstacles, a vertex V is a critical vertex if V is a leading vertex, i.e., if the ray emanating from O through V at time t_0 is tangent to the polygon and no points of the polygon are to be found when the tangent line is swept in the direction of the motion of the polygon (Fig. 3.16). A trailing vertex of a slowly-moving obstacle is never a critical vertex (Fig. 3.16). The same definition applies to a moving line segment, except for the degenerate case (as in Fig. 3.6c).

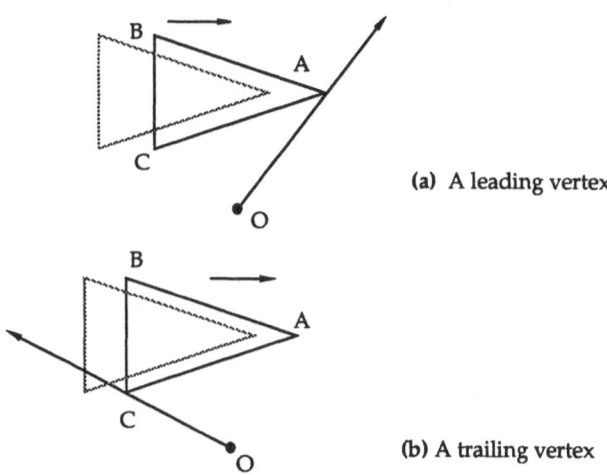

(a) A leading vertex

(b) A trailing vertex

Fig. 3.16. A leading vertex and trailing vertex

Proposition 5. Suupose that *PlanMotion* successfully generates a motion in an environment containing fast-moving obstacles.

(i) If every corner of the resulting motion is either a critical vertex of a fast-moving obstacle or a vertex of a slowly-moving obstacle, then the motion is time-minimal in that homotopic path-class, although the motion may not be globally time-minimal.

(ii) If every corner of the time-minimal motion in every path-class from O to G is a critical vertex of an obstacle, then a time-minimal motion from O to G is a shortest path from O to G.

Proof: (i) Suppose that the generated motion is not time-minimal. Then, there must be a time-minimal motion and the path must be shorter in the same path class. In order for the path to be shorter than the generated motion, it must cross the trajectory of a non-critical vertex of a slowly-moving obstacle at a time later than its accessible time along the generated path. But, this contradicts the Time-Minimal Motion theorem as applied to the path class.

(ii) This claim is easy to see by noting that the motion generated by *PlanMotion* is the shortest of all motions in the same homotopic path-class. For example, when all obstacles are growing (Fig. 3.17), a time-minimal motion is a shortest path. ◊

When a time-minimal motion only visits critical vertices, the motion is shortest in that path-class. However, it may not be a shortest path in a global sense. In general, time-minimal motions are not shortest except for some special cases such as Fig. 3.17.

Procedure *PlanMotion* may not find a motion in an environment containing obstacles that move faster than the robot even when there exists a motion. This is due to the fact that the search space defined by the accessibility graph is not complete when the environment contains obstacles that move faster than the robot. One possible remedy would be to consider the trajectory of a fast-moving obstacle. We divide the accessible portions of the trajectory into a number of non-overlapping strips and regard each strip as time-dependent obstacles. See more discussions in Section 5.3. If the speeds of the obstacles in the environment are equal to that of the robot, and *PlanMotion* generates a motion, then the resulting motion is time-minimal.

From the discussions in this chapter, it follows that *PlanMotion* can be modified to handle polygonal convex obstacles that grow and shrink. An obstacle is said to be *growing* if each vertex V_i's position at time t can be expressed as $c(t-t_0) \cdot \vec{v_i}$, where P is a fixed point inside the obstacle, v_i is a growing vector of V_i, t_0 is a start time, and c is a positive constant representing a growing ratio (See Fig. 3.17). A *shrinking* obstacle can be defined in a similar manner with a negative constant c. (There could be many other ways to define growing and shrinking obstacles.) For the case of shrinking obstacles, the speeds of all vertices must be smaller than $v_{\max}$ to preserve the time-minimal property of the resulting motion. For growing obstacles, each vertex of the polygon is a critical vertex. We also assume that the growing and shrinking obstacles are sufficiently distant from each other so that they do not overlap before the robot reaches the destination point. (Alternately, we could assume that the obstacles grow and shrink alternately. See Section 4.4 for more discussions on such "piecewise linear motions" of the obstacles.)

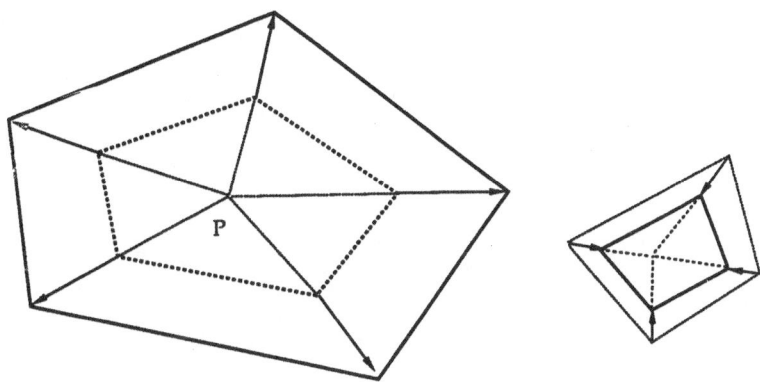

Fig. 3.17. Growing and shrinking obstacles

The time-minimality property for this case can be confirmed by using an argument similar to the one used to prove the Time-Minimal Motion theorem. It can also be confirmed that the theorem holds when the obstacles are growing and shrinking while moving at slow speeds. The concept of growing obstacles may be used to model an obstacle that is moving at an uncertain speed — the area possibly occupied by the obstacle grows as time passes.

The above formulation may be relevant for a ship navigating on the sea where obstacles (e.g., islands) may grow with tide changes. For related work on time-minimal routing problems of a vessel moving in time dependent environments, see (Perakis and Papadakis 1989; Papadakis and Perakis 1990). A related problem of "transient obstacles" (obstacles that exist in the environment only for certain intervals of time) is discussed in detail in Section 5.1. Another generalization is to allow deforming obstacles, that is, a vertex moves in an arbitrary fixed direction (See Fig. 3.18). In this case, the motion of an edge of the obstacle is no longer linear, and its corresponding collision front may have an inflection point. Figure 3.19 is an example of an edge whose endpoints are pulled towards opposite directions. The collision front of the edge is no longer a portion of a quadratic curve and it has an inflection point.

The Time-Minimal Motion theorem can be extended to handle obstacles moving in the plane that is subdivided into regions each of which has its own maximum speed for the robot. Here we have to assume that the robot can move faster than any of the obstacles in each region to preserve the time-minimal property. The proof follows essentially the same pattern as the proof of our theorem. However, it requires to solve the weighted region problem (Mitchell 1988; Rowe and Richbourg 1990) to find the accessible point of a vertex of an obstacle polygon.

While there is much research on shortest paths in static environments, little is known about shortest paths in dynamic environments. When the start point is not intersected by any trajectory (as in Fig. 3.13), the shortest path may be obtained by a straight line motion. Also, it is not known at present how short a time-minimal motion is.

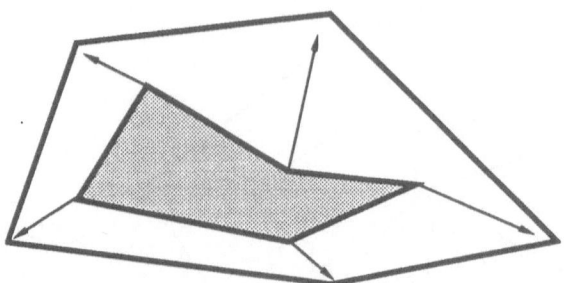

Fig. 3.18. A deforming obstacle

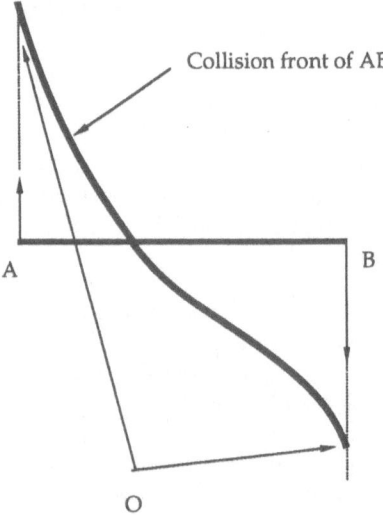

Fig. 3.19. A collision front with an inflection point

If the obstacles are permitted to touch each other, then the solution to the problem may call for some modification depending on whether or not the point robot may move through between two obstacles that are in contact. If the point robot is allowed to move through contact points, then no modification is necessary to our solution. If the point robot is allowed to be on a contact point but not allowed to move through it, then the point robot may have to wait until the two obstacles in contact separate (Fig. 3.20) before it can move through between them. Such an instance can be modelled as a splitting obstacle (Fig. 3.21) and splitting points can be used as a (moving) subgoal. Motion planning amidst splitting and merging obstacles is treated in more detail in Section 4.6.

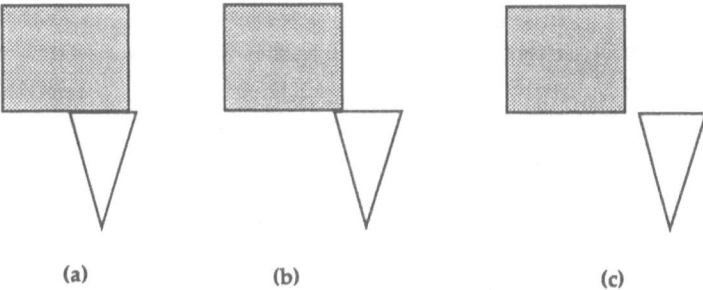

Fig. 3.20. Obstacles in contact

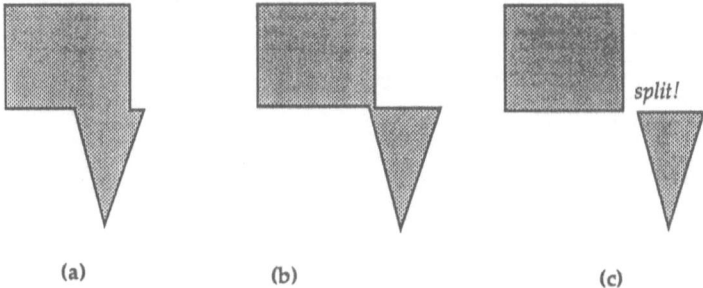

Fig. 3.21. A splitting obstacle

3.7 Summary

We have studied the problem of moving a point robot among a set of obstacles moving at constant velocities in the plane. We have discussed the case where the robot can move faster than any of the obstacles and the destination point. Making use of the concept of accessibility, we have demonstrated an $O(n^2 \log n)$ algorithm to find a motion, and proved that a time-minimal motion is a sequence of edges in the graph. It is known that in a stationary environment the shortest path is a sequence of edges in the visibility graph. In this sense, the accessibility graph is a logical extension of the visibility graph.

Our theorem (Time-Minimal Motion) implies that when dealing with slowly-moving obstacles, a point robot must keep moving at its top speed in order to reach the destination point at the earliest time, i.e., it will never pay to decelerate or wait for an obstacle to pass by. This may seem counter-intuitive, since we can sometimes avoid moving obstacles by decelerating to let them pass by first. Four factors may account for this discrepancy. First, our robot is a point, while a real moving object is not a point. Second, our robot is subject only to a speed bound, while a real moving object is usually subject to an acceleration bound as well. Third, humans sometimes prefer to take a safer motion rather than a fast but dangerous motion. Fourth, our robot can move faster than any of the obstacles, while in a real world some obstacles may move faster than the robot. If these factors are taken into account, a different strategy may result. Some of these ideas will be discussed further in the following chapters.

Chapter 4
Time-Minimal Motion: Applications

We have shown some basic properties of accessibility in Chap. 3. In this chapter, we describe a number of extensions and applications that make use of the concept of accessibility. Some results can be derived using the Time-Minimal Motion theorem proved in Chap. 3 by making some modifications to, or observations about, Propositions 1 and 3. For example, we show that some speedup is possible for the case in which all the obstacles are convex. Also, we further extend the use of accessibility to deal with more complex classes of dynamic environments. They involve time-minimal motion when the destination point can move faster than the robot, motion planning in the presence of obstacles that have piecewise linear motions, motion planning in the environment that contains rotating obstacles, motion planning among obstacles that split and merge, etc.

4.1 Concave Obstacles

So far we have assumed that each obstacle is convex. This condition can be relaxed to allow concave obstacles. In other words, when procedure *PlanMotion* is executed in an environment that contains concave obstacles as well as convex obstacles, the resulting motion is still time-minimal. This can be confirmed by noting that a concave polygon can be decomposed into convex polygons. A concave obstacle is thought of as comprising of a collection of separating convex obstacles whose split times (Section 4.6) are set to infinity. Thus, a point robot never moves along edges inside a concave polygon. It follows that in this case also, a time-minimal motion does not contain a motion segment along which the robot moves at a speed less than v_{max}.

Next, we show that a time-minimal motion never visits a concave vertex. Suppose that a motion α visits a concave vertex, say V (Fig. 4.1a). We construct an alternative motion α' by modifying part of motion α near the concave corner V such that motion α' does not visit V. Let P be a point on α before α passes V, and let Q be a point on α after α passes V. Motion α' is constructed by substituting a straight motion PQ for part PVQ of motion α. The rest of motion α' is identical with motion α. Note that between P and Q of motion α', the speed is less than the maximum speed of the robot, since PQ is a straight line segment.

We can make part PQ of motion α' collision-free by choosing both P and Q to be sufficiently close to vertex V. Since no two obstacles touch, there must be a minimum clearance distance between any two obstacles, say δ. Take both P and Q within distance

δ from V. Then the entire straight motion PQ is within distance δ from V and is thus collision-free. To see this, let C be the location of the concave vertex V when motion α passes V. Let A and B be the locations of V when α passes P and Q, respectively. Let δ_1 and δ_2 be the lengths of AP and BQ, respectively, where $\delta_1, \delta_2 \leq \delta$ (Fig. 4.1b). Note that V moves from A to B at a constant speed while α' moves from P to Q at a constant speed. It is simple to show that the moving point on α' is always found within distance δ from V on AB. Thus motion segment PQ is collision-free.

Using this modification, we can convert any motion, say α, that visits concave vertices into a motion, say α', that does not visit any of the concave vertices and that arrives at the destination point at the same time as α. By the Time-Minimal Motion theorem, no motion that contains a segment along which the speed is less than $v_{\max}$ is time-minimal. It follows that any motion that visits concave vertices is never time-minimal. Thus, we have obtained the following result:

Proposition 6. Procedure *PlanMotion* generates a time-minimal motion even when some of the moving obstacles are concave, and a time-minimal motion does not visit concave vertices.

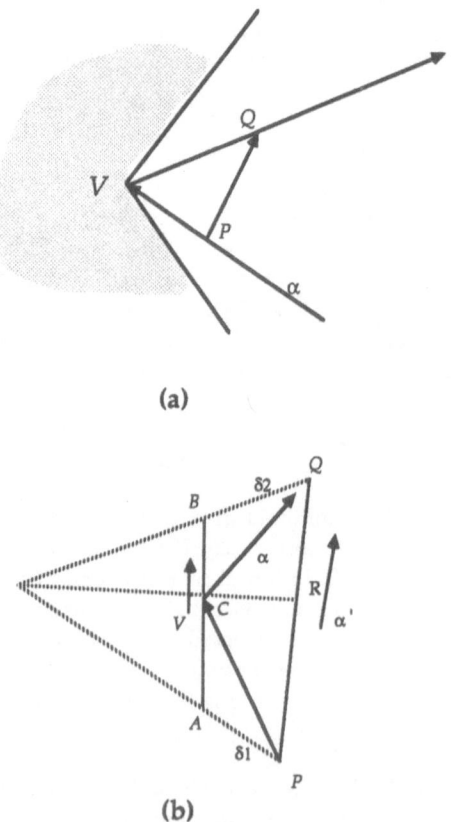

(a)

(b)

Fig. 4.1. A non-convex vertex (shaded)

4.2 Convex Obstacles

4.2.1 Convex polygonal obstacles

In Section 3.5, we obtained a time complexity of $O(n^2 \log n)$ for computing a time-minimal motion. When all the obstacles are convex, this complexity can be improved. A vertex V of a polygon P is called an *extremal visible vertex* from O, if the ray emanating from O through V is tangent to P (see Fig. 4.2a). A vertex V of a possibly-moving polygon P is called an *extremal accessible vertex* from O, if the ray emanating from O through the accessible point of V is tangent to the set of accessible points of all points on P generated at O. The following proposition relates visibility and accessibility and is useful in computing extremal accessible vertices of a slowly moving convex polygon.

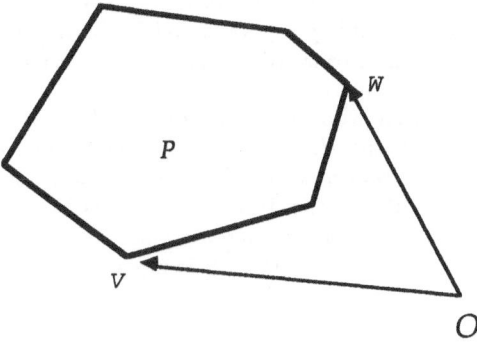

(a)   V and W are extremal vertices from O.

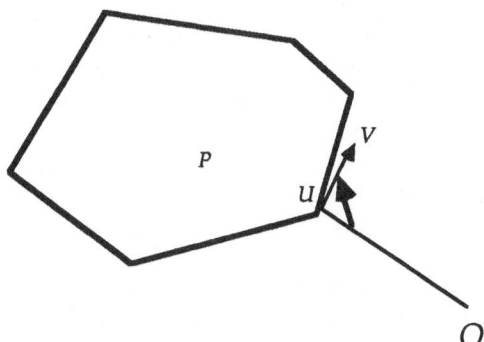

(b)   A shortcut is indicated as a thick line.

Fig. 4.2. A concave obstacle

Proposition 7. Let P be a convex polygon that starts moving at time t_0 and let R be a point robot that starts moving at time t_0 from O. Let O be outside of P at time t_0. Let P be the only obstacle in the environment. Suppose that R moves faster than P.

(i) A point V on P is accessible from O by R, if and only if V is visible from O at time t_0.

(ii) Let V_1 and V_2 be the two extremal visible vertices of P from O. Let V_1' and V_2' be the accessible points of V_1 and V_2, respectively. Then, V_1' and V_2' are the two extremal accessible vertices of P from O.

Proof: Property (ii) can be shown by noting that the collision front is a portion of either a line or hyperbolic curve and that O is in the same side as one of the foci of the curve. For any pair of vertices of P, say A and B, the angular order (say, in a counter clockwise direction) of the accessible points of A and B about O along the collision front of AB is the same as the angular order of A and B about O along line segment AB.

   Property (i) is proved by showing that V is not accessible from O if and only if V is not visible from O. If a point, say B, on P is not visible from O at time t_0, then there must be a point, say A, on P that is visible from O at time t_0. Note that O, A, and B are collinear. Recalling that this is the degenerate case of the collision front discussed in Section 3.4 (see Fig. 3.6c), O, the accessible point of A, and the accessible point of B are also collinear in this order. Therefore, B is not accessible from O. The converse is similar. $\Diamond$

   Observe that a time-minimal motion visits only extremal accessible vertices of a polygonal obstacle. If the robot passes a non-extremal accessible vertex, it is always possible to shortcut the motion near the vertex as indicated in Fig. 4.2b. The same argument used to avoid a concave vertex discussed in the previous section applies here. In other words, a motion that passes through a non-extremal accessible vertex is not time-minimal. Therefore, we only need to consider extremal vertices of a polygon when constructing the accessible graph. This means that there are at most $2k$ vertices to be considered at a current point, where k is the number of polygons in the environment. Using the argument in Section 3.5, it takes $O(k \log k)$ time to determine extremal vertices that are accessible from a current point; this gives us the following proposition.

Proposition 8. When all the obstacles are convex, it takes $O(nk \log k)$ time to compute a time-minimal motion, where n and k are the total numbers of vertices and convex polygons, respectively, in the environment.

   When k is considerably smaller than n, this achieves a good speedup. For an environment that contains only stationary convex polygons, Rohnert (1986) shows that it takes $O(k^2 + n \log n)$ time to find a shortest path between two arbitrary points with an $O(n + k^2 \log n)$ preprocessing time. He determines all the support lines between any two convex polygons. A support line is a line that is tangent to both polygons. This technique does not seem to be useful for moving obstacles, since support lines between two obstacles change as the obstacles move.

4.2.2 Circular obstacles

Parker (1988) considers motion planning among moving circles. She computes points on a circle, called tangent points, at which the point robot tangentially meets the circle when the robot moves along a straight line. These points correspond to extremal accessible points of the circle in our definition. After the robot reaches a tangent point, the motion is extended along the straight line until the robot clears the obstacle. This extension is necessary in order to avoid collision with an obstacle that moves faster than the robot. This process is repeated until the destination point is reached.

When the robot can move faster than any of the circular obstacles, it is possible for the robot to follow the border of a circular obstacle. Then, the robot can alternate between two kinds of motions — a border following motion and a straight-line motion that leaves and meets obstacles tangentially. The resulting motion resembles the motion that would be used by the robot when the accessibility approach is extended to circular obstacles. In fact, when a circle is approximated by an n-gon with a large n, the type of motion described above will be produced by procedure *PlanMotion*. A time-minimal motion for circular obstacles is obtained by a limiting process in which n tends to infinity. It is simple to compute extremal accessible points of a circular obstacle as they correspond to extremal visible points of a circle as can be deduced from Proposition 7 (Fig.4.3). However, it seems more complex to find a tangent point exactly on a circle at which the robot leaves the circle.

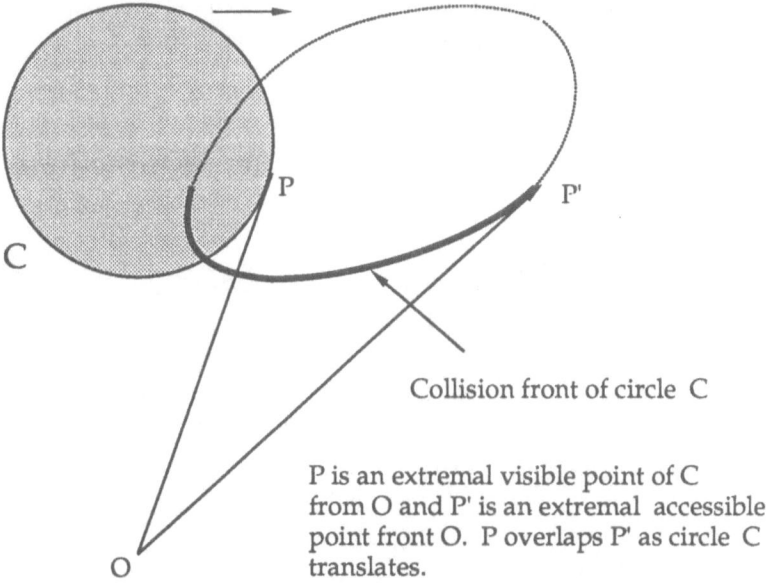

Collision front of circle C

P is an extremal visible point of C from O and P' is an extremal accessible point front O. P overlaps P' as circle C translates.

Fig. 4.3. Accessible points of a circular obstacle

4.3 Start Point and Destination Point

Previously, the robot always starts from a given point at a given time and the destination point was defined to move at a fixed speed less than v_{max}. In the following sections, we relax some of these restrictions and show that the Time-Minimal Motion theorem still holds.

4.3.1 Fast moving destination point

When the destination point moves faster than the robot, it is possible that the robot will not be able to reach the destination point. This gives rise to a decision problem: given an environment and a destination point in motion, determine if it it possible to reach the destination point. We show that this decision problem can be solved by applying procedure *PlanMotion*. If all vertices in the scene have been visited before the destination point is reached, then the procedure reports that it is not possible to reach the destination point. To correctly conclude that the destination point is unreachable, the base case of the main proof of the theorem (Section 3.4) needs to be revised so as to handle a fast moving destination point. Note that this is the only part of the proof (besides a part of Proposition 3 which has been already taken care of in page 40) that involves the motion of the destination point.

The following is a revision of the base case of the proof. Suppose that there are no obstacles (stationary or moving) in the scene. Let v_G and v_R be the speeds of the destination point and the robot, respectively. Let I and O be the points at which the destination point and the robot, respectively, are found initially at time t_0. Let X be the point at which the robot meets with the destination point. Since the distance travelled by the robot in a certain time interval is proportional to the speed of the robot, $IX : OX = v_G : v_R$ (where $v_G > v_R$). The set of points that satisfy the above equation with respect to X forms a circle (usually called an Apollonius circle), say C (Fig. 4.4).

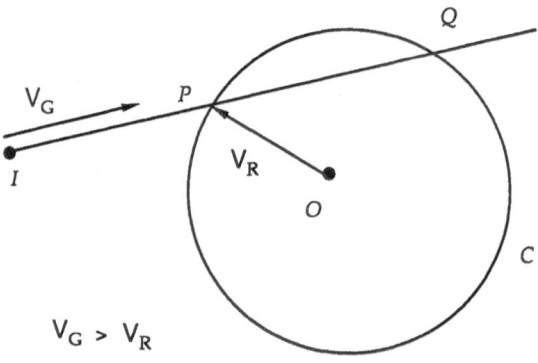

Fig. 4.4. A fast-moving destination point

There are three cases, depending on the number of common points shared by the trajectory of the destination point and the circle C. If the trajectory intersects C twice, say at P and Q, then the robot can reach the destination point at either P or Q (see Fig. 4.4). In this case, we define the one with the younger accessible time to be the accessible point of the destination point. Let P have the younger accessible time. Note that an Apollonius circle with a smaller value of v_R lies inside C. Therefore, a point robot with a lower speed cannot reach the destination point earlier than the accessible time of P. If the trajectory of the destination point is tangential to C, then the destination point is accessible only when the point robot moves in the direction of the tangent point. It should be clear that no other motions can reach the destination point. When the trajectory does not intersect C, it is not possible to reach the destination point. In summary, the motion of the point robot (if there is any) is time-minimal when it moves straight to the destination point.

Thus, we have established that the time-minimal motion is obtained when the robot moves in the direction of the destination point at its maximum speed. Noting that the rest of the proof of the Time-Minimal Motion theorem does not rely on the assumption about the relative speeds of v_R and v_d, we have shown that the theorem also holds for the case in which the destination point moves faster than the robot.

4.3.2 Piecewise linear motion of the destination point

Secondly, we show how to relax our original assumption that the number of steps in a motion of the destination point is bounded. Let n_{goal} be the number of steps made by the destination point (each step of which has a constant moving direction and speed) and n_{obs} be the number of obstacle movements. There is a total of $n_{obs} + n_{goal}$ movements in the scene. Here we are dealing with two kinds of movements – one is distributed over the two-dimensional space and the other is distributed over time. Since the destination point is accessible only at one location (assuming that the robot can move faster than the destination point), the size of the accessible vertex set is $n_{obs} + 1$. However, it takes $O(n_{obs} + n_{goal})$ time to determine the elements of the accessible vertex set. This can be reduced to $O(n_{obs} + \log n_{goal})$ time by using a binary search to determine the accessible point for the destination point, assuming the initial data for movements of the destination point is sorted in time. Normally, where $n_{goal} < (n_{obs})^c$ (for some constant c), this does not affect the total computation time of $O(n^2 \log n)$.

4.3.3 Piecewise continuous motion of the destination point

We have assumed up to now that the destination point always has continuous motion. Here, we consider the more general problem in which the destination point is piecewise continuous, i.e., the destination point may jump from one place to another, or it may even be non-existent for some time interval. This happens, for example, when the destination point is temporarily covered by the obstacles. The robot is required to reach the destination point when it is not covered by any of the obstacles.

First, we consider the restriction that the destination point must be reached within a given time interval. This problem can be readily solved by applying the Time-Minimal

Motion theorem. Procedure *PlanMotion* is run to see if the arrival time lies within the given time interval.

Second, we consider the point of the obstacle edge at which the destination point exits (or the point at which the destination point reappears). While the destination point is covered by an obstacle, we treat the exit point, say E, as the destination point. If it is possible to reach E, the robot just waits at E, while moving together with E, until the destination point exits from E. Of course, after it exits from E, the destination point itself is the point to be reached until it is again covered by another obstacle.

4.3.4 Disjoint start points

We have so far assumed that we are given a single start point and start time. A more general problem is that of determining a minimal time motion, given k disjoint start points, each with its own start time. We wish to determine the start point from which the robot arrives at the destination point at the earliest time.

We compute accessible vertices for each of the given start points and start times. When a vertex of a polygon is accessible at different times, we take the one with the earliest accessible time and do not consider the rest of the motions. Those motions never arrive at the destination point earlier than the motion with the earliest accessible time. Recall that according to the Time-Minimal Motion theorem, a motion that contains a segment along which the speed is less than the robot's maximum speed is never time-minimal. For this reason, the computation of accessible vertices takes place at each vertex at most once. Therefore, it takes $O((k + n)n \log n)$ time to compute the motion that reaches the destination point at the earliest time.

The same argument applies to determining time-minimal motions from a single start point to k destination points. It takes the same amount of time to compute all the fastest motions to all k points.

4.3.5 Starting from a line segment

We now consider the case that a set of starting points form a line segment and all points on the line segment have an identical start time. In other words, the robot can start any point of a given line segment. For stationary obstacles, Asano, Asano, and Imai (1987) consider a related problem of finding a shortest path between two disjoint simple polygons in the plane. As in the case of stationary obstacles, a time-minimal motion departing from an internal point of the segment begins with a motion segment that is perpendicular to the start line segment; for otherwise it is always possible to shortcut the motion. For example, suppose that vertex V is accessible from P on the start segment and that PV is not perpendicular to the segment. Then, V is accessible from P' at an earlier time, where P'V is perpendicular to the segment (Fig.4.5). The rest of the computation is the same as *PlanMotion*. We have more discussions on this issue in Section 5.1.

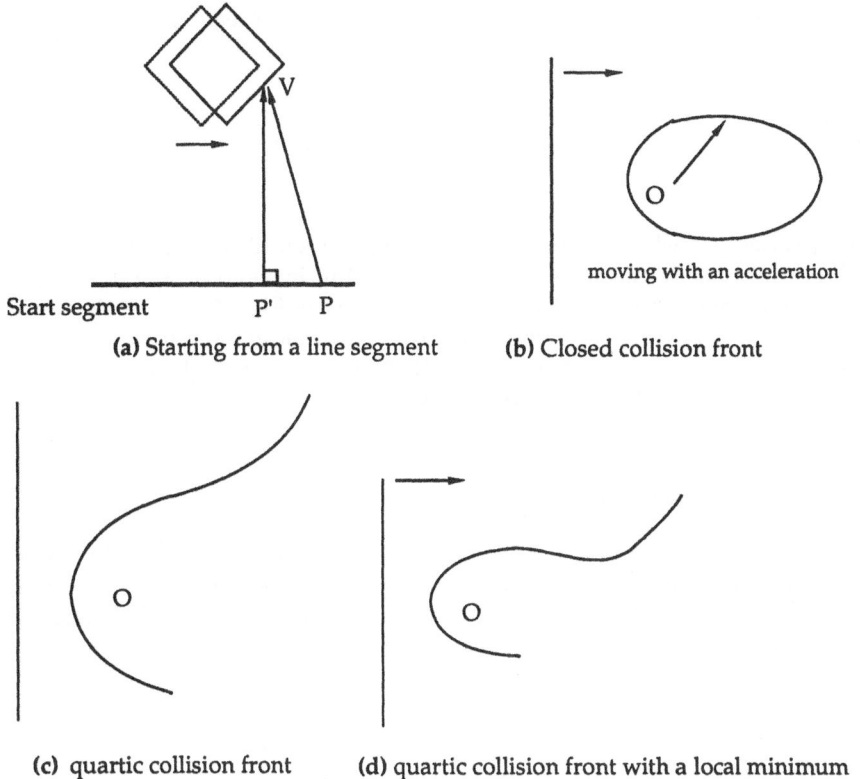

Start segment   P'   P

(a) Starting from a line segment   **(b)** Closed collision front

moving with an acceleration

(c) quartic collision front   **(d)** quartic collision front with a local minimum

Fig. 4.5. Various shapes of collision fronts

4.3.6 Starting with an acceleration

We have so far assumed that the robot has a certain speed when it departs from the start point. We now consider the case that the robot starts moving at speed zero and keeps accelerating at a constant rate until it reaches a certain speed. Earlier discussions on the collision front generalizes to this case. However, the collision front is no longer a portion of a conic section.

Let m be a line parallel to the y-axis moving at speed v in the positive x-direction. Suppose m is initially found at $x = x_0$ at time $t = 0$. Let $A(x, y)$ be an accessible point of a point on m from the origin. Assuming that R can reach A before R reaches its maximum speed, x and y must satisfy the following equations:

$$\frac{1}{2}\alpha t^2 = \sqrt{x^2 + y^2}$$

$$\frac{x - x_0}{v} = t$$

where α is the acceleration of R. Eliminating t, we have

$$\left(\frac{\alpha}{2}\left(\frac{x - x_0}{v}\right)^2\right)^2 = x^2 + y^2.$$

When R attains its top speed before it reaches P, the first equation must be replaced by

$$1/2\alpha t_1^2 + v_{\max}(t - t_1) = \sqrt{x^2 + y^2}$$

where t_1 is the time when R attains the maximum speed. The resulting curve is quartic and it can take one of the three shapes illustrated in Fig.4.5b, c, and d, depending on the value of α relative to v. A closed collision front as in Fig.4.5b means that line m will hit R before R accelerates to a speed fast enough to move away from m. The shapes of the curves in Fig. 4.5c and d indicate that an endpoint of the collision front may correspond to an internal point of the line segment.

4.4 Piecewise Linear Motion of the Obstacles

A straight-line motion may not be sufficient to describe the motion of the obstacles. A somewhat more general description is a piecewise linear motion — i.e., the motion consists of a finite number of time intervals during each of which the obstacle moves in a fixed direction with a constant speed. Intuitively, such an obstacle has a zig-zag motion.

4.4.1 Extension

It is simple to extend the concept of accessibility to this situation. We can define a movement for line-segment L as (L, d_L, v_L, TI_L), where TI_L represents the time interval during which L moves in direction d_L at speed v_L. When the motion of the obstacle is piecewise linear, the collision front becomes a finite set of connected segments of quadratic curves. Note that points where two curves meet may now correspond to an internal point of L. Let us use the term *internal accessible point* to denote such an accessible point. Internal accessible points are also used to define vertices in the accessibility graph. Note that at the instant at which the robot arrives at an internal accessible point, the number of movements to be considered in the environment decreases by one.

Example. Figure 4.6 contains an example. Edge L moves in direction d_1 until it overlaps CD, after which it moves in direction d_2 (Fig. 4.6a). Points A and B are the locations of vertices V_1 and V_2, respectively, when L starts moving. Point P is the accessible point of vertex V_1 (Fig. 4.6b). Point Q would have been the accessible point of vertex V_2, if L did not change its direction when it overlapped CD. The collision front corresponding to the movement of L from AB to CD is indicated by curve segment PX (indicated as a thick curve). In this case, P serves as an accessible point as before, while Q no longer serves as an accessible point. Instead, X is an internal accessible point that is to be a vertex of the accessibility graph. Note that X corresponds to an internal point of L. There may be a collision front corresponding to the movement of L after CD, depending on the direction of the movement (i.e., d_2).

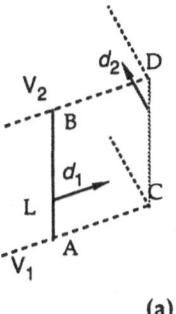

(a)

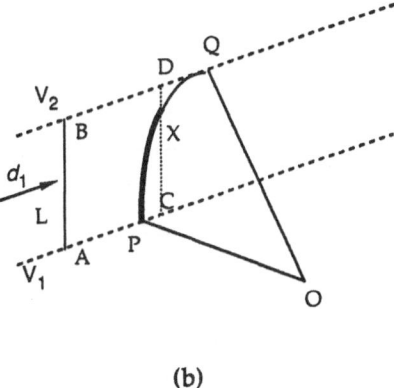

(b)

Fig. 4.6. A piecewise linear motion

4.4.2 Optimality

The time-minimality of the motion defined above can be shown by revising the proof of Proposition 3. In that proof, we used two auxiliary motions, σ_1 and σ_2 (Section 3.4). Those motions are such that a point moving along them is always coincident with a point on the obstacle. When an obstacle has piecewise linear motions, these auxiliary motions are also piecewise linear. Figure 4.7 illustrates such a situation. In Fig. 4.7a, L moves in direction d_1. The line segment L changes its direction of motion when L overlaps AB. P and Q are the accessible points of V_1 and V_2, respectively. Figure 4.7b shows the auxiliary motions, σ_1 and σ_2.

A motion τ_1 (or τ_2) is now defined as follows: τ_1 (τ_2) is identical to motion σ_1 (σ_2) until π_2 becomes accessible. This happens when the obstacle changes its direction. After π_2 becomes accessible, τ_1 (τ_2) moves in the direction of π_2. It can be shown that τ_1 (τ_2) is collision-free in a manner similar to the proof of Proposition 3.

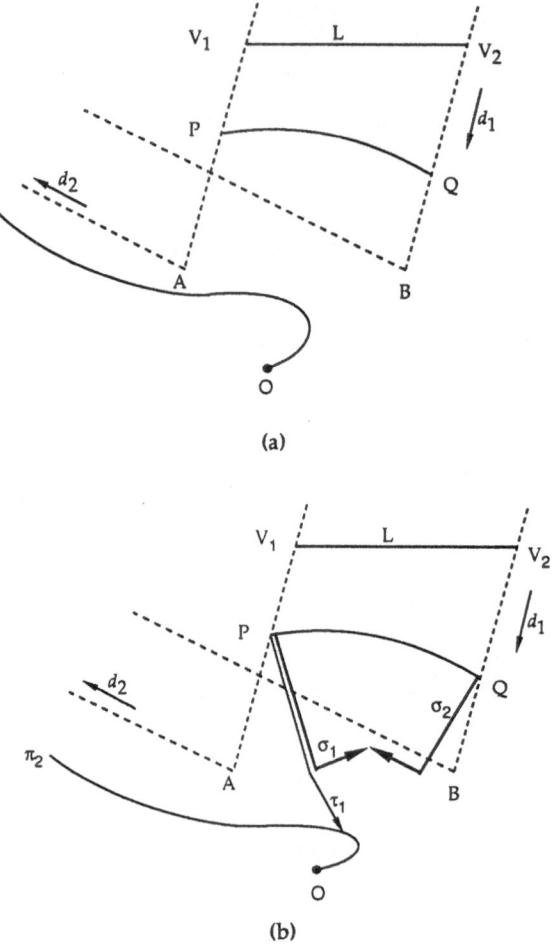

Fig. 4.7. Auxiliary motions

4.4.3 Complexity

We now discuss the time complexity of motion planning with piecewise linear movements of obstacles. Let n be the number of edges in the environment and let m_i be the number of movements made by edge L_i. Then the total number of movements in the environment is $m_1 + m_2 + \cdots + m_n$. Let $m = \frac{m_1 + \cdots + m_n}{n}$, the average number of turns made by the obstacles.

Suppose that we need to determine the accessible point of an edge, say L, from a given current point, say A. Let $M_1, M_2, \cdots,$ and M_p constitute L's movements, i.e., L has p movements in its lifetime. We wish to know in which movement L is accessible. Note that L is accessible only once from a given current point. If L's movements are given in chronological order, it takes $O(\log p)$ time to determine the movement in which L is accessible by using a binary search. Otherwise, it takes $O(p)$ time.

The above process must be performed for all edges. It takes a total of $O(\log m_1 + \log m_2 + \cdots + \log m_n)$ time, i.e., $O(n \log m)$ time,[1] to compute the accessible points for all edges. Observing that the rest of the process is the same, it takes $O(n(n \log m + n \log n))$ = $O(n^2 \log(mn))$ time to compute a time-minimal motion in such a piecewise linear environment. Thus we have proved

Proposition 9. It takes $O(n^2 \log(mn))$ time to compute a time-minimal motion in an environment containing polygonal moving obstacles that have piecewise linear motions.

4.4.4 Comparison with other approaches

At this point, let us compare our approach with some past work in the field of motion planning among moving obstacles. In particular, we consider how 'fast' the final motion is. Our approach differs from those of Kant and Zucker (1986) and Erdmann and Lozano-Pérez (1987). Lee and Lee (1987) use an approach that is similar to (Kant and Zucker 1986).

Kant and Zucker decompose the process of motion planning into two phases, "where" and "when." (See Section 2.2.2). In the first phase, they determine "where to go", i.e., they plan a path among stationary obstacles. In the second phase, the speed along this path is varied to make the trajectory collision-free with the moving obstacles. Their algorithm becomes inefficient, and may even fail to generate a path, when a part of an obstacle remains coincident with the path determined in the first phase. This is because the path is fixed in the second phase; thus the robot is not allowed to circumnavigate moving obstacles. Also, since the path is fixed in the first phase, their method cannot easily incorporate a moving destination point.

Erdmann and Lozano-Pérez (1987) represent the movements of the obstacles as a set of slices in space-time. These slices represent configuration spaces at particular times. The times are those at which some moving obstacle changes its velocity. A motion consists of a series of motion segments that starts at a vertex of an obstacle in one slice and terminates at a vertex of an obstacle in the next slice. Between two vertices, the moving object (the robot) makes a straight movement with a constant speed. As a result, along a final motion, the point robot changes its velocity only at vertices of the obstacles when some obstacle's velocity changes. Their approach is complete when the topology of the free space does not change (i.e., the obstacles do not merge or split) and requires $O(rn^3)$ time, where n is the total number of edges in the environment and r is the number of slices constructed.

Our approach determines "where" and "when" to go at the same time. As a result, our approach generates a collision-free motion even in situations where the approach of Kant and Zucker fails. A motion generated by our method also consists of straight motion segments, but they do not necessarily terminate at a vertex of an obstacle.

---

[1] $\log \frac{m_1 + \cdots + m_n}{n} \geq \frac{\log m_1 + \cdots + \log m_n}{n}$

Our approach is complete only when the topology of free space does not change. For example, we can imagine a 'gate' on the route to the destination which opens only for a specific short period of time. The planner must be able to generate a path such that the robot arrives at the gate just in time for the opening. In particular, the planner must at least be able to generate a point-wise time-minimal path. We discuss this issue in detail in Section 4.6.

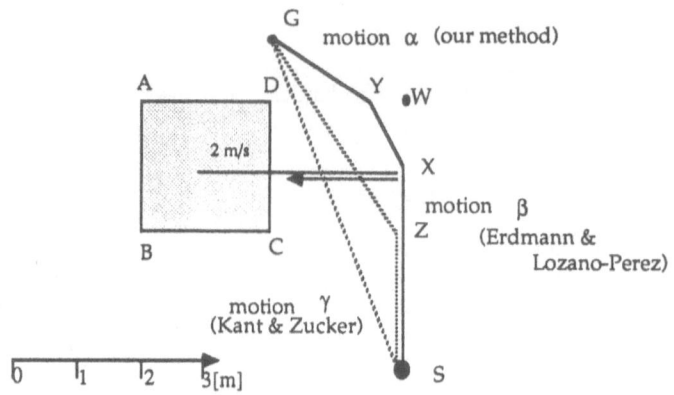

(a) Three motions for a scene containing one moving obstacle.

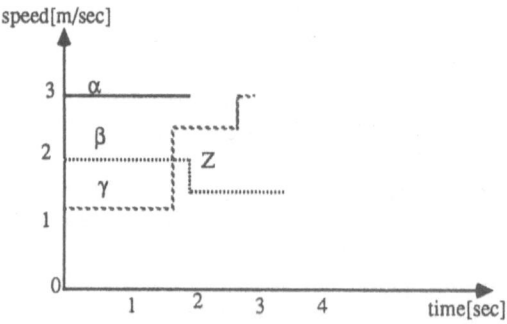

(b) Time-speed profile of the three motions.

Fig. 4.8. Comparison of motions

Example. Figure 4.8a shows how the above three approaches negotiate a moving obstacle. Points S and G represent the start and destination points. Object ABCD is an obstacle of size 2m by 2m whose initial speed is 2 m/s moving towards the right. Obstacle ABCD changes its direction of motion towards the left when its right edge reaches point X and also reduces its speed to 1 m/s. Three motions which are the outputs of the above mentioned approaches are illustrated. We impose a speed limit of 3 m/s on the robot. Motion α is the one planned by our algorithm. Motion β is generated by vertex-to-vertex transitions as implemented by Erdmann and Lozano-Pérez. The first vertex-to-vertex transition can be either S to C at Z or S to D at W. The latter possibility is eliminated because of the speed bound. Motion γ would be generated using Kant and Zucker's approach. It is a straight line, since there are no stationary obstacles in the scene. The second phase determines the speed along this straight line. Note that along motion γ the robot gains speed after passing vertex C while moving towards the left, and again after passing vertex D. Figure 4.8b is the time-speed profile for these motions. Motions β and γ terminate at the destination later than motion α. This indicates that the motions generated by their corresponding algorithms are, in general, not time-minimal.

4.4.5 Repeated motions

At times, the motion of an obstacle may be defined as a repeated motion. An obstacle starts moving at an initial position P at time t_0, comes back to the initial location P at time $t_0 + \delta$, and repeats the same process again and again. Although this description is finite, the number of movements is infinite (see Fig. 4.9a). In such a case, the determination of the movement in which the obstacle is accessible requires some care. Let a *cycle* be the set of movements made by the obstacle after it leaves P and before it returns to P. We first need to determine the cycle in which the obstacle is accessible. This can be done by estimating an accessible time of location P. We then need to check the cycle that contains the estimated accessible time. Therefore, we only need to check at most the number of movements that constitute one cycle to determine where the obstacle is accessible.

Another related dynamic problem is one in which the motions of the obstacles are described by procedures. For example, we can define a motion of an obstacle by a command like the ones used in turtle geometry (Abelson and diSerra 1982), such as "move in direction X at Y m/s for Z seconds, then move in direction X+x at Y+y m/s for Z+z seconds, and repeat the process." If a latest time by which the robot is to reach the destination point is specified, then the number of movements to be considered becomes finite, thus making the problem solvable. Otherwise, analysis of the problem is complex except for cases in which the motion of the obstacle makes some special pattern. For example, in Fig. 4.9b, the motion of vertex V is characterized by the discrete step made by every fourth turn of V. We call such a motion as a *characteristic motion* of a point. If it is possible to find a meeting point of the characteristic motion, then the meeting point of the point itself can be easily located.

Yet another variant is the case that the obstacle is composed of several overlapping obstacles each of which has its own piecewise linear cyclic motion. Figure 4.9c contains an example where an edge intersects at most one other edge of the composed obstacle. As long as connectivity between parts does not change as they move, our method can be extended to handle this type of composed obstacles. We discuss the case of splitting and merging obstacles in Section 4.6. Figure 4.9d is an example of a conveyor along which one can move faster or slower depending on the direction of motion. Figure 4.9e contains a case in which one must cross a river. In such cases, we need to determine the entry and exit points to and from the obstacle. Optimization of the path amidst such obstacles is discussed in terms of the weighted region problem (Mitchell and Papadimitriou 1990).

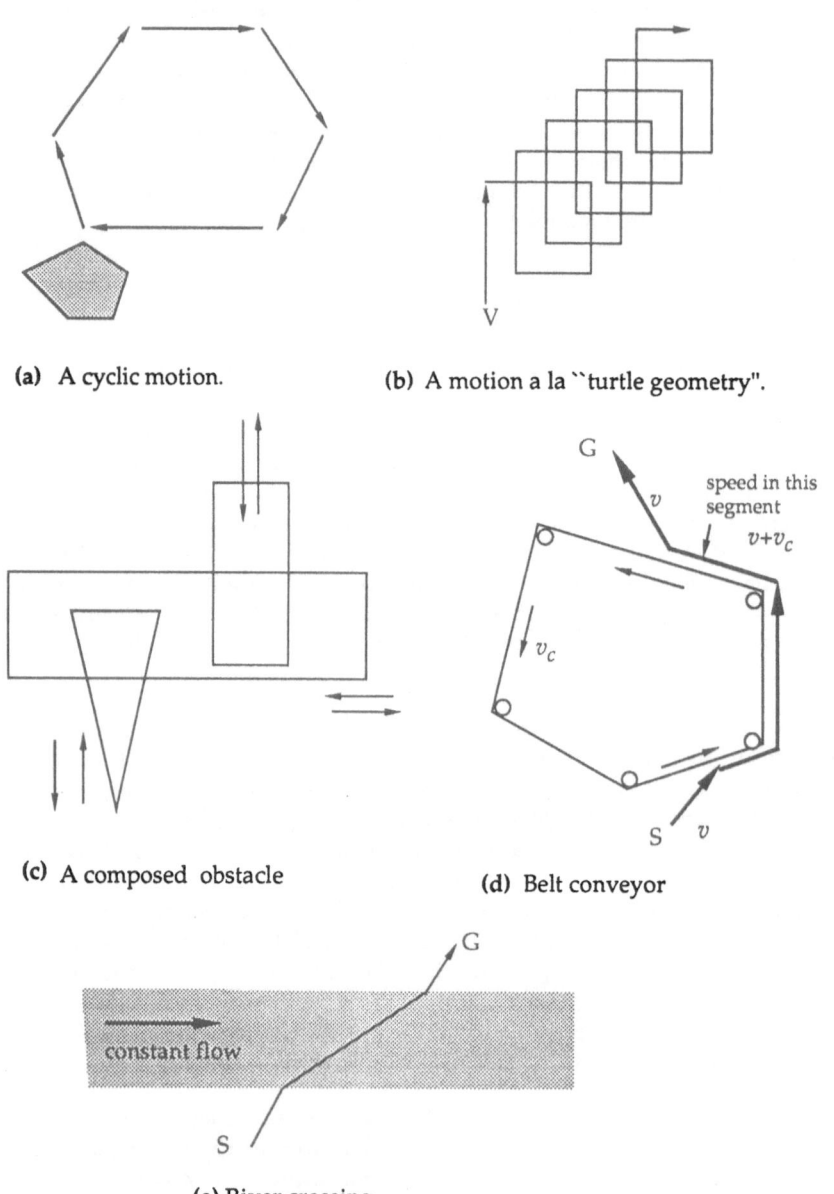

(a) A cyclic motion.   (b) A motion a la "turtle geometry".

(c) A composed obstacle   (d) Belt conveyor

(e) River crossing   .

Fig. 4.9. Variants of repeated motion

(f)

Fig. 4.9.

Now we described a method for finding a meeting point of a moving point that has a particular type of recursive motion, say Hilbert curve (Fig. 4.9f). In such a case, the point follows some fixed pattern of motion of various sizes (or levels). At each level, a characteristic motion which terminates in finite time can be defined. We first look at an arbitrary level in the recursive motion for the meeting point. If the meeting point is found to be at that level or a lower level of motion, then we need to move down the level in order to locate the meeting point exactly at a level below in a recursive manner. If the motion is not accessible at that level, we need to go up the level to locate the meeting point.

4.5 Nonlinear Motion of the Obstacles

We have assumed up to now that the motions of the obstacles are either linear or piecewise linear. In this section, we examine a few simple cases that do not have this restriction.

4.5.1 Accelerating obstacles

First, we consider an obstacle that moves with an acceleration. The motion of an object that moves with an acceleration (or deceleration) can be approximated by a series of piecewise linear movements. Approximation can be made arbitrarily close to the motion with acceleration by using a large number of pieces. In other words, the motion with an acceleration may be viewed as a motion where successive approximate motions by piecewise linear movements converge when the number of pieces approaches to infinity. Viewed as such, it is considered that the time-minimal property is also preserved at convergence as long as the speed of the obstacles do not exceed the maximum speed of the robot. Realistically, however, it remains to be resolved how many pieces are to be used to approximate such a motion of the obstacle.

In general, the x and y components of the motion of V are given in the form:

$$x(t) = at^2 + bt + c$$

$$y(t) = a't^2 + b't + c'$$

It requires solving a polynomial equation of a higher degree to find the accessible point. Some numerical method (such as a bisection search for the root) must be employed.

4.4.2 Rotating obstacles

Next, we show a heuristic method for handling an obstacle that follows a circular trajectory. In this case, different points on the obstacle may move at different speeds. We assume that the robot can still move faster than the fastest moving point on the obstacle. Suppose that a point V (V is a point on a moving object) is initially at $A(x_0, y_0)$ and the center of rotation is $C(x_c, y_c)$ (Fig. 4.10). The accessible point $X(x, y)$ of the rotating point from the origin can be computed as follows:

$$\frac{\sqrt{x^2 + y^2}}{v} = \frac{\theta}{\omega}$$

$$|CA| = |CX|$$

$$\theta = \frac{\cos^{-1}(\vec{CA} \cdot \vec{CX})}{|CA| \cdot |CX|}$$

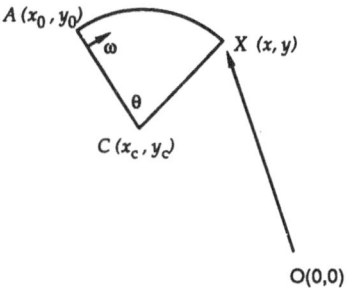

Fig. 4.10. A circular trajectory

where ω is the angular velocity of V. It seems complicated to solve the above equations for X exactly. Instead, a binary search with respect to X may be used to find a location of X that is arbitrary close to the exact solution to the equations.

In the case of translational motion of the obstacles, once the robot moves to a vertex of an obstacle, it is always coincident with some point on the obstacle until it leaves the obstacle. Let us call this motion "contact motion." When the obstacle's motion is piecewise linear, contact motion is also piecewise linear. However, the motion of the obstacle is nonlinear, its contact motion may not necessarily be linear. Suppose that the robot moves to a vertex V of the obstacle that is following a circular trajectory. Four cases need to be considered. When V is the leading vertex and the robot motion is inbound (Fig. 4.11a) or V is the trailing vertex and the robot motion is outbound (Fig. 4.11c), the robot has a contact motion with the obstacle and its trajectory is nonlinear. Otherwise (Figs. 4.11b and 4.11d), the robot can move from V to a vertex, say V' of the same obstacle without being in contact with the obstacle. This is due to the fact that for any object that follows a circular trajectory, the speed of a point on the object is faster when the point is further from the center of the rotation.

For the special case that the obstacle edge is collinear with the center of rotation, a simple solution is possible. Let AB be an edge that rotates about O at an angular speed ω. Let AB be always collinear with O and let A be the further endpoint from O. Suppose that the robot is initially found at $A(r,0)$ (in polar coordinate). The robot is always coincident with some point on AB (i.e. contact motion), while moving from A to B at a constant speed (Fig. 4 11d). When the robot is X (ρ, θ) at time t, v can be decomposed into the ρ component and the θ component. Thus, (ρ, θ) must satisfy:

$$\sqrt{|\dot{\rho}|^2 + (|\rho|\omega)^2} = v$$

$$\theta = \omega \cdot t$$

We get $(\rho, \theta) = (\frac{v}{\omega} \cos \omega t, \omega t)$, from which we can compute the time at which the robot reaches B.

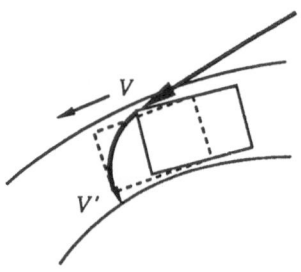

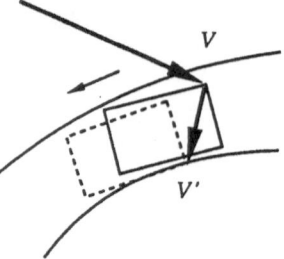

(a) V is the leading vertex of the polygon and the robot motion is inbound. The robot is always coincident with some point on the obstacle polygon between V and V'.

(b) V is the trailing vertex of the polygon and the robot motion is inbound. The robot leaves the obstacle at V adn meet the obstacle again at V'.

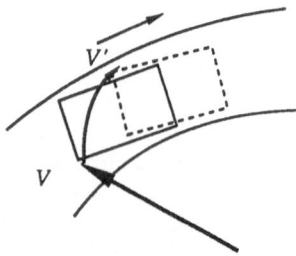

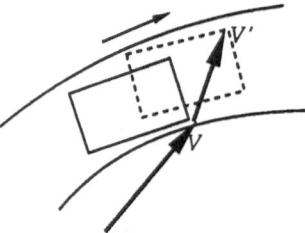

(c) V is the trailing vertex of the polygon and the robot motion is outbound.

(d) V is the leading vertex of the polygon and the robot motion is outbound.

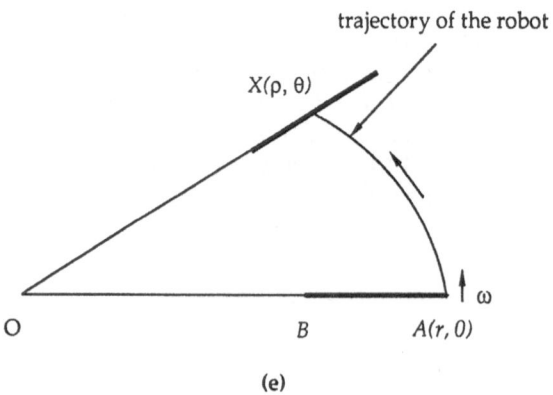

(e)

Fig. 4.11. Rotating obstacles

4.6 Splitting and Merging Obstacles

In this section, we study motion planning in the presence of moving obstacles that are permitted to overlap (i.e., pass through) each other arbitrarily. In other words, we allow two obstacles that are initially disjoint to come to contact, overlap each other for a certain period of time, cease to overlap, and move away from each other. We assume that each obstacle is a convex polygon that moves in a fixed direction at a constant speed, and that the robot is a point that is subject only to a speed bound. We present a method of determining whether or not there is a collision-free motion for the robot from an initial position to a final position, and of finding such a motion, if it exists, that takes the robot to the final destination in the shortest possible time.

The problem of overlapping obstacles has the following applications. The first one is planning a motion for a finite-sized robot among moving obstacles. One formulation for the problem has been to use configuration spaces. In a configuration space, the obstacles are expanded by the size of the robot. As a result of the expansion, configuration space obstacles may overlap. In a time-varying environment, it is possible that two configuration space obstacles that do not overlap in their initial positions do overlap for a certain period of time, then cease to overlap and move away from each other. This happens even when the physical obstacles do not overlap at all. The algorithm described in this section will be able to handle such a situation. In our formulation, the motions of two splitting obstacles can act as a gate-opening for a point-robot in configuration space when the robot needs to pass between the two obstacles. In this formulation making use of a two-dimensional configuration space, a resulting motion for the robot is translational, i.e., the robot is to follow a path without rotation. Some omnidirectional mobile platforms, e.g., (Killough and Pin 1990; Reister 1990), are able to follow paths such as generated by this algorithm.

Our formulation has another application. We can view obstacles as search lights projected on the ground. The projections of the lights sweep the ground in a scheduled manner. Given the schedule of the search lights, our motion planning algorithms provide a way for a culprit to move from one place to another without being detected by any of the lights.

4.6.1 Splits and merges

As discussed in Chap. 3, if obstacles do not overlap, the robot need only move in the directions of vertices of the obstacles at its maximum speed. This is still true in an environment containing obstacles that overlap but do not split or merge (over a given period of time). (Proposition 1 needs some care. When an edge intersects other edges, the edge is divided into segments by the intersection points. These segments are treated as 'edges' in Proposition 1.) When obstacles split or merge, connectivity relationship between the obstacles changes. These events are critical in motion planning: a split may create a new passage for the robot and a merge may close a passage (Fig. 4.12a) or even crush the robot (Fig. 4.12b). When the robot cannot escape from being crushed, the planner needs to report that there is no collision-free motion.

We define splits and merges in terms of movements (or edges in motion). A merge of two edges means that two disjoint edges begin to cross each other. It is possible that when a merge takes place, the robot is confined into a closed area (Fig. 1.2, page 5) or crushed between the two closing obstacles. This means that no matter what action it takes, the robot cannot escape from being crushed. In terms of accessibility, the event is indicated by crossing collision fronts (Fig. 4.12c).

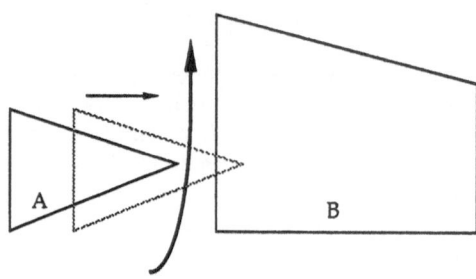

(a) Obstacle A eventually overlaps with obstacle B.
   When A overlaps B, the pathway indicated by the thick arrow disappears.

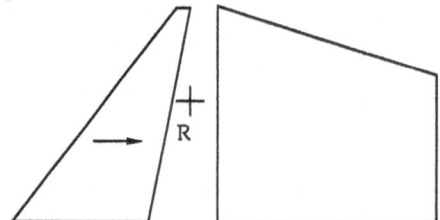

(b) It is possible that the robot (R in the figure) is crushed no matter what action it takes.

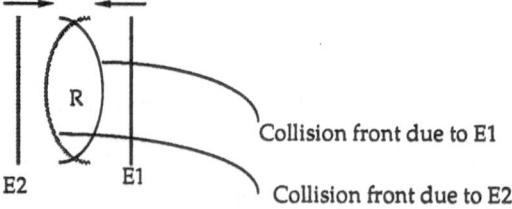

(c) A case in which the robot (R) cannot escape from being crushed.

Fig. 4.12. Merges of edges

A split of two edges, when intersecting edges cease to intersect, requires special handling. Such an event should not be missed, since a new pathway may be opened. For example, suppose that edges E_1 and E_2 intersect. A split occurs when a vertex of E_1 passes E_2 (or vice versa). The location at which the split takes place is called a *split point*, and the time at which it occurs is called a *split time*. Note that even when a split of two edges occurs, the two obstacles having those edges as sides may still overlap. A *merge point* and a *merge time* are defined in a similar manner. The following proposition illustrates the importance of a split point.

Proposition 10. Suppose that an environment contains only one split and that it is possible to reach the destination point passing through the split point at its split time. If a motion is late for the split time, then the motion is never time-minimal.

Proof: Let A and B be the two obstacles that have just split (Fig. 4.13a). Suppose that vertex P of A and point Q of B are at the split point, S. Let α be a motion that passes S at its split time. The point robot moving with motion α is at S at its split time. On the other hand, motion β is behind motion α, i.e, β is not at S at its split time, but passes through the passage created by the split at a time later than the split time. We prove that motion β is never time-minimal, assuming that the environment contains only one split.

Consider an elastic net between P and Q. As P and Q move, the net is always stretched tautly between P and Q. It is easy to show that a mobile point that is located at S at the split time can move to any point on the net at any time (Fig. 4.13b). If the motion vectors of P and Q are $\vec{u}$ and $\vec{v}$, respectively, the motion vector of a point on the net, w, can be represented as $\vec{w} = s\vec{u} + (1-s)\vec{v}$ for some constant s, where $0 \leq s \leq 1$. Note that the magnitude of $\vec{w}$ is less than or equal to $\max(|\vec{u}|, |\vec{v}|)$.[2] A similar argument applies when a third obstacle intercepts the net and stretches the net in the direction of its movement.

We can construct an alternative motion, say α', that joins motion β exactly at the time when motion β crosses the net. Let T be the point at which β crosses the net. Motion α' departs from S at its split time and moves to T at a velocity as defined by $\vec{w}$. Thus the speed of α' is slower than the maximum speed between S and T. The rest of motion α' is defined to be identical with β. Note that after the split made by P and Q, the environment does not contain any splits; thus the Time-Minimal Motion theorem holds. Motion α' is not time-minimal, since its speed between S and T is less than $v_{\max}$. Motion α' arrives at the destination at the same time as β. Therefore, motion β is not time-minimal. $\Diamond$

Proposition 10 does not imply that the robot must always be at a split point at its split time in order to be time-minimal. Consider an environment in which there are two splits. The robot may not be at the first split point at its split time, but may still catch up at the second split point at its split time. Such a motion can still be time-minimal in a global sense. However, it may well be that a motion that is late for the first split cannot arrive at the second split point until after its split time. Note that

---

[2] Assume $|\vec{u}| \leq |\vec{v}|$, without loss of generality. $|\vec{w}|^2 = s^2|\vec{u}|^2 + 2s(1-s)\vec{u} \cdot \vec{v} + (1-s)^2|\vec{v}|^2 \leq |\vec{v}|^2$ Thus, $|\vec{w}| \leq |\vec{v}|$.

if it is impossible for the robot, if it departs the first split point at its split time, to reach the second split point at its split time, then it is certainly impossible for a robot that is not at the first split point at its split time to reach the second split point in time. For this reason, it is always a good idea to locate the robot at a split point at its split time, whenever possible.

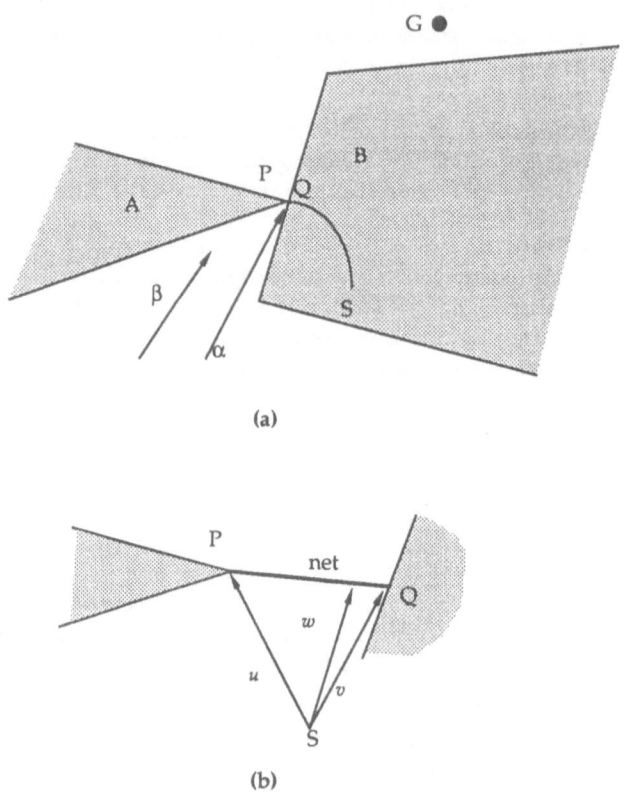

(a)

(b)

Fig. 4.13. A split point

4.6.2 Subgoals

How can a robot arrive at a split point exactly at its split time? To insure this, when obstacles overlap, we introduce auxiliary points on an edge which can serve as subgoals in the process of motion planning. A subgoal represents a collision-free motion of a possibly moving point that converges to a split or merge point. Two types of subgoals are used. Note that when we discuss splits or merges, we are speaking about edges rather than obstacles.

Subgoal Type 1 (edge-vertex intersection): A split or a merge occurs when an edge meets with a vertex of another edge. Let Y be a point on an edge that intersects with a vertex of another edge. We consider Y as a subgoal, since it converges to the split (or merge) point. We aim the robot R at Y. Once it reaches Y, the motion of the robot is identical with that of Y until it reaches the split (or merge) point. It is always possible to follow Y because the speed of Y is the same as that of the obstacle on which Y is found.

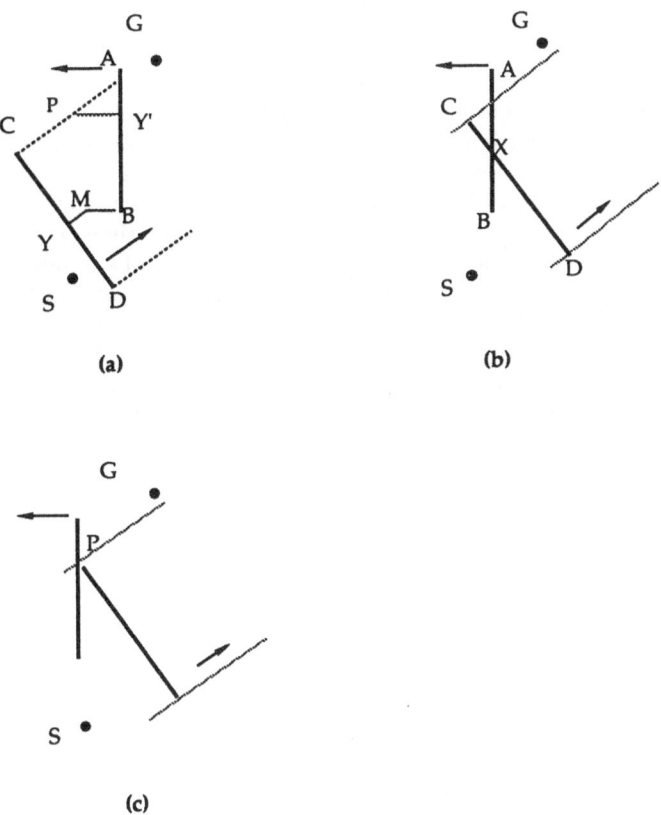

Fig. 4.14. Intersecting edges

Subgoal Type 2 (edge-edge intersection): Let X be the intersection point between two intersecting edges. As the edges move, the intersection point X also moves straight toward the split (or merge) point at a constant speed. We treat X as a subgoal; in other words, the robot is directed toward X. After it reaches X, the motion of the robot is identical with X until it reaches the split point. However, it is possible that X moves faster than the maximum speed of the robot (depending on the angles between the two edges). In such a case, X cannot serve as a subgoal.

Example. Figure 4.14a contains two edges that are about to intersect. Let S be the point at which the robot R is initially found, and let G denote the destination point. The merge point and the split point of edges AB and CD are indicated by M and P, respectively. Point Y on edge CD passes through the merge point M, and point Y' on edge AB passes through the split point P. Thus Y and Y' are both subgoals. When the two edges intersect, the intersection point (indicated by X in Fig. 4.14b) is also a subgoal. After the robot (R) leaves S, it is aimed at Y. After it reaches Y, its motion is identical with that of Y until it comes to the merge point M. After M, it follows the intersection point X until it comes to the split point P. After R reaches P, it is moved straight to the destination point G (Fig. 4.14c). If the robot were to move from G to S in the same environment, R would be directed toward Y' to reach the split point P.

Figure 4.15 illustrates a Type-1 subgoal between two polygons. Rectangle ABCD moves in direction d and triangle FHE is a stationary obstacle. Vertex F is a split point whose split time is the instant at which point Y on edge BC passes vertex F. Point Y is a subgoal and γ indicates Y's trajectory. Evidently, there are other ways of moving a robot from a current position to a split point at its split time. For example, motion π, a straight-line motion from S to F in Fig. 4.15, seems to be a natural choice for R's motion in approaching the split point. Along SF, R moves at a constant speed such that R can reach the split point exactly at its split time. This motion π can also be followed by R. Our strategy is to first move to a subgoal with maximum speed, and then to follow the motion of the subgoal. This choice of motion for the robot makes it easier to design an algorithm.

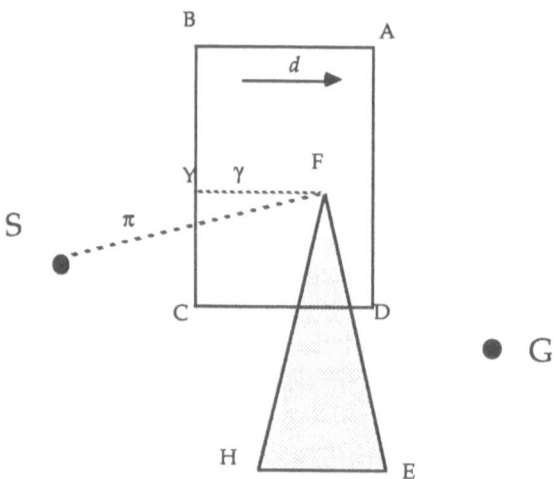

Fig. 4.15. Example of Type-1 subgoal

Figure 4.16 illustrates a Type-2 subgoal when two obstacles split. Polygons ABCD and EFHJ are about to separate. Edges AD and FH and edges DC and FH split. At the split time, the split point V coincides with vertex D and lies on edge FH. The intersection point X of edges FH and AD is a Type-2 subgoal. In this example, V (Type-1 subgoal) cannot serve as a subgoal as it is not accessible from S, the current location of the robot. The intersection point of edges DC and FH is also a subgoal, but this point is not accessible from S either. The procedure to determine accessible subgoals from the current robot location is described in the next section.

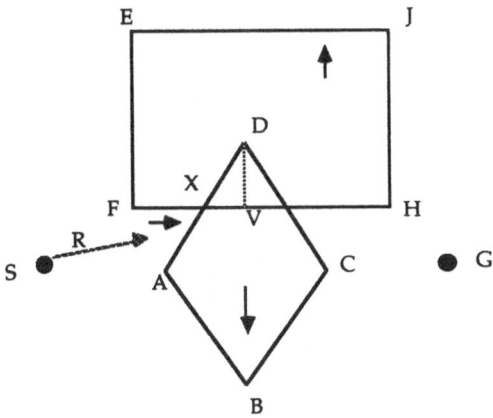

Fig. 4.16. Example of Type-2 subgoal

Also in this example, there are other ways of moving R from S to V other than following X. Observe that X moves the slowest of all points that converge to the split point V. This means that if it is not possible to follow X, then it is certainly not possible to follow other points that converge to the subgoal.

Note that the two types of subgoals may chain, as shown in the example in Fig. 4.17. Here, polygon ABC intersects stationary polygon DEFHIJ. Suppose that the robot (initially located at S in Fig. 4.17a) needs to reach point G. There are two subgoals that are accessible from S, i.e., Y (Type 1) and the intersection point of edges AC and DE (Type 2). Both subgoals converge to vertex E, where a split of edge AC and DE takes place (Fig. 4.17b). Next, we consider the intersection between edges AC and EF. Their intersection point is a Type-2 subgoal (Fig. 4.17c) until a split of edges AC and EF occurs. Finally, the intersection point of edges AC and FH serves as a Type-2 subgoal (Fig. 4.17d). In summary, we can consider this chain of intersection points as a path that eventually leads the robot to the split point of the two obstacles at its split time.

As shown in Chap. 3, when obstacles do not overlap, the robot can reach the final destination without having to visit the same vertex of an obstacle more than once. However, in a situation that allows overlaps among obstacles, the robot may have to visit the same vertex many times. Figure 4.18 illustrates such a situation. Triangle ABC is an obstacle that is moving towards the right. Triangles DEF and HJK are stationary obstacles. Point O is the starting point of R. Figure 4.18a shows the moment when R arrives at vertex C. After leaving vertex C, R moves to F, and meet with C again (Fig. 4.18b). Next, R moves to vertex K (Fig. 4.18c), after which it meets with C again (Fig. 4.18d).

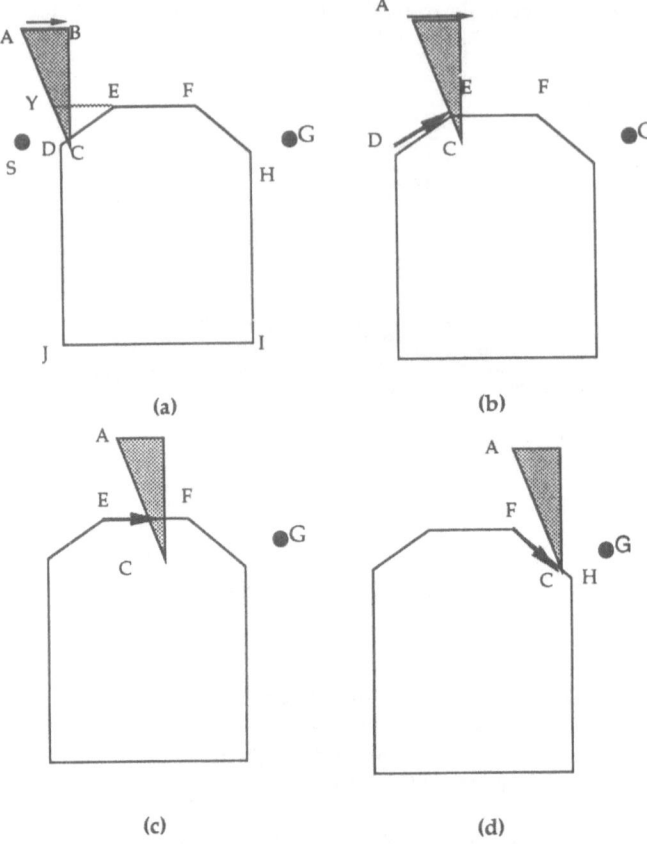

Fig. 4.17. A subgoal chain

In general, a vertex of an obstacle can be treated as a new vertex after it has passed through the inside of an obstacle (e.g., vertex C in Fig. 4.18). Let us call a vertex *live* when it is not covered by any of the obstacles, and let a *live period* of a vertex be a time interval during which the vertex is live. In Fig. 4.18, vertex C has the following three live periods: The period before C intersects edge FD; the period after C intersects edge FE and before it intersects edge HK; and the period after C intersects edge JK. The robot does not have to visit the same vertex more than once while the vertex is in the same live period.

So far we have introduced two types of subgoals and defined motions to be followed when a split occurs. As noted earlier, there are other ways of moving the robot to a split point at its split time. We treat the motion defined in this section as a canonical form for motion planning. It can be shown using an argument similar to Proposition 10 that whenever there exists a motion that reaches the split (merge) point at its split (merge) time, there is a canonical motion to reach the same split (merge) point.

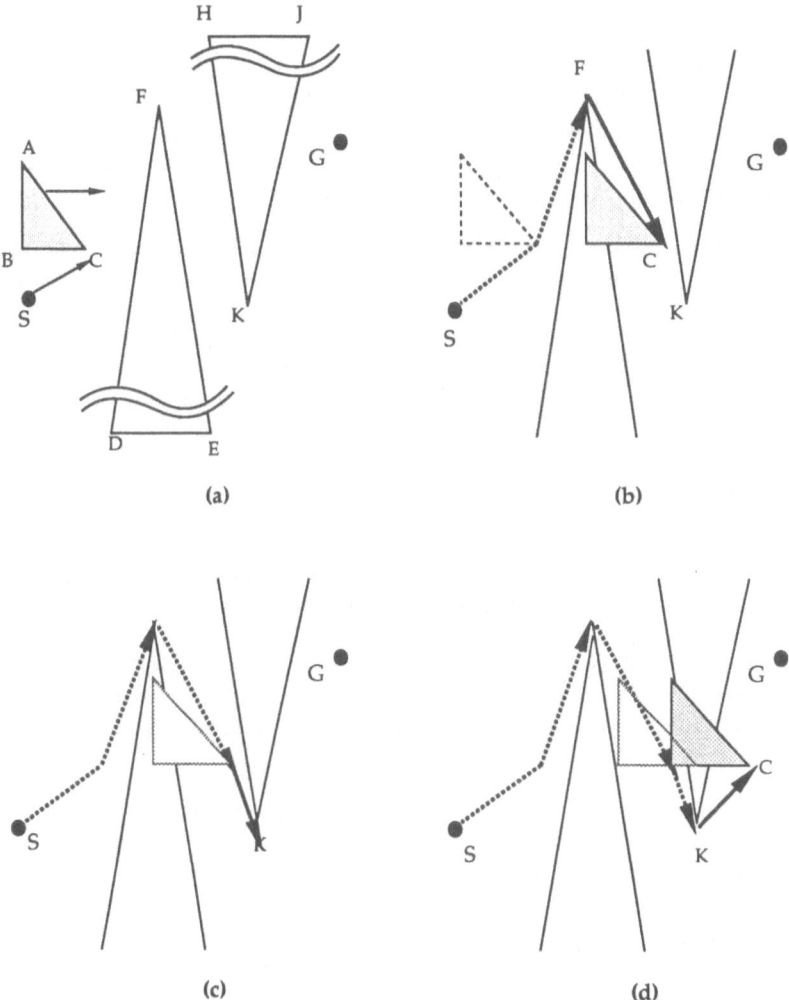

Fig. 4.18. The robot visits the same vertex more than once

In our approach, a motion from a given start point to a destination point takes place as follows. After the robot leaves its start point, it moves to one of the subgoals in a shortest time. After it reaches a subgoal, it follows the motion of the subgoal to its split (or merge) point. After the split (or merge) time, the robot moves to another subgoal in a shortest time. This process is repeated until the robot eventually reaches the final destination point.

4.6.3 Algorithm

We now describe an algorithm to find a collision-free motion and analyze its complexity. Let n be the number of vertices in the environment. Let k be the total number of merges and splits that occur between a vertex and an edge. The value of k depends on the nature of the obstacles. It is zero when obstacles do not overlap at any instant of time. In the worst case, k is $O(n^2)$, since every obstacle can overlap every other obstacle.

The idea behind our algorithm is as follows. If obstacles do not overlap, the (point) robot need only move in the directions of vertices of the obstacles along a straight line at its maximum speed. If obstacles do overlap, the robot also needs to move in the directions of the two types of subgoals. In the following, we use the term 'target' to collectively refer to either a vertex or a subgoal. After the robot reaches a subgoal, it moves with it until it comes to a split or merge point. At a split or merge point, it needs to change its direction towards its next target (a vertex of an obstacle or another subgoal) until it reaches its final destination point. During this process, the robot may encounter the same vertex of an obstacle more than once. We now give a description of the algorithm.

1. Enumerate all the subgoals. This can be done naively by checking each vertex against all the edges in the environment. By doing so, all the split and merge points and split and merge times are determined. At the same time, we can determine the live periods of each vertex. A vertex has up to $O(n)$ live periods, since a vertex can be covered by obstacles at most $O(n)$ times. Note that since the total number of live periods of vertices does not exceed the total number of merges and splits, it is $O(k)$.

   When a vertex of an obstacle intersects an edge, the intersection point on the edge becomes a subgoal. Since there are k such intersections, the number of subgoals is $O(k)$. It is also necessary to identify the trajectory of a subgoal. Since a subgoal is always on an edge, its motion is determined by that edge. However, it is necessary to determine when and where the subgoal starts. To determine the starting point, the trajectory is checked against all edges in the environment. This takes $O(n)$ time per subgoal.

2. There is a total of $n + k$ targets (vertices and subgoal). Let $N = n + k$. Sort the accessible points of the targets in clockwise order with respect to the current point. This takes $O(N \log N)$ time.

3. Rotate a ray emanating from the current point about the current point. The ray halts each time it intersects the accessible point of a target. Check whether this target is accessible from the current point. This can be done using a balanced binary tree (e.g., a 2-3 tree) as described in Section 3.5. After $O(N \log N)$ time, all targets accessible from the current point are determined. If no targets are accessible, then the current point is a dead end.

4. Maintain a priority queue of targets, where priority corresponds to the accessible time of the target. Choose the target whose associated time is the earliest, say Y. If Y is the destination point, then stop. If Y is a vertex, repeat steps (2), (3), and (4)

with Y as the current point. If Y is a subgoal, pick the split (merge) point Z and the split (merge) time associated with Z, and repeat steps (2), (3), and (4) with Z as the current point.

5. Repeat steps (2), (3), and (4) at most N times.

Examples. Figure 4.19a illustrates an example of our motion planning algorithm. Four rectangles and triangles JHK are stationary while triangle ABC and DEF are moving in the indicated directions. The broken lines show the trajectories followed by the two triangular obstacles. Point O is the starting point of the robot R and G is the final destination point. There are a number of subgoals in the scene, but only two of them, X and Y, are accessible from O. Also, there are a number of accessible vertices. Other subgoals, which are not accessible from O, are located at intersection points of the broken lines (trajectories of the moving obstacles) with stationary obstacles.

Figure 4.19b illustrates a motion that aims at the vertex L. In this case, after entering the passage between the two left rectangles, the robot is doomed to be crushed between the obstacles. Figure 4.19c illustrates the consequences of a motion that aims at X. At X, the robot waits until vertex C passes by, and enters the passage between the rectangles. In this case the robot is also doomed to be crushed, because triangle DEF will make it impossible for the robot to get through the passage.

Alternatively, the robot can aim at the subgoal Y (Fig. 4.19d). In this case, it waits at Y until vertex F passes through it. (Notice that Y is a stationary subgoal since the rectangle on which Y occurs is stationary.) After F passes Y, the robot follows the subgoal formed by edge EF and the bottom edge of the lower-right rectangle. Since there are no further obstacles in its path, the robot can reach G by following the north-east corner of the upper left rectangle. If the left two rectangles extend infinitely to the left, and the right two rectangles extend infinitely to the right, then it is easy to see that the suggested motion is also time-minimal.

When dealing with a finite-sized robot, motion planning is performed in terms of a configuration space. The number of vertices in the configuration space is $O(n)$, assuming that the robot has a bounded number of vertices (Kedem and Sharir 1985). We create configuration space obstacles from the given set of physical polygonal obstacles and the given polygonal robot. See (Lozano-Pérez 1983; Whitesides 1985) for a detailed algorithm. It takes $O(n_i + m)$ time to create a configuration space for an obstacle with n_i vertices and a robot with m vertices. Therefore, it takes $O(n_1 + \cdots + n_l + ml)$ time to create the configuration space from an environment that contains l obstacles. This amounts to $O(n)$ time, assuming that the number of vertices of the robot is bounded. After the configuration space is created, the rest of the process is the same as above.

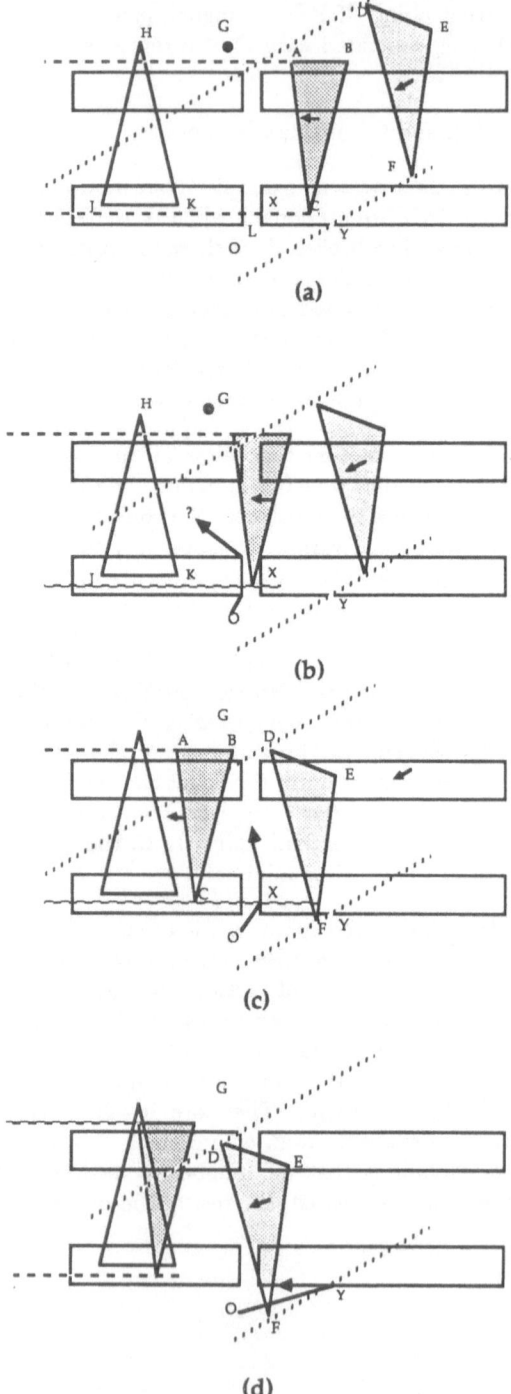

Fig. 4.19. Splitting and merging obstacles

Example. Figure 4.20 is a simple example of motion planning for a triangular robot (R) among two rectangular moving obstacles (P and Q). The five parts of Fig. 4.20a show the motion in configuration space, and the five parts of Fig. 4.20b show the corresponding motion in physical space. R first moves to X (Fig. 4.20a(ii) and (iii)), a subgoal. After R reaches X, it stays on X until it reaches Y, which is a split point (Fig. 4.20a(iv)). After P and Q have separated, R moves in the directions of real vertices in the scene until it reaches the destination point G (Fig. 20a(v)). Note that in Fig. 4.20b (ii) and (iii), R touches both of the obstacles P and Q.

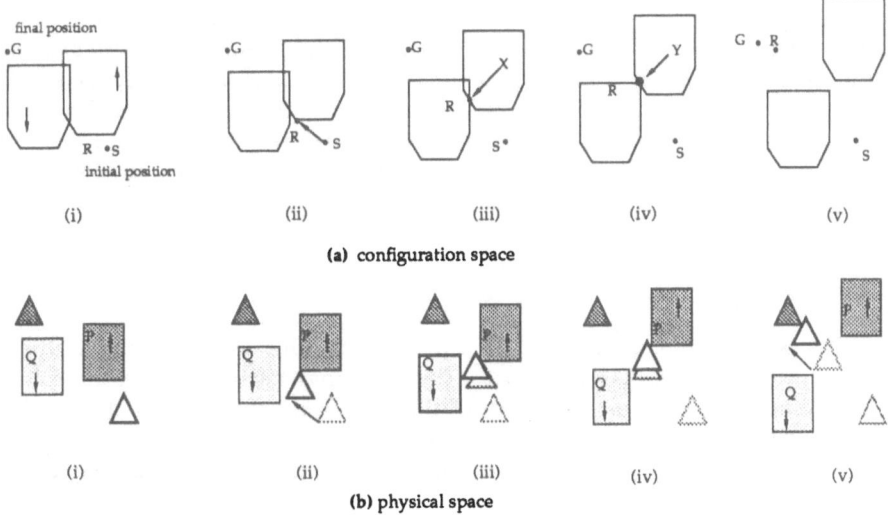

Fig. 4.20. Motion planning in a time-varying environment

Subfigure (i)–(v) in (a) show a motion in configuration space, while subfigures (i)–(v) in (b) show the corresponding motion in physical space.

4.6.4 Analysis

The computation time required at each step of the algorithm was indicated in the description of the step. It consists of three major components, i.e., determination of all split and merge points ($O(n^2)$ time), determination of all subgoals ($O(nk)$ time), and path search ($O(N^2 \log N)$ time), where $N = n + k$. Altogether, it takes $O(n^2) + O(nk) + O(N^2 \log N) = O((n + k)^2 \log(n + k))$ time to produce a motion. The value of k can be as large as n^2 in the worst case where each and every edge intersects all other edges. However, normally where each edge intersects only with a bounded number of other edges, k is expected to be much smaller than n^2. Kedem and Sharir (1985) have studied the complexity of motion planning among stationary obstacles under translation. They developed an algorithm that runs in time $O(n \log^2 n)$, where n is the total number of vertices of the obstacles. Bhattacharya and Zorbas (1988) have proposed a new approach that takes $O(n \log n)$ time to compute a translational motion among stationary convex polygons.

4.6.5 Moving obstacles with uncertain velocities

Our approach can be easily adapted to an environment with uncertainty. Such a situation arises due to errors in the measurement of the motion of the objects. For example, the notion of accessibility can be extended to handle some amount of uncertainty in the speed of the obstacles. Consider a line segment L which moves in a constant direction at speed v, where $v_1 \leq v \leq v_2$ for some known v_1 and v_2. We can create two collision fronts, C_1 and C_2, which correspond to the movement of L at speeds v_1 and v_2, respectively. A collision front of L at velocity v must lie between C_1 and C_2. We use the term *collision area* to denote the area which is swept by L and bounded by $C1$ and $C2$ (Fig. 4.18). The extremum points of this area (e.g., points A and B in Fig. 4.18) can be used as accessible points in the procedure to find a motion among obstacles with uncertain speeds. In such a case, the collision fronts of two obstacles may overlap even when the obstacles themselves do not overlap. When we wish to plan a motion under such uncertainty, our approach can be used, since it allows overlaps between obstacles.

Another source of uncertainty is the robot itself. Due to errors in the driving mechanism or disturbances along the path, the robot may have a range of uncertainty in its own velocity. The dynamic nature of the environment aggravates the problem: once the robot falls behind a planned path, it may become increasingly hard or even impossible for the robot to catch up with the original path. This is because a small delay at an early stage of the path can easily grow to be an insurmountable delay at a later stage, since the delay increases with time. To some extent, we can prevent this from happening by incorporating the uncertainty in the robot's velocity and defining a collision area similar to that shown in Fig. 4.21. In stationary environments, Donald (1988) has considered the problem of planning motion in the presence of some uncertainty in the velocity of the robot.

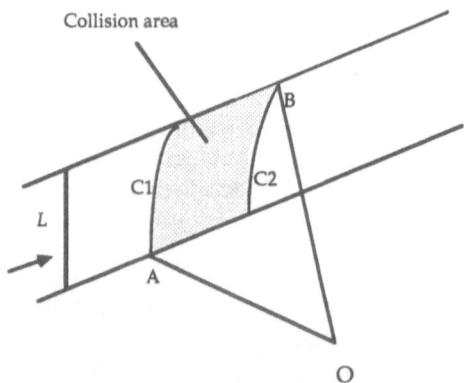

Fig. 4.21. Collision area

4.7 Heuristics in time-varying environments

Heuristics play an important role in accelerating search processes. Usually, an estimation function is used to evaluate how close a given state is to the goal state in the search space. When there are several choices for the next move at a given state, a heuristic function is applied to each of the candidates, and the one with the best evaluation is chosen as the next state. The other choices of states are placed on a queue for later consideration. A search algorithm is called admissible when it guarantees a shortest path from the current state to the final state (Nilsson 1980). Usually, in motion planning in a static environment, the following estimation function h is used:

$$h(CP) = f(CP) + g(CP),$$

where $f(CP)$ gives the distance from the start point to the current point (CP), and $g(CP)$ is a heuristic evaluation of the path from the current point to the destination point, G.

In a time-varying environment where we wish to optimize time, we can use the time from location X to location Y in place of the distance from X to Y. We can let f be the time elapsed from the start time to the current time, and g be the accessible time from CP to G. Since g never overestimates the time from CP to G, a search with the heuristic function h is admissible. We executed our algorithm with this heuristic function; as a result, the execution time for the data of Fig. 3.11 was reduced from 3.6 seconds to 0.6 seconds. Note that a naive choice of heuristic function will make the search algorithm non-admissible. For example, we could simply let g be the distance between CP and G divided by the point robot's speed. The search algorithm with this heuristic function, however, is not admissible. In a situation in which G is in motion, it is possible that h overestimates the time from CP to G. Sedgewick and Vitter (1985) have studied heuristics for searching for a shortest path in Euclidean graphs.

4.8 Unexpected Obstacles

We have assumed that all information about the obstacles is known a priori by the robot. In this section, we consider the case where the robot may encounter obstacles unexpectedly on its way to the destination point. We develop a model of robot navigation based on visual information in an environment that contains unknown moving obstacles. The robot is assumed to be equipped with a sensor that is capable of detecting the speed and location of a moving obstacle. When the robot detects a moving obstacle, it may have to revise its motion plan in light of its current knowledge about the environment.

We consider the following situation. The environment contains a number of stationary and moving obstacles. The objective is to plan a motion to reach a given destination, while avoiding collision with any of the obstacles. We assume that the robot has a visual or auditory sensor that is capable of detecting an obstacle when it is not occluded. Upon detecting an obstacle that was not known previously, the robot must plan its motion appropriately to avoid a collision with the obstacle. We also assume that moving obstacles do not change their motions locally. In other words, the robot can assume that a moving obstacle keeps moving at the same speed in the same direction. This means that once the robot detects an obstacle, its motion becomes predictable.

Here is our strategy. Upon detecting a moving obstacle, the robot computes its collision front. When the collision front does not intersect the robot's current motion, it does not collide with the new moving obstacle. When the collision front intersects the robot's motion, it must avoid the predicted collision before the robot actually reaches the intersection point. The robot considers all collision fronts of currently known obstacles. Then, it makes a best decision based on its current knowledge of the environment.

It is possible that the robot detects a second moving obstacle while it moves along its replanned motion. The robot must then again revise its motion taking the two obstacles into account. Figure 4.22 contains such an example. The robot moves along an initially planned path STG. At A, an unexpected obstacle P becomes visible. AV' is the revised path. At B, another moving obstacle Q becomes visible, which requires the robot to change its course of motion again. This strategy works when the total number of moving obstacles (known plus unknown) in the environment is finite. In such an environment, the robot must plan while moving. Therefore, we must take latency time into account in planning a motion, i.e., it is important to guarantee that the robot be safe while it is computing a new path upon detecting a new obstacle.

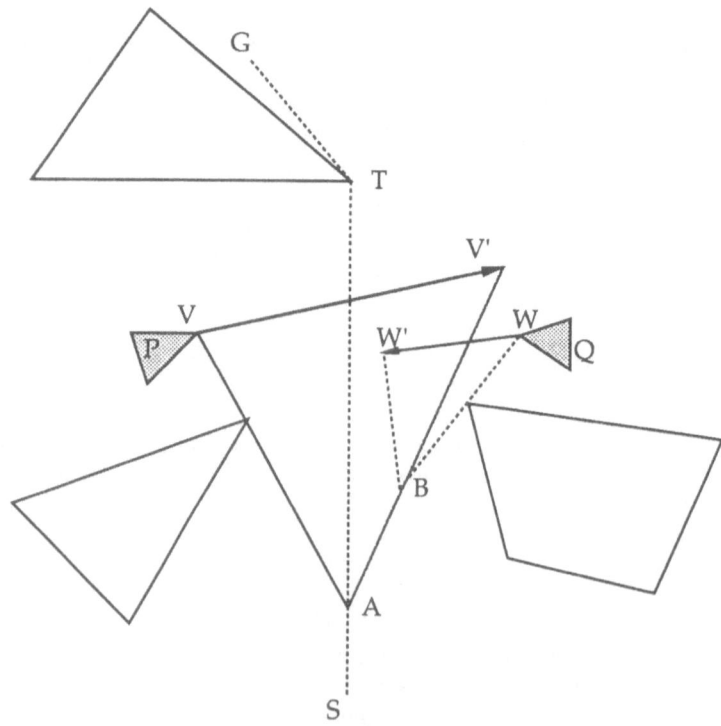

Fig. 4.22. Unexpected obstacles

For a stationary environment, Lumelsky has developed a framework for planning motion among unknown obstacles using a tactile sensor (Lumelsky and Stepanov 1987) or a visual sensor (Lumelsky and Skewis 1990). Chattergy (1985) has proposed another heuristic strategy for robot navigation among unknown stationary obstacles using a visual sensor.

Exact detection of a moving object using visual or auditory sensors is not an easy problem. Ultrasonic sensors have been used to detect objects mostly in a static environment for navigation (Elfes 1989; Borenstein and Koren 1988; Kuc and Viard 1991). Each ultrasonic sensor has a conic field of view. Distance between the sensor and an object found in the cone is computed based on the travel time of the echo (time-of-flight). Motion detection using vision is a subject of active investigation (Moravec 1983; Thorp *et al* 1989).

We show a simple method using range information obtained by an array of ultrasonic sensors to detect motion of a moving object in the plane. Ultrasonic sensors are arranged on the platform (mobile robot) as illustrated in Fig. 4.23. Each sonar detects an object when it enters its conical field of view. The box is an object wrapped with a bubble wrap so that it is better detected. The box is moved toward the right. Suppose that the box is the only moving object in the plane and there is no other objects near the platform.

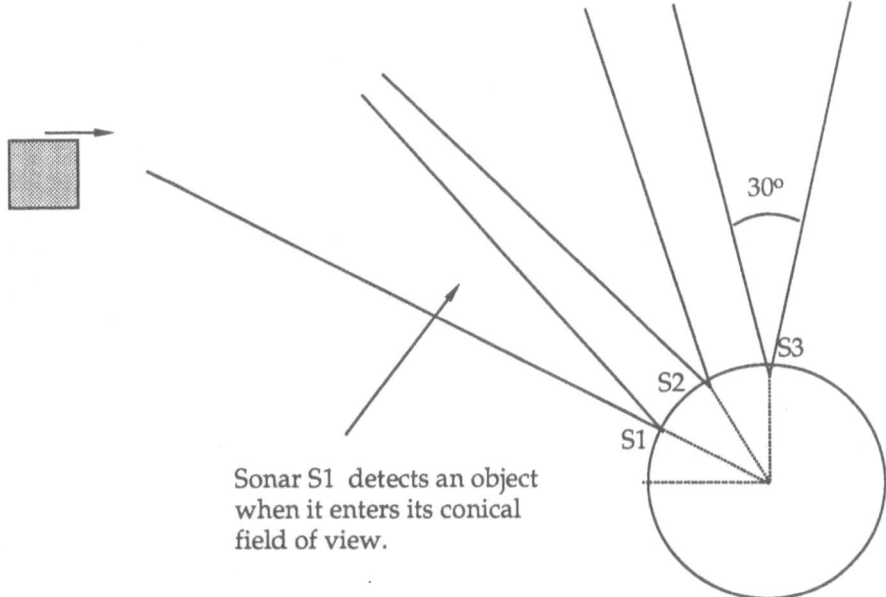

Sonar S1 detects an object
when it enters its conical
field of view.

Fig. 4.23. Detecting a moving object

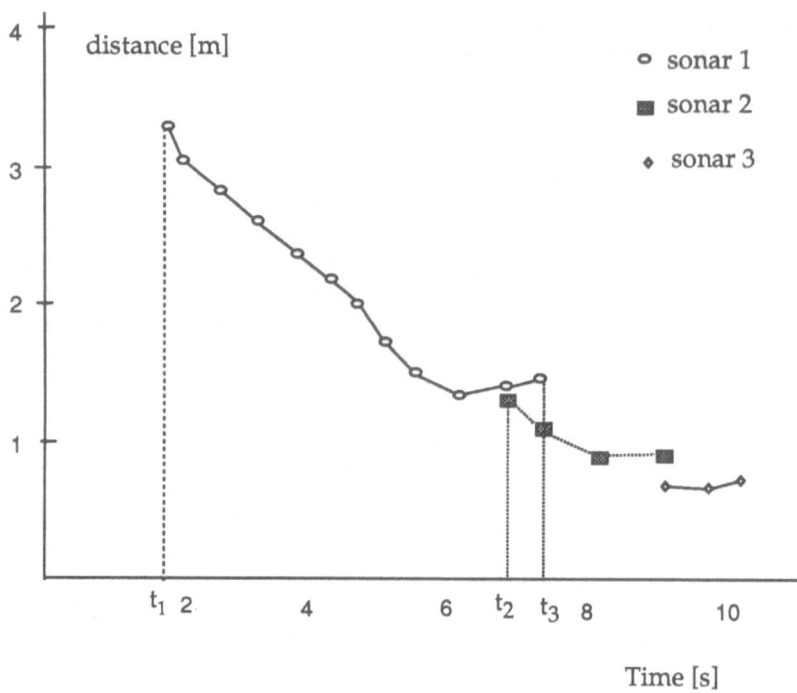

Fig. 4.24. Sensor readings

Figure 4.24 contains range data measured by the three sonars S1, S2, and S3 fixed in the front part of the platform. Initially, readings of all sonars show some high values and they drop as the moving object enters their fields of view. The readings before the drops are omitted in Fig. 4.24. The object enters the field of view of sensor S1 at time t_1 and exits its field of view at time t_3 and so on. If we assume that the box moves in a fixed direction at a constant speed, it is possible to detect the motion of the object from these data. When the platform is in motion, the values must be interpreted appropriately to reflect the motion of the platform.

Although motion detection is possible, this method has some restrictions. It takes a while before reliable motion is detected. This is due to accuracy of sonar data as well as time it takes for an object to pass through the field of view. As the field of view takes on the shape of a cone, the farther the object is from the platform, the more difficult it is to detect the motion of the object. Also, if there is more than one moving object, a problem arises as to finding a match between the readings and the objects. Accuracy of data can be improved by using range sensors of better quality such as infrared sensors. The second problem can be remedied by rotating the platform so that the field of view of a sonar sweeps through the moving object. Another method for object detection using a conic mirror is introduced in (Yagi *et al* 1991).

4.9 Summary

We have demonstrated the usefulness of the accessibility graph by solving a number of relevant problems of motion planning in an environment containing moving obstacles, and analyzing their complexity. The accessibility approach has been extended to handle concave obstacles, a destination point that can move faster than the robot, piecewise linear motion of the obstacles, etc. Throughout the chapter, the motion of the robot has been translational. Note that it is simple to incorporate non-holonomic motion for the point robot. Figure 4.25 contains an example where the motion is subject to a minimum turning radius. Given a minimum truning radius and an angle with which the point robot meet with a vertex, its meeting point can be computed in a manner analogous to the method in Section 4.5.

In navigation, we may wish to require some minimum clearance distance between the robot and the obstacles in order to increase the safety of the motion. The problem of finding a motion that satisfies this clearance can be readily solved by growing each obstacle by the minimum clearance distance, and then using our algorithm for obstacles that split and merge. However, it remains to be investigated how much safety is to be considered for each obstacle. Also, it remains to be solved whether it is possible to reduce the computational cost of motion planning by examining the types of overlaps produced by configuration space obstacles.

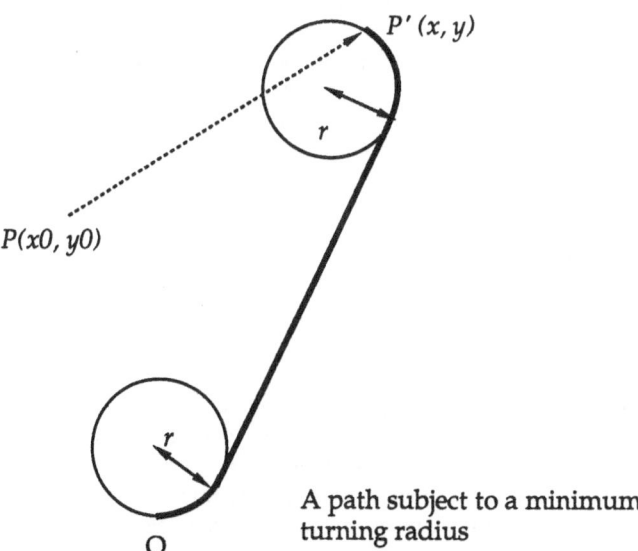

A path subject to a minimum turning radius

Fig. 4.25. Motion with a minimum turning radius

Chapter 5
Time-Minimal Motion: Generalizations

This chapter contains two topics. In Section 5.1, we extend the accessibility approach to the case of disappearing and appearing obstacles in the plane. In Section 5.2, the concept of accessibility is generalized to three dimensions.

5.1 Transient Obstacles

Most of the prior approaches to motion planning problems assume that the obstacles always exist in the environment, whether they are stationary or in motion. In this section, we consider the case that the environment contains obstacles whose existing periods are dependent on time, i.e., they may disappear and reappear in the environment. Such an obstacle is called a "transient obstacle" in this section.

This formulation allows us to model a number of time-varying situations that can arise in application domains.

1. A traffic light is such a dynamic obstacle on the road.

2. For robot navigation, an area that the robot is not allowed to pass through for a certain period of time is a transient obstacle.

3. For a mobile robot that must work on an aircraft carrier or in an airport, aircraft (such as helicopters) that land and take off may be modeled as appearing and disappearing objects.

4. In certain situations, some other agent (e.g., a crane) picks up one of the objects in the workspace and puts it back at some other location in the same environment. From a mobile robot in the plane, these objects may be viewed as disappearing from the scene and appearing again in the environment. Such a situation may arise when two robots operate simultaneously in the same workspace.

5. A fast-moving obstacle can be approximated by a series of transient obstacles. This makes it possible to give a near time-minimal solution amidst fast and slowly moving obstacles in polynomial time.

5.1.1 Statement of the problem

We consider the following motion planning problem in two dimensions. The environment contains a set of polygonal obstacles, a start point, and a destination point. Each obstacle is a polygon that exists in the scene for a certain interval of time $[t_1, t_2]$, where $t_1 < t_2$. Here, t_1 can be $-\infty$ and t_2 can be $+\infty$. For the interval $[t_1, t_2]$, the obstacle is fixed at a certain location in the environment. For ease of explanation, we classify obstacles into the following four types, depending on whether or not t_1 and t_2 are finite:

Type 1 (Disappearing obstacle): The obstacle exists in the scene for an interval of time $(-\infty, t_{disappear}]$, where $t_{disappear} < \infty$.

Type 2 (Appearing obstacle): The obstacle exists in the scene for an interval of time $[t_{appear}, \infty)$, where $-\infty < t_{appear}$.

Type 3 (Temporary obstacle): The obstacle exists in the scene for an interval of time $[t_{appear}, t_{disappear}]$, where $-\infty < t_{appear} < t_{disappear} < \infty$.

Type 4 (Permanent obstacle): The obstacle is permanently fixed in the environment.

When an obstacle is moved around in the plane by pick-up and put-down operations, it may appear and disappear in the scene many times. An obstacle that exists in the scene during k intervals of time (either at the same location or different locations in the plane) is treated as k different obstacles in our formulation. The obstacles are disjoint, that is, no two obstacles are allowed to overlap at any time. However, different obstacles are allowed to occupy the same area in the plane for different periods of time. We assume that the description of the obstacles (shapes, locations and time intervals in which the obstacles exist in the environment) is completely given ahead of planning. The robot is assumed to be a point subject only to a maximum speed bound. Given a start point and a start time, our problem is to determine a time-minimal motion for the point robot from the start point to the destination point such that the motion is collision-free, i.e., the point robot is always outside of any of the obstacles, or establish that there is no such motion. The destination point is assumed to be outside of any of the obstacles at all times.

Our strategy to cope with these types of dynamic obstacles is to compute reachable regions from a given start point. The reachable region is the set of points that can be reached from the start point within a certain time. This bears some resemblance to propagation of a wavefront from a start point. The process is also called the "continuous Dijkstra paradigm" and has been applied to a number of shortest path problems (Mitchell, Mount, and Papadimitriou 1987; Mitchell 1988; Mitchell and Papadimitriou 1990; Mitchell 1990b; Rowe and Richbourg 1990). The idea is as follows: The wavefront originates at a start point and grows outward in all directions at a fixed speed. Whenever the wavefront meets an obstacle, i.e., a barrier in the scene, it halts at that point and starts growing outward again when the obstacle is lifted, i.e., when it disappears from the scene. For each obstacle, we keep track of the earliest time when it is swept by the wavefront. A fastest motion to any point in the plane can be thus obtained by tracing the wavefront back to the start point. To simulate this process, we use two types of plane sweep techniques. One is to cope with the wavefront that originates from a point, and the other to cope with the wavefront that originates from a line segment.

To formulate our problem, we extend the concepts of accessibility and collision fronts, which were introduced in Section 3.2. We first give an algorithm to cope with transient obstacles, and then show that the algorithm can uniformly handle moving obstacles as well as transient obstacles.

5.1.2 Disappearing obstacle

First, we consider the case that the wavefront meets an obstacle that disappears from the environment. After the obstacle has disappeared from the scene, the point robot is allowed to pass through the region that was previously occupied by the obstacle.

For ease of explanation, let us first consider the case that there is only one line segment as an obstacle in the environment. Consider an environment that contains a line segment L, a start point O, and a destination point G. Let A and B be the two endpoints of L, and let $t_{disappear}$ be the time associated with L to indicate the time at which L disappears from the environment. Suppose that R, the point robot, starts moving from O at time t_0 at a speed v. (In the following, we adopt the convention that $t_0 = 0$.) After it starts moving, it keeps moving in a fixed direction at the same speed until it reaches an obstacle vertex or edge (or it may never meet any obstacles).

Accessibility from a point: A point V (V is either the destination point or a point on an obstacle edge) is said to be *accessible* from O, if there exists a direction of the motion such that R meets V before it disappears. When there is more than one obstacle in the environment, this motion from O to V must be collision-free for V to be accessible from O. Here, it is essential that for a point V to be accessible, V must exist in the scene when R reaches V. In other words, V is not accessible if V does not exist in the scene when R passes the point. The time at which R reaches V is called the accessible time of V and denoted by $t(V)$. The set of accessible points corresponding to all points in L forms a line segment which is a subset of L.

This subset of L is called the *collision front* of L (with respect to O, t_0, and v). Note that this definition is consistent with the definition in Section 3.4, where accessibility to an object that has a piecewise linear motion is defined. If L is the only obstacle in the scene, and its endpoints, A and B, are both accessible from O (i.e., if R is directed toward A, R can reach A before L disappears, and the same for B), then all points on L are accessible, since it takes less time to move to an internal point of L than to one of the endpoints. In this case, the collision front for L is L itself. Otherwise, only a portion of L is accessible from O. The rest of L is not accessible as L disappears before R can reach that part of L. Therefore, the collision front is a portion of L. This portion can be easily identified by intersecting L by the circle centered at O with its radius equal to $v \cdot t_{disappear}$. When there is more than one obstacle in the environment, it is possible that only a portion of a collision front is actually accessible.

These concepts are illustrated in Fig. 5.1. (In the examples in Fig. 5.1., the line segment L is assumed to be the only obstacle in the scene.) The endpoint A of line segment L is accessible from O (Fig. 5.1a), while endpoint B is not since L disappears from the scene before R can reach B (Fig. 5.1b). In this case, there must be such a point, say X, on L that R passes exactly at the same time as L disappears (Fig. 5.1c). In other words, line segment L disappears just when R passes X, i.e., $t(A) < t_{disappear} = t(X) < t(B)$. The circular arc indicates the location of the wafefront at time $t_{disappear}$. Notice that all points that lie between A and X are accessible, while all points between X and B are not accessible. Therefore, the collision front of L is AX. Note that point X is an internal point of L and serves as one of the endpoints of the collision front.

Figure 5.1d shows an effect of disappearing obstacle in motion planning. The rectangle disappears from the scene at a certain time after the point robot departs from O. The portion of the rectangle indicated by the broken lines is not reachable from O. As a result, it becomes possible to pass through the area (the internal area of the rectangle) which was previously occupied by the obstacle before it disappeared from the scene.

From a motion planning point of view, we must consider motions that start from the start point, move to some internal point on the collision front, stay at that spot until the obstacle disappears, and start moving again toward the destination point as soon as the obstacle disappears. It is possible that this type of motion reaches the destination point at an earlier time than motions that pass through endpoints of the line segment. For example, Fig. 5.1e shows such a motion that goes "through" a collision front. The point robot moves from O to H, stays there until the edge disappears, and starts moving again toward G after L disappears. Motion OHG may indeed reach G earlier than, say motion OAG, depending on the location of G relative to AX. (In this example, motion OHG is time-minimal if $t_{disappear} + \frac{HG}{v} < \min(t(A) + \frac{AG}{v}, t_{disappear} + \frac{XG}{v})$.) In such a case, motion OHG with HG being perpendicular to L is the time-minimal motion in the environment. Note that motion OAG passes A at time $t(A)$ (the accessible time of A) while any motion through an internal point of the line segment, i.e., a point in (A, X], departs from that point at $t_{disappear}$ (the disappearing time of the line segment.)

The above example indicates that a time-minimal motion to the destination point can actually go "through" any internal point on a line segment. Moreover, for the case that there is more than one obstacle in the environment, it is possible that the point robot goes "through" internal points of edges all the way to the destination point without ever visiting a vertex of the obstacles. This is in contrast to the approach that makes use of the visibility graph for a set of stationary obstacles, where the robot is always moved from a vertex of an obstacle to another vertex. Of course, if there is no appearing or disappearing obstacles in the scene, a time-minimal motion is a squence of vertex-to-vertex transitions as defined in the visibility graph.

This gives rise to a problem of determining accessible points from a segment. In addition to vertex-to-vertex transitions, we would also like to use a line segment as a set of points where the point robot can start moving. Let us call such a segment a *start segment*. As described earlier, a start segment is a subset of an obstacle edge. Let S be a start segment which is a subset of an obstacle edge L. All internal points on a given start segment S have exactly the same start time, i.e., the disappearing time of the line segment. An endpoint of S also has the same start time if the endpoint is an internal point of L. Otherwise (if the endpoint of S is an obstacle vertex), its start time is the

accessible time of the vertex. We define "accessibility from a start segment" by using
the concept of "accessibility from a point" defined earlier.

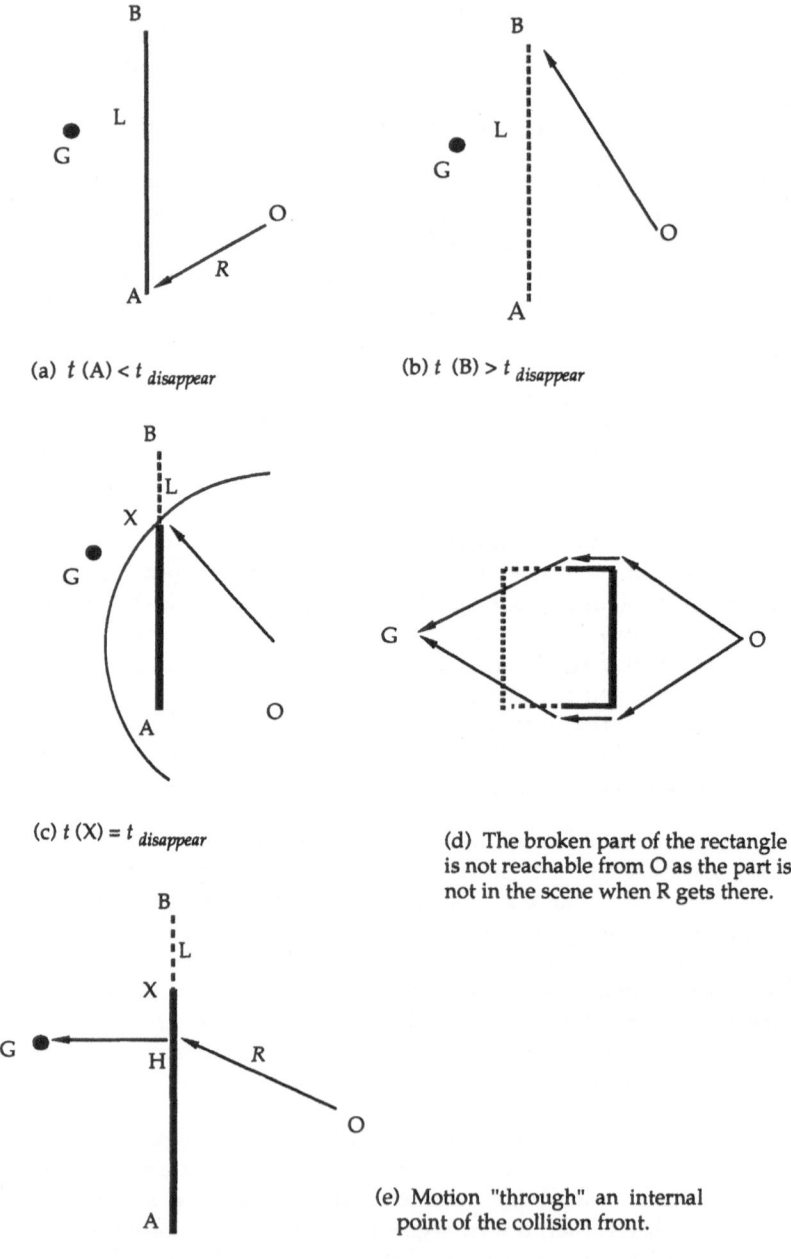

(a) $t(A) < t_{disappear}$

(b) $t(B) > t_{disappear}$

(c) $t(X) = t_{disappear}$

(d) The broken part of the rectangle
is not reachable from O as the part is
not in the scene when R gets there.

(e) Motion "through" an internal
point of the collision front.

Fig. 5.1. Disappearing obstacles

Accessibility from a line segment: Given a start segment S and a start time t_0, a point V (V is either the destination point or a point on an obstacle) is said to be *accessible* from S if V is accessible from an internal point, say H, on S such that VH is perpendicular to S, or V is accessible from one of the endpoints of S. The time at which V is reached from S is called the accessible time of V and denoted by $t(V)$. When V is accessible both from an internal point and an endpoint of S, we adopt the younger accessible time as $t(V)$.

Here, for the reason which we describe later, when a motion starts from an internal point of a line segment, we only consider motions whose initial segments are perpendicular to the line segment. The concept of collision front is define in a similar manner.

Figure 5.2 shows some intuition behind the above definition. Figure 5.2a shows the region that can be reached from a given start segment AX within a certain time $t = t_c$. Note that the start time for A is earlier than the start time for (A, X). The wavefront represents the set of farthest points that can be reached from [A, X] within time t_c, i.e., any point outside of the wavefront is not reachable from any point on AX within time t_c. The wavefront contains two types of border, i.e., circular parts C1 and C2 which correspond to waves emanating from the two endpoints X and A, respectively, and line segments D1 and D2 which are parallel to AX and correspond to the set of points that are reached from internal points of AX. These portions of the wavefront are called "subwaves." As can be seen from the above example, a subwave can emanate from two types of "sources", i.e., a point and an open line segment. These are respectively called a *point source* and a *segment source*. A collision front on an disappearing obstacle in Fig. 5.1e has a total of three sources, i.e., two point sources and a segment source.

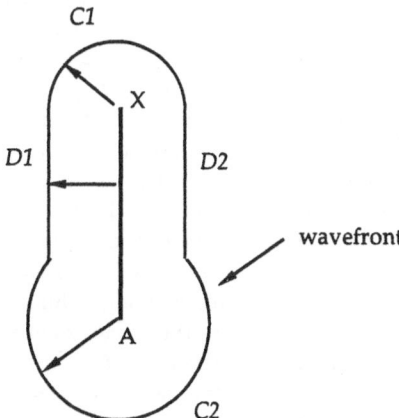

(a) The reagion that can be reached from segment AX.

Fig. 5.2. Accessible points from a start segment

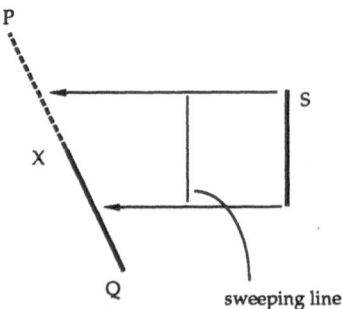

(b) Only portion QX is reachable from start segment S.

Fig. 5.2.

When the wavefront meets an obstacle, the part of the obstacle edges intersected by the wavefront becomes a new collision front. The wavefront may not meet some portion of the obstacle because the obstacle disappears before the wavefront can reach that portion (as illustrated in Fig. 5.2b). In such a case, the collision front corresponding to that part does not exist.

5.1.3 Appearing obstacles

We now consider an obstacle that appears in the environment at a certain time. We associate a time t_{appear} with the obstacle to denote such an appearing time of the obstacle. An obstacle of Type 3 (temporary obstacle) has characteristics of both Type 1 (disappearing obstacle) and Type 2 (appearing obstacle). We treat a Type-3 obstacle as an appearing obstacle until it appears in the scene, and then consider it as a disappearing obstacle immediately after it has appeared. Before t_{appear}, the point robot is allowed to traverse the area that is to be occupied by the obstacle. After t_{appear} (and before the obstacle possibly disappears), the robot is not allowed to pass through the obstacle. Also, the robot is not allowed to remain inside the obstacle at any time. We define accessibility as in the case of disappearing obstacles as follows: A point V is said to be accessible from O, if R can move to V with a straight line motion from O at a given constant speed v. The point V must exist in the scene when R reaches the point. Here, we can observe a situation contrasting to the case of disappearing obstacles. Consider an environment that contains a line segment, say L, as a single obstacle and O as the start point for the point robot R. If the closest point on L from S is accessible, then all points in L are accessible. Otherwise, only some portion of L is accessible. The concept of collision front is defined similarly as in the case of appearing obstacles.

Figure 5.3 illustrates the concept. We assume that L is the only obstacle in the scene in this example. In Fig. 5.3a, endpoint A of L is not accessible from O, since L has not appeared in the scene yet when R passes A. Note that in our definition, endpoint A is not accessible even though it is possible to reach A by reducing the speed of the point robot. Such a point is called *passable*. The set of passable points are called a passable segment. On the other hand, endpoint B of L is accessible from O, since L is already in the scene when R reaches B (Fig. 5.3b). In such a case, there must be a point in L, say X, where R passes just as L appears, i.e., $t(A) < t_{appear} = t(X) < t(B)$ (Fig. 5.3c). Therefore, XB forms the collision front of L. Segment AX, the set of passable points from O, is the passable segment generated about O. For the case of appearing obstacle, the collision front can consist of two segments (See Fig. 5.3d). When a line segment appears, disappears and reappears, the collision front can consist of at most four segments. In general, if a line segment exists in the scene for k disjoint intervals of time, its collision front may consist of at most $2k$ segments. We treat this case as k disjoint obstacles.

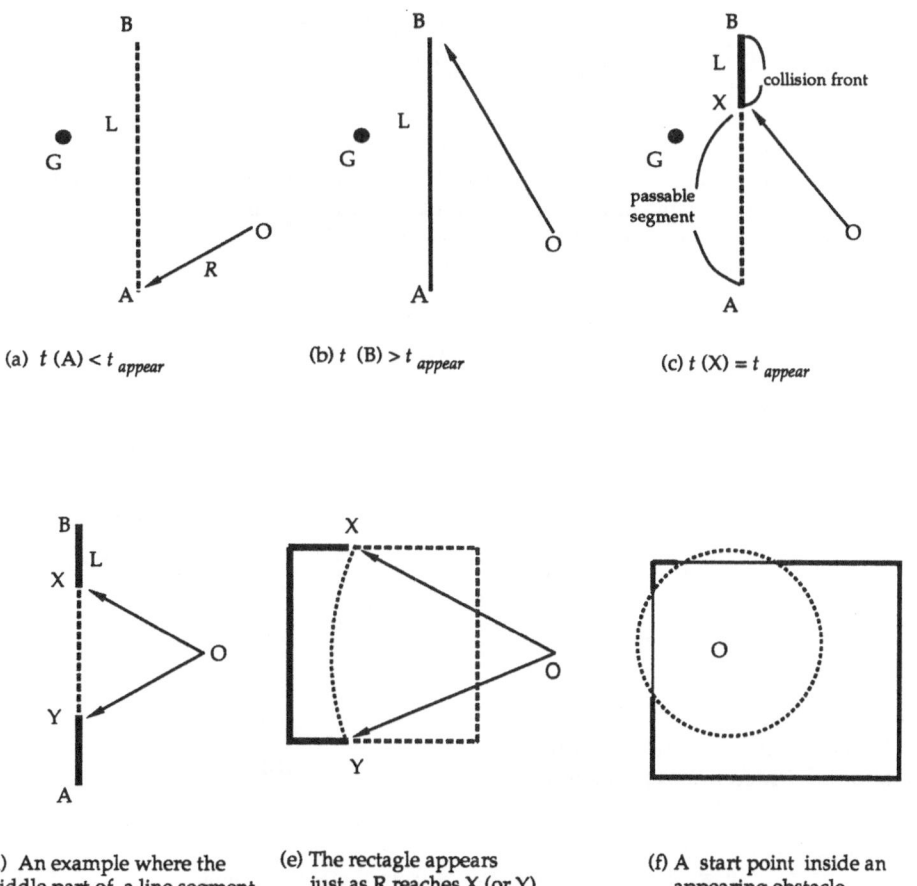

(a) $t(A) < t_{appear}$

(b) $t(B) > t_{appear}$

(c) $t(X) = t_{appear}$

(d) An example where the middle part of a line segment is passable, but not accessible.

(e) The rectagle appears just as R reaches X (or Y).

(f) A start point inside an appearing obstacle.

Fig. 5.3. Appearing obstacles

Appearing obstacles need some care. If the point robot is inside an obstacle when it appears, the robot is said to be crushed, in which case it does not survive. For this reason, we need to consider the directions of motion for the robot such that the robot is outside the obstacle when it appears. Figure 5.3e shows a case of an appearing rectangle and Fig. 5.3f shows a case that the start point is inside an appearing obstacle. If the robot moves from O to any point on the segments indicated by the thick lines, the robot is crushed when the rectangle appears. In such a case, the arcs of the circle inside the rectangle may be called as collision fronts generated about O. The wavefront terminates here and we do not keep those motions that are terminated before reaching the destination point. (Alternately, we could allow the robot to move in the interior of an obstacle even after it had appeared. Then the thick lines in Fig. 5.3e and Fig. 5.3f are collision fronts generated about O.)

The collision front from a start segment is defined in a similar manner to the case of disappearing obstacles (see Fig. 5.4a). As with the case for disappearing obstacles, the collision front varies for the initial location of the start point/segment, start time, and the speed of the point robot. For appearing obstacles, it is not necessary to consider motions that end at internal points of a collision front, since a motion that is once blocked by an appearing obstacle cannot reach the destination point earlier than motions that pass through endpoints of the collision front. In other words, an appearing obstacle and a permanent obstacle cannot have a segment source. A collision front of a transient obstacle or a disappearing obstacle gives rise to a segment source and two point sources.

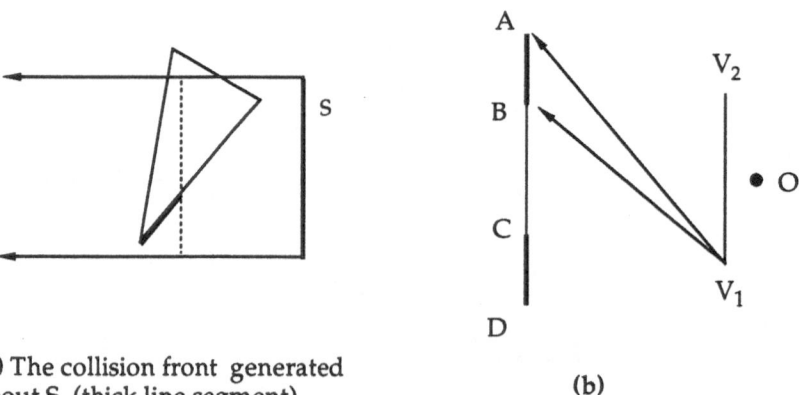

(a) The collision front generated about S (thick line segment).

(b)

Fig. 5.4. Accessible points from a start segment

5.1.4 Propagation of the wavefront

In our algorithm, we propagate the wavefront according to the following two rules. From now on, let v be the maximum speed of the robot.

Rule 1: When the wavefront hits a point P on an obstacle B, the wavefront propagates from P in the following two ways: (i) If P is a point source, then the wavefront propagates in all directions in free space through P at speed v with either $t(P)$ or $t_{disappear}$ as the start time, depending on whether ot not P is a vertex of B, respectively. (ii) If P is a point in a segment source, and B is going to disappear at time $t_{disappear}$, then the wavefront propagates through P at speed v with $t_{disappear}$ as the start time. Its direction of propagation is perpendicular to the obstacle edge in which P is found. When the obstacle B does not disappear after $t(P)$, the portion of the wavefront that hit internal points of edges of B terminates at that point.

The second rule tells what to do when a point on an obstacle is swept by more than one wavefront at different times.

Rule 2: When a point V on an obstacle is reached more than once by subwaves, we only retain the one that passes V at the earliest time. The wavefront is propagated through V with the youngest accessible time as its start time. Subwaves that reach V at later times are not propagated through V. This rule applies even when point V is on an obstacle that does not exist when a wavefront passes through it.

Figure 5.4b illustrates how Rule 2 applies. An edge AD is a temporary obstacle and edge $V_1 V_2$ is a permanent obstacle. Suppose that segments AB and BD are the collision front and the passable segment generated about V_1, respectively. Likewise, segments CD and AC are the collision front and the passable segment generated about V_2, respectively. Clearly, points on segment AB have younger accessible times when they are reached from V_2 than when they are reached from V_1. (Segment AB is a portion of the passable segment generated at V_2.) Therefore, we do not consider AB as a start segment. The same argument applies to points on CD. As a result, there is no start point or start segment in [AD].

In the above example, one might wonder if there are points in the plane that could be reached from V_1 through [AB], but not from V_2. If so, we would miss some time-minimal motions. According to the claim which we show later, any point that is reachable from V_1 through [AB] are reachable from V_2 at an earlier time. Because of this rule, wavefront propagation takes place at most once for any accessible point in the plane. This process is repeated until the wavefront reaches the destination point. We show that by repeating the process described above, the wavefront can indeed reach any point in the plane in minimum time.

In our algorithm, the point robot is always at the forefront of the wavefront, as the wavefront is propagated at the maximum speed of the robot. This is important as can be seen in the example if Fig. 5.1e. In Fig. 5.1e, if the point robot is not on the collision front at $t_{disappear}$, the motion is never time-minimal. However, it does not imply that the point robot must always be on a collision front when the obstacle disappears in order for the motion to be time-minimal. Consider an environment in which there are two disappearing line segments. The point robot that is not on the first collision front at its disappearing time may still catch up at the second collision front before it disappears. Such a motion can still be time-minimal in a global sense. However, it may well be that a motion that is late for the first disappearing time cannot arrive at the second collision front until after its disappearing time. Note that if it is impossible for the point robot, if it departs the first collision front at its disappearing time, to reach the second collision front at its disappearing time, then it is certainly impossible for a point robot that is not at the first collision front at its disappearing time to reach the second collision front in time. For this reason, we always locate the robot at a collision front at its disappearing time, whenever possible.

Now, we formally justify the above argument as well as Rule 1. For this purpose, let us first define the canonical motion. The canonical motion represents a motion that follows Rule 1 and is always at the forefront of the wavefront.

A motion segment from P to Q (P is either the start point or a point on a collision front, and Q is either the destination point or a point on a collision front) is said to be *canonical* when one of the following holds:

(i) (Starting from a point source): P is an endpoint of a collision front or the start point. The point robot departs from P at time $t_{disappear}$ if P is an internal point of the line segment, or at $t(P)$ if P is an endpoint of the line segment, or the start time if P is the start point. The robot moves straight from P to Q at speed v.

(ii) (Starting from a segment source): P is an internal point of a collision front. The point robot departs from P at time $t_{disappear}$ and moves straight from P to Q at speed v. The motion segment PQ is perpendicular to the collision front.

(iii) (Waiting motion): P and Q are the same point on a collision front. The robot stays at P until the disappearing time of the obstacle.

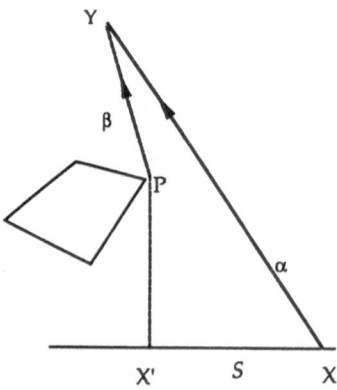

Fig. 5.5. Canonical motion

A motion is said to be *canonical motion*, when it consists of a series of canonical motion segments. In Fig. 5.5a, motion α departs from X on S and moves straight to Y. This motion is not canonical, since XY is not perpendicular to S. On the other hand, motion β moves straight to an obstacle vertex P such that X'P is perpendicular to S, and then moves to Y again along a straight line. Motion β is canonical and reaches Y earlier than motion α. Below, we show that for any non-canonical motion, there is a canonical motion that reaches the same point at the same time or earlier.

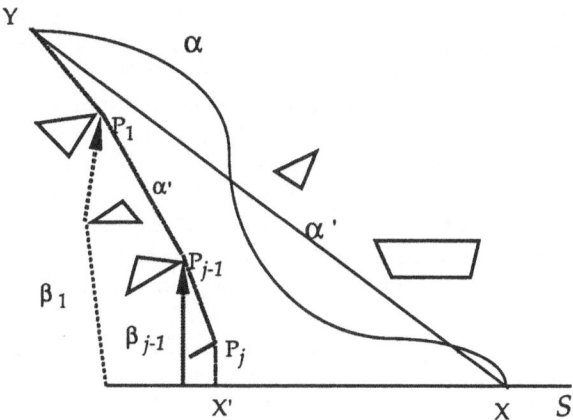

Fig. 5.6. Illustration of Proposition 9

Proposition 9. Let X be a point on a segment S, and Y be an arbitrary point in the plane. If there exists a motion starting from X on S at time t_1 and terminating at Y at time t_2 (where $t_2 > t_1$), then there exists a canonical motion from a point X' on S (X' and X may be different) starting at time t_1 and terminating at Y at time t_2' such that $t_2' \leq t_2$.

Proof: Let α be a motion starting from X at time t_1 and terminating at Y at time t_2. There are two cases depending on whether or not α crosses any of the collision fronts that are generated by repeatedly applying the wavefront algorithm starting from segment S (S contains three sources).

(Case 1): Motion α does not cross any of the collision fronts.

We first stretch the motion α tautly among the collision fronts in free space. In doing so, we regard all collision fronts as just two dimensional obstacles in the plane while ignoring the timing information. Let α' be the sequence of line segments created as a result of the stretch. Note that the total length of α' is shorter than α. Let α' pass through $X, C_1, C_2, \cdots, C_k, Y$, where C_i's are endpoints of collision fronts (timing information through C_i's is ignored for now). Let us first discuss the case where $k = 0$ (i.e., $\alpha' = XY$, as in Fig. 5.6). If XY is perpendicular to S, then α' is a canonical motion and the arrival time at Y is clearly earlier than that of α. Otherwise, we slide the start point of α' (let it be X', initially coinciding with X) along S in the direction such that the length of α' is shortened while fixing Y, until either $X'Y$ becomes perpendicular to

S (in which case $X'Y$ is a canonical motion and we are done) or X' coincides with an endpoint of S (in which case $X'Y$ is a canonical motion and we are done) or segment $X'Y$ hits an endpoint of some collision front. If $X'Y$ hits an endpoint of a collision front , say P_1, we do the same operation on line segment $X'P_1$, i.e., we fix P_1 and slide X' along S in the direction such that the length of $X'P_1$ is shortened. We repeat this process until we obtain a sequence of line segments YP_1, P_1P_2, P_2P_3, $\cdots$, P_jX', where either P_jX' is perpendicular to S or X' is an endpoint of S.

Motion $X'P_j$ (starting X' at time t_1) is a canonical motion by definition. We now check if $t(P_{j-1})$ is younger than the arrival time at P_{j-1} along motion $X'P_jP_{j-1}$. (Note that the arrival time at P_{j-1} along a canonical motion $X'P_jP_{j-1}$ must not be earlier than $t(P_{i-1})$ by Rule 2.) Although $X'P_jP_{j-1}$ is a canonical motion, there may be another canonical motion from S to P_{j-1} that arrives at P_{j-1} earlier. If so, let β_{j-1} denote such a canonical motion to P_{j-1} (i.e., the one that arrives at P_{j-1} at $t(P_{j-1})$). Otherwise, we adopt motion $X'P_jP_{j-1}$ as β_{j-1}. Thus we have β_{j-1} to move to P_{j-1} at an earliest time. We now repeat the same operation at P_{j-2}. If motion β_{j-1} plus its extension $P_{j-1}P_{j-2}$ does not arrive at P_{j-2} at $t(P_{j-2})$, then there must be another canonical motion to P_{j-2} from S. We adopt such a motion and call it β_{j-2}. We repeat this process until we come to P_1. By construction, the arrival time at P_1 along a canonical motion β_1 is younger than the arrival time that would be resulted from following the sequence of motion segments α'. By connecting P_1 to Y, we have a canonical motion from S to Y that reaches Y at an earlier time than α. The case that $k > 0$ is handled similarly.

Now let us consider the case that α' passes through C_i's. In this case also, we produce a canonical motion from S to Y that arrives at Y earlier than α.

(Case 2): Motion α crosses collision fronts.

Suppose that α crosses collision fronts, say $F_1, \cdots, F_k$, in this order. In this case, F_k must disappear at a time earlier than the time at which α passes through F_k. We can create a canonical motion from F_k (starting a point on F_k at its disappearing time) to Y that arrives at Y earlier than α, as can be seen from the proof of Case 1. Let this canonical motion start from Q on F_k. The fact that Q is on F_k implies that there exists a canonical motion from S to Q. By concatenating a canonical motion from S to Q, a waiting motion at Q (see above definition (iii)), and a canonical motion from Q to Y, a canonical motion from S to Y is constructed. $\lozenge$

Now we justify Rule 2. Rule 2 tells us that if there is more than one motion that reaches the same point at different times, motions that come late may be ignored. Suppose that two canonical motions α and β pass a point P on an obstacle at times t_1 and t_2, respectively, where $t_1 \leq t_2$. Let AP and BP be the last motion segments of motions α and β before P, respectively. We show that for any point, say Q, after P along motion β, there exists a canonical motion to Q such that the motion arrives at Q at an earlier time than motion β. Such a motion can be obtained by revising motion α as follows. We stretch an elastic string tautly from A to P. One end of the string currently at P is gradually moved to Q along motion β, while fixing A. See Fig 5.7. (Here we assume that A is a point source. A similar argument applies to the case that A is a point in a segment source, in which case the end of the string currently at A

also needs to be moved along the segment so that the initial segment of the string is always perpendicular to the segment.) In doing so, the string may be bent at corners of collision fronts (generated in the process of creating the motion represented as the string), if necessary. Clearly, the distance from A to Q along the string is shorter than the distance from A to Q via P, i.e., it is also shorter than the distance from B to Q along motion β. If motion β crosses a collision front (generated in the process of creating the motion represented by the elastic string), Proposition 9 can then be used to show that there exists a motion to reach any point after the collision front on motion β earlier than β starting from a point on the collision front.

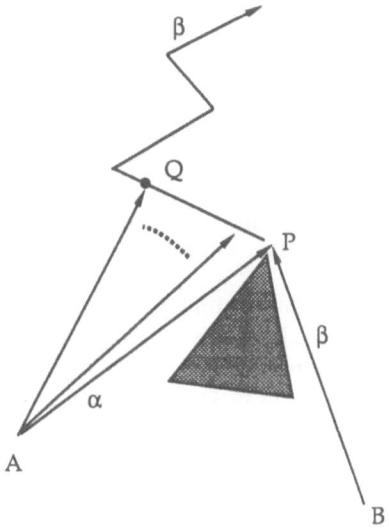

Fig. 5.7. Illustration of Rule 2

For an environment that contains more than one line segment, each line segment has its own collision fronts. However, it is possible that only a part of the collision front is reachable from a source since some collision front may occlude those behind it. The set of accessible points (i.e., collision fronts) from a point source as well as from a segment source is determined as follows.

(Collision fronts from a point source:) First, we describe how to determine the set of accessible points from a start point O. This is done by using a technique similar to that used to determine the visibility of a given set of line segments, and was described in Section 3.5. By using an angular sweep about O, it takes $O(n \log n)$ time to determine the set of accessible points from O.

(Collision fronts from a segment source:) Next, we describe how to determine the portion accessible from a given segment source S. This is done by a plane-sweep technique. The sweep line initially coincides with S and starts moving at time t_0 at speed v in the direction perpendicular to S. The portion of a line segment, say L, that is intersected by the sweep line before L disappears is the set of accessible points from

S. The sweep line halts each time the line intersects an endpoint of a collision front, and checks whether or not the collision front associated with the endpoint is accessible from S. This can be achieved by maintaining the active collision fronts based on their distances from S. This process also takes $O(n \log n)$ time.

A line segment, say L, may be reached from more than one source at various times. In such a case, Rule 2 is applied to retain the appropriate portions. The resulting portions are used as sources on L.

5.1.5 Algorithm and analysis

We now describe how to compute a motion from the start point. We use a priority queue of sources where the start time of each source serves as the source's priority.

1. Insert the start vertex into the queue.

2. Remove a source, say S, from the queue whose associated accessible time is the youngest. If the queue is empty, then report that a motion does not exist and exit.

3. If the source U in step (2) is the destination point, then report the motion and exit. Otherwise, insert all segments of the collision fronts generated about U based on Rule 1 into the queue. When the line segment is reached from more than one source (in this case, different parts of the same line segment are accessible from those sources), retain appropriate collision fronts based on Rule 2. Repeat steps (2) and (3).

Now we analyze computation time required in the above process. Usually, in an algorithm that makes use of wavefront propagation, its computation time is measured in terms of two quantities, T, the total number of events (the number of times the wavefront intersects obstacle vertices or edges), and W, the amount of work required on an event. The total computation time is given by multiplying the two quantities, T and W.

First we analyze the number of events. The total number of events is measured by the total number of sources created in the process. We show that accessible points on an edge can be divided into at most $O(n)$ connected segments (thus at most $O(n)$ sources per edge), where n is the total number of vertices in the environment. Note that an obstacle can divide the wavefront into a small fixed number of subwaves. (See Fig. 5.3d for a case that an appearing obstacle gives rise to three pairwise concave subwaves.) Recall that a subwave is a connected portion of the wavefront consisting of either a single arc (emanating from a point source) or a line segment (emanating from a segment source). We can divide motions into motion classes based on which subwaves a motion has followed. Due to Rule 2, an obstacle can split at most one subwave (the one that arrives at the obstacle at the earliest time) into a small fixed number of (pairwise concave) subwaves. Therefore, the total number of subwaves at any given time is $O(n)$. Thus, an obstacle edge has at most $O(n)$ sources. This means that the number of events T is bounded by $O(n^2)$.

Figure 5.8 contains a scene where the total number of events is indeed $O(n^2)$. Vertical line segments represent obstacles in the scene. Thick lines are reachable segments from O, which is located sufficiently far from the obstacles so that the rays emanating from O are considered almost parallel to each other when they hit the obstacles. The short line segments in the right divide the wave from O into $O(n)$ subwaves. The next longer vertical line segments are disappearing obstacles and they disappear as soon as the subwaves hit them. Thus, each of them has $O(n)$ sources. Hence, the total number of sources in the scene is $O(n^2)$.

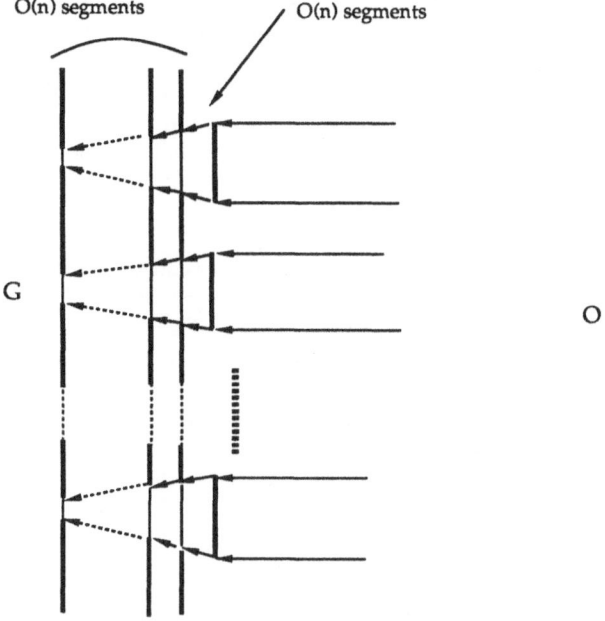

Fig. 5.8. $O(n^2)$ segments

The set of accessible points from a source can be determined in $O(n \log n)$ time by the plane sweep techniques described above. (In case of an appearing obstacle, we retain passable segments as well.) One propagation from a source gives rise to a total of $O(n)$ candidate sources. A linear list is associated with each edge to store these candidate sources. A new candidate source is checked with an existing list and the list is maintained appropriately. This can be achieved in $O(\log n)$ time by using binary search on a linear list associated with the edge. Thus it takes $O(n \log n)$ time to store all candidate sources. In summary, when the wavefront starts from a source, a plane-sweep ($O(n \log n)$ time) is performed to determine the collision fronts generated about the source, which is followed by maintenance operations that retain appropriate collision fronts ($O(n \log n)$ time). Therefore, the required computation at a source W takes $O(n \log n)$ time. Since the total computation time is obtained by $T \cdot W$, we have established the following result:

Proposition 10. It takes $O(n^3 \log n)$ time to find a time-minimal motion to the destination point in the presence of transient obstacles.

We have studied the problem of motion planning in the presence of obstacles that appear and disappear in the environment. A method is proposed to determine the portions of the plane that are reachable from the given start point by plane-sweep techniques. This leads us to an algorithm to generate a time-minimal motion. When the environment does not contain any transient obstacles (i.e., all the obstacles are stationary and permanent obstacles), our algorithm generates a path that would be generated by using the visibility graph on the set of stationary obstacles. In this sense, our approach is a generalization of shortest path computations using the visibility graph. As a result of our algorithm, the robot's speed alternates between $v_{\max}$ when the robot is in motion and zero when the robot is in a waiting mode. This sudden change in speed can be reduced as follows: after the initial motion is determined, an appropriate travel speed at each moving mode is recomputed such that the robot reaches the waiting location just in time for the next moving mode (i.e., adjust the speed such that the robot does not have to wait any more).

It should be noted that our approach can be extended to handle an environment containing slowly moving obstacles as well as transient obstacles (Fig. 5.9). This is because motion planning amidst both types of obstacles can be formulated consistently by using the concept of accessibility. The time-minimal property can be shown by applying the Time-Minimal Motion theorem in Section 3.4 and Proposition 9. Furthermore, transient obstacles may be used to approximate fast-moving obstacles. See Section 5.3 for more discussions.

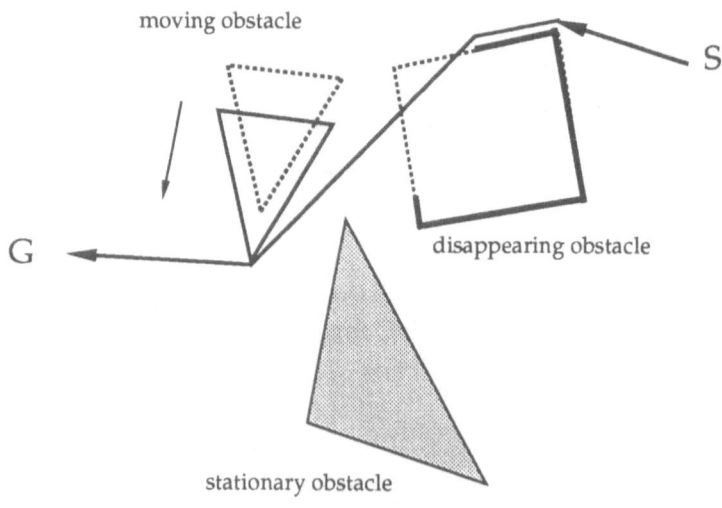

Fig. 5.9. A dynamic environment

5.2 Moving Obstacles in Three Dimensions

In this section, we consider motion planning in the presence of a set of moving polyhedral obstacles in three dimensions. The motions of the obstacles are linear, i.e., all obstacles are moving in fixed directions at constant speeds without rotation. We consider a point robot which can move in any direction in space with a single constraint that it cannot move faster than a given speed bound. All obstacles are *slowly moving*, i.e., their speeds are strictly slower than the maximum speed of the robot. This condition is essential in some part of the following discussions. In other words, the point robot can have any motion in space as long as its maximum speed (which is faster than that of any of the obstacles) does not exceed a given limit. We further assume that the obstacles are disjoint at all times, i.e., they do not collide with each other. The destination point also moves along a known (piecewise) linear trajectory and is assumed to be collision-free at all times. The speed of the destination point is also assumed to be slower than the maximum speed of the robot. As a consequence of this assumption, the destination point is shown to be always reachable. If the speed of the destination point is faster than the maximum speed of the robot, then there are cases that the destination point is not reachable. Our method may be extended to solve this problem as well. The problem that we set out in this section is: Given a start location, a start time, motions of the polyhedral obstacles, and a trajectory of the destination point, find a motion to reach the destination point in a minimal time.

5.2.1 Properties of shortest paths

Solving our problem draws on some techniques used in finding a shortest path amidst stationary polyhedral obstacles. For the case of stationary polyhedra in three dimensions, a shortest path that avoids passing through the interiors of the obstacles is known to have the following three properties (Sharir and Schorr 1986; Akman 1987):

1. A shortest path π from X to Y is a serial chain of line segments (i.e., π is a polygonal arc) that bends at internal points of edges or at non-convex vertices of the polyhedral obstacles. In other words, π can be represented as a sequence of one or more line segments $\pi = (\pi_0, \pi_1, \cdots, \pi_p)$ such that each π_i is a line segment $P_i P_{i+1}$, where $P_0 = X$ and $P_{p+1} = Y$. Each P_i ($i = 1, \cdots, p$) is either an internal point of an obstacle edge or a non-convex vertex of an obstacle.

2. Suppose that a shortest path π passes through an internal point of an obstacle edge e. The path π enters and leaves e at equal angles.

3. If π is a shortest path from X to Y that passes through interior points of a given sequence of edges $\xi = (\xi_1, \xi_2, \cdots, \xi_p)$, then π is the unique shortest path from X to Y that is constrained to pass through ξ in this order.

Unlike the two-dimensional case, shortest paths bend also at interior points of edges of the input polyhedra rather than just vertices. When all polyhedra are convex, shortest paths never bend at vertices of the obstacles. Using the above three properties, the problem of finding a shortest path amidst polyhedra can be solved (Sharir and Schorr 1986). The problem is decomposed into two subproblems: (i) given a sequence of edges, find a shortest path that is constrained to pass through the edge sequence, and (ii) determine the sequence of edges and (non-convex) vertices through which a shortest path passes.

Both problems are known to be computationally hard to solve exactly. Fastest algorithms known so far solve subproblem (i) in singly-exponential time (Reif and Storer 1985; Canny 1988a) and subproblem (ii) is known to be NP-hard (Canny 1988a). Subproblem (ii) can be simply solved by examining all possible permutations of sequences of edges and vertices, and compute the length of a shortest path constrained to pass through each of these sequences. For subproblem (i), Sharir and Schorr (1986) describe two methods (numerical computation and algebraic computation) to obtain a shortest path by making use of the above three properties.

The numerical method for subproblem (i) begins with an arbitrary polygonal path passing through a given sequence of edges. Then, the path is iteratively shortened by picking one of the contact points that does not satisfy the second property regarding equal entry and exit angles and replacing it by another point on the same edge that satisfies the property. Since the path is strictly shortened after each iteration, the path is converged to the desired shortest path by this process. However, as Mitchell and Papadimitriou (1990) point out, it is not known in analytical terms how fast the path converges to the desired shortest path, although in practice the process is observed to be extremely fast.

The algebraic computation gives an exact shortest path as a solution of a system of n equations with respect to n contact points at the given edges. Sharir and Schorr (1986) show that it takes doubly-exponential time to solve the system by elimination in the number of edges of the input polyhedra in the environment. This complexity has been improved to a singly-exponential time by using more efficient reduction of the system (Reif and Storer 1985; Canny 1988a). Papadimitriou (1985) shows an approximation method to compute a shortest path in three dimensions.

For the case that the number of input polyhedra is a fixed number, a shortest path can be computed in polynomial time in the number of total edges in the polygons and exponential in the number of polyhedral obstacles (Sharir 1987; Baltsan and Sharir 1988). Gewali, Ntafos, and Tollis (1990) consider restricted cases of the problem in which polyhedral obstacles are all vertical. They show an algorithm that runs in $O(n^{6k-1})$, where k and n represent the numbers of vertical obstacles and vertices of the obstacles, respectively. For the special case that the number of polyhedra is one, Mount (1985) shows an algorithm that runs in $O(n^2 \log n)$ time to find a shortest path between two points on the surface of the polyhedron. Mitchell, Mount and Papadimitriou (1987) study a related problem of finding geodesic paths on the surface of a polyhedron.

Regarding motion planning in the presence a set of moving polyhedra, relatively little is known. Reif and Sharir (1985) have established in their seminal paper that the problem is PSPACE-hard in the presence of rotating obstacles. They also show a decision algorithm that runs in $O(2^{n^{O(1)}})$ time and in $n^{O(\log n)}$ space. They observe that just avoiding slowly moving obstacles is possible.

5.2.2 Properties of time-minimal motions

We show in this section that a time-minimal motion among slowly moving polyhedra exhibits the following three properties that are analogous to the above three properties for shortest paths.

Property 1: A time-minimal motion π from X to Y consists of a serial chain of straight motion segments that bends either at internal points on obstacle edges or vertices of the polyhedra (See Fig. 5.10). Motion π is traversed at the maximum speed of the point robot throughout π from X to Y. In other words, π can be represented as a sequence of one or more motion segments $\pi = (\pi_0, \pi_1, \cdots, \pi_p)$ such that each π_i is a straight line motion from P_i to P_{i+1} traversed at the robot's top speed, where $P_0 = X$ and $P_{p+1} = Y$. For each $i = 1, \cdots, p$, P_i is coincident either with an internal point on an obstacle edge or a vertex of an obstacle.

Property 2: Suppose that a time-minimal motion π passes through an internal point of an edge e_i. The motion π enters and leaves the boundary segment of the collision front generated by e_i at equal angles.

Property 3: If $\pi = (\pi_0, \pi_1, \cdots, \pi_p)$ is a time-minimal motion from X to Y starting X at time t_0 that passes through interior points of a given sequence of moving edges $e=(e_1, e_2, \cdots, e_p)$, then π is the unique time-minimal motion from X to Y starting X at time t_0 that is constrained to pass through e in this order.

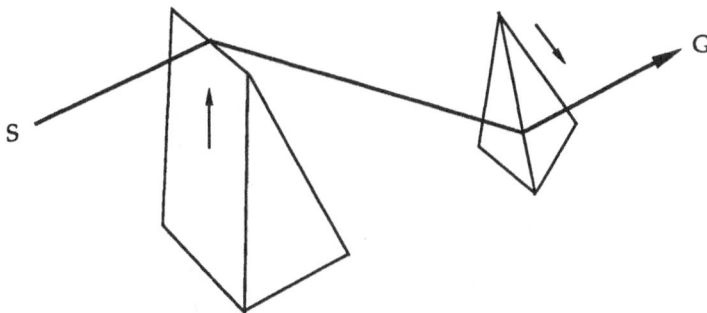

Fig. 5.10. A polygonal path

The concept of collision front in Property 2 is a generalization of that of two dimensions to three dimensions and is defined below. In proving the first property, we use techniques similar to those used in proving the Time-Minimal Motion theorem in Section 3.4.

In the following discussion, we consider only the case that every obstacle is a plane polygon[1] (i.e., a face). More general cases (e.g., polyhedra) are thought of as consisting of a collection of faces (i.e., polygons) with the property that two faces can intersect only at their common edge. We call such an object a wall. A *wall* is defined by the union of a finite set of plane polygons such that every edge of a polygon is shared by

---

[1] A polygon is called a plane polygon in three dimensions when all of its vertices are coplanar.

one or zero other polygon and no subset of polygons has the same property. Here we mean by a polygon (or a face) the union of its boundary and interior. Intuitively, if we remove some faces from a polyhedra, the resulting object is a wall. When removing a face, its boundary edge is removed only when it is not shared by other face of the same wall. A polyhedron is also a wall by this definition. Fig. 5.11 contains an example of a wall. Without loss of generality, we assume that each face has been made convex by introducing some additional edges on the face.

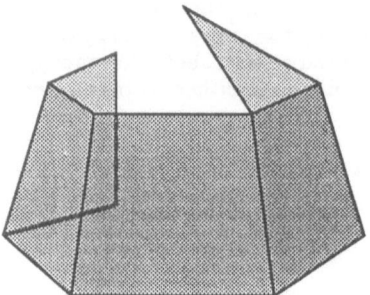

Fig. 5.11. A wall

While the robot is moved in space, it is not allowed to penetrate any part of a wall. When our argument is generalized from a collection of faces to a set of walls, a wall is considered as comprising of faces to be separated at a time that is set to infinity. This is equivalent to disallowing a point robot to move from one side of a wall to the other through an edge.

A *face movement* is defined as a tuple (F, d_F, v_F) that represents a motion of a face F moving in direction d_F at speed v_F. An *edge movement* is defined for an edge by a tuple (E, d_E, v_E) in a similar manner. Now let us extend the concepts of accessibility and collision front to three dimensions.

Accessibility (3D): Consider a set of face movements $M = \{M_1, M_2, \cdots, M_n\}$ and G, the destination point. Let R be a point robot located initially at O at time t_0. Suppose that R starts moving at time t_0 at a speed v. After R starts moving, it is moved in a fixed direction at constant speed v. A point V (V is either the destination point or a point on a face of a wall) is said to be *accessible* at X from O, if there exists a direction of the motion of R such that R meets V without being intercepted by any other movement. The meeting point X is called an accessible point of V and the meeting time is called the accessible time of X and denoted by $t(X)$.

Collision Front (3D): Consider an environment that contains only one face movement, say (F, d_L, v_F). Let O be as defined above. The set of accessible points from O corresponding to all points in F forms a curved surface. We call this surface a *collision front* due to F generated about O (with respect to the robot's staring time and speed). When there is more than one face in the environment, there will be more than one collision front and it is possible that only some portion of the faces is accessible.

Fig. 5.12 contains some examples of three-dimensional collision fronts for a single moving face.

Proposition 11. A three-dimensional collision front for a slowly moving face is a portion of either a hyperboloid, cone, or plane. For the case of hyperboloid, the start point is on the axis of the hyperboloid. For the case of cone, the start point coincides with its vertex.

Proof: Without loss of generality, we consider a face F that is always parallel to the x-y plane as it moves. Let v_F and v be the speeds of F and the robot, respectively. Let O denote the start location of the robot. Let α be the plane that moves vertically (in the direction of the z-axis) at the speed equal to the z-component of v_F. Hence, α always contains F as it moves. Let u denote the z-component of v_F. Let α coincide with $z = a$ ($a \geq 0$) at the start time.

We first classify the motion of moving face into the following four types. A face F is called (i) *receding* when α moves away from O after the start time (i.e., $a > 0$ and $u > 0$), (ii) *proceeding* when α approaches to O after the start time (i.e., $a > 0$ and $u < 0$), (iii) *coplanar* when α is coplanar with O (i.e., $a = 0$), and (iv) *degenerate* when the direction of the motion of α is coplanar with α (i.e., $u=0$). The case that α is stationary are treated as type (iv) for convenience.

We now show the proposition for these cases. We consider the set of accessible points corresponding to all points on α.

(Case 1): Receding face.

Suppose that a point P at (x, y, a) on α at the start time (time 0) is accessible from the origin $(0,0)$ at point A at (x, y, z). Refer to Fig. 5.12a. Then, x and y must satisfy

$$t(A) = \frac{z - a}{u} = \frac{\sqrt{x^2 + y^2 + z^2}}{v} \tag{5.1}$$

The above equation defines a quadratic relationship over x, y, and z. Considering $v > v_F \geq u$, the collision front of plane α is one side of a hyperboloid (with two sheets). It is easy to see that the collision front due to F is the intersection of the hyperboloid and the trajectory of F; thus the collision front of F is a portion of the hyperboloid.

(Case 2): Proceeding face.

By using the same argument as above with the difference that the value of u is negative, we can see that the collision front is a portion of the other sheet of the hyperboloid defined by Equation (5.1).

(Case 3): Coplanar face.

When $a = 0$, i.e., F is coplanar with O, the set of accessible points corresponding to all points on α forms a cone (Fig. 5.7b). This can be seen by just letting a to be 0 in Equation (5.1). Therefore, the collision front due to F is a portion of a cone whose vertex coincides with O.

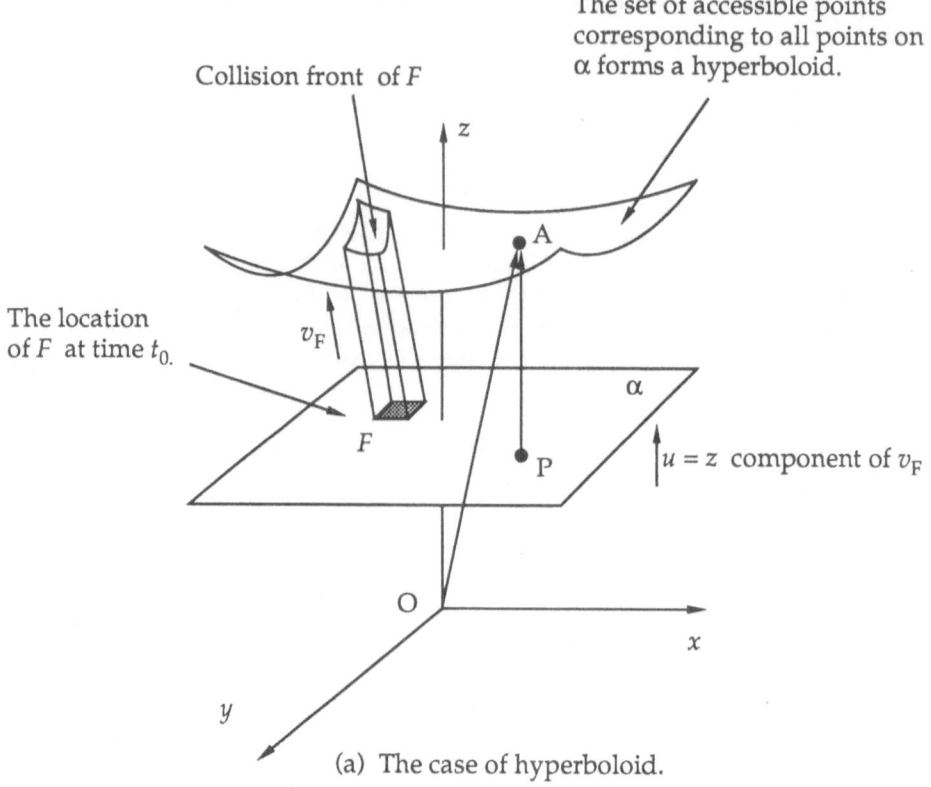

Collision front of F

The set of accessible points corresponding to all points on α forms a hyperboloid.

The location of F at time t_0.

v_F

F

A

α

P

$u = z$ component of v_F

O

x

y

z

(a) The case of hyperboloid.

Fig. 5.12. Examples of collision fronts on three dimensions

(Case 4): Degenerate face.

When $u = 0$, it is simple to see that the collision front due to F is a subset of plane α (Fig. 5.12c).◊

The set of accessible points corresponding to all points in a boundary edge of a face is called the *boundary segment* of the collision front generated by the moving edge. The following proposition regarding the shape of a boundary segment is simple to confirm.

Proposition 12. A boundary segment of a collision front is a portion of either a hyperbola, a parabola, or a line.

Proof: Note that a boundary segment is a conic section. ◊

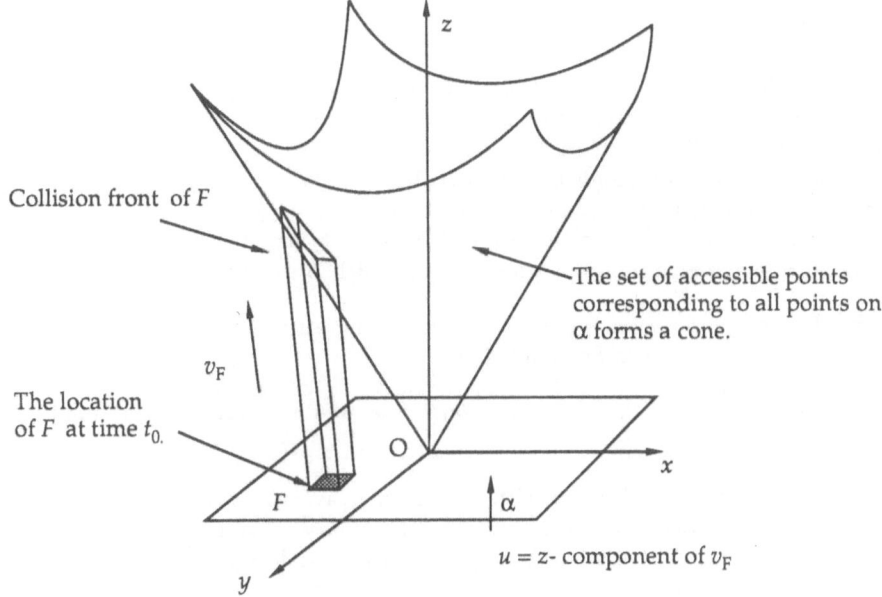

Collision front of F

The set of accessible points corresponding to all points on α forms a cone.

v_F

The location of F at time t_0.

O

F

α

x

y

$u = z$- component of v_F

(b) The case of cone.

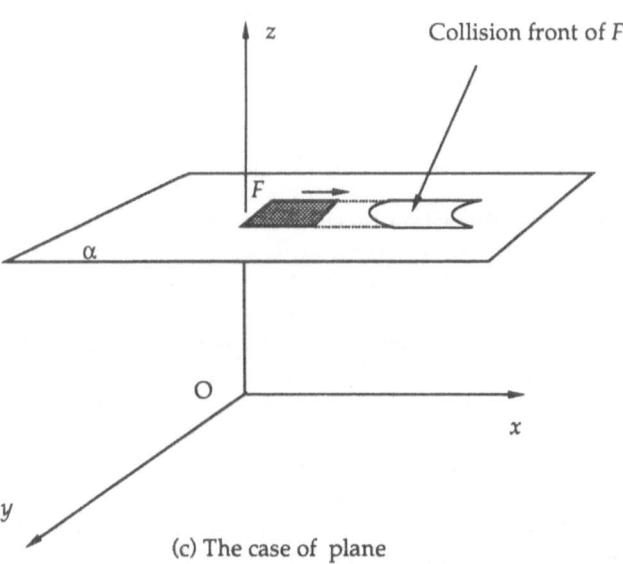

z

Collision front of F

F

α

O

x

y

(c) The case of plane

Fig. 5.12

The following Propositions 13 and 14 are generalizations of Propositions 1 and 3, respectively, and used to prove Property 1 of time-minimal motions. These propositions can be proven by using arguments similar to those used to prove Propositions 1 and 3. From now on, let v_{max} denote the maximum speed of the point robot.

Proposition 13. Given a set of face movements M and a destination point G, suppose that point R and an internal point on edge E (or on vertex V) are at location X at time t_1. Let F_E be the set of faces that are incident on E (or on V, respectively). Let M_E be the set of movements of elements of F_E. If there exists a motion, say α, starting from X at time t_1 and terminating at G at time t_2 ($> t_1$) in $M - M_E$, then there exists a motion, say α' in M, starting from X at time t_1 and terminating at G at time t_2. Motion α' contains a motion segment along which R's speed is less than v_{max}.

Proof: The proposition can be proven by using an argument closely parallel to the proof of Proposition 1 in Section 3.4. $\Diamond$

As in the proof of the two-dimensional case, we divide all motions from O to G into the following two groups.

Group 1 - motions that start with a segment traversed at speed v_{max} in a constant direction through a point on a boundary of some collision front generated at O. The motion after passing the initial segment is arbitrary but must eventually reach G.

Group 2 - the other motions.

Proposition 14. Suppose that G is not accessible from O. Let π_2 be a collision-free motion from O to G. Let π_2 be in Group 2. There exists a collision-free motion from O to G in Group 1, say π_1, that is identical to π_2 starting at some point J. The speed along some portion of π_1 before J is less than v_{max}.

Proof: This proposition can be proven by essentially the same technique as the one used to prove Proposition 3. Thus, we only sketch the proof here.

As candidate for π_1 in Proposition 14, we construct a set of motions τ's. All τ's begin with a straight line segment OP traversed at v_{max}, where P is a point on a boundary segment generated at O. Let P on face F. After reaching P, each of τ's moves at a speed infinitesimally less than v_{max} and heads for the earliest point J on π_2 that it can reach (Fig. 5.13). It can be shown that there is at least one such collision-free τ that can reach π_2. In doing so, we consider a set of auxiliary motions σ's, each starting from a point, say Q, on the boundary segments generated about O at $t(Q)$. Each of the motions σ's moves at a constant speed $v_i < v_{max}$ (i indicates the edge on which Q is found) in the direction perpendicular to the edge in which Q is found, such that it is always coincident with some point in the face F. The role of motions σ's is exactly the same as that of the two motions σ_1 and σ_2 in the proof of Proposition 3 in Section 3.4. The rest of the proof of the proposition is done by applying a similar argument of the proof of Proposition 3. $\Diamond$

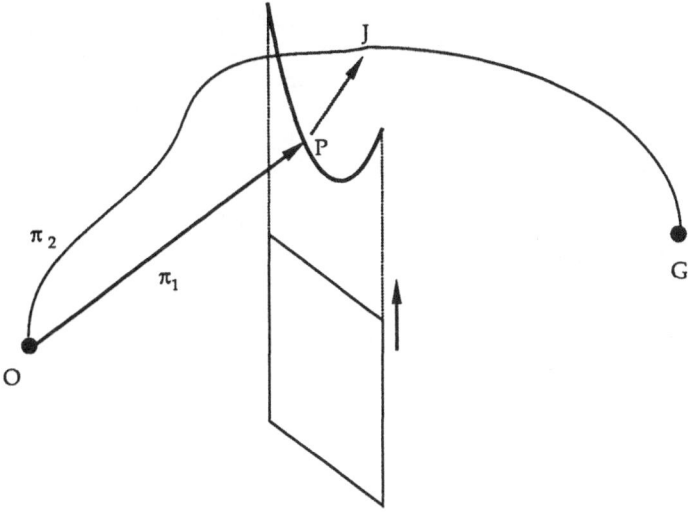

Fig. 5.13. Illustration of Proposition 13

Proposition 15. For an environment that contains a set of slowly moving walls, a time-minimal motion π from X to Y consists of a serial chain of straight motion segments. The robot keeps moving at $v_{\max}$ along the time-minimal motion and changes the direction of the motion either at internal points on edges or at vertices of the polyhedra.

Proof: This proposition is to show Property 1 described earlier in this section. The main flow of the proof is essentially identical to that of the proof of Theorem 1 in Section 3.4. As in the proof of Theorem 1, we consider the environment with n face movements M and a destination point G. We show the proposition by induction on n. Note that when $n = 0$, the proposition holds. Now we assume that the proposition holds for $n = k > 0$. We have the following observations for the case $n = k + 1$:

Observation 1. Suppose that R is coincident with a point, say P, on one of the obstacles. Then a time-minimal motion from P to Y satisfies Property 1 described earlier.

Observation 2. For any motion in Group 2, a better motion in Group 1 exists.

(Proof of Observation 1): Let F_P be the set of faces that are incident on the point P, and let M_P be the set of face movements of elements of F_P. We remove M_P from the environment, resulting in a set of walls with a total number of face movements less than before. By the induction hypothesis, a time-minimal motion exists from P to G that satisfies Property 1. This motion can be shown to be collision-free also in M by using Proposition 13, thus a time-minimal motion in M.

(Proof of Observation 2): Assume that there exists a motion α in Group 2. Using Proposition 14, it can be shown that there exists a motion β in Group 1 that moves from O to a point on one of the boundary segments generated about O and turns to rejoin motion α with a speed less than $v_{\max}$. Motion β is not time-minimal, since it contains a motion segment traversed at a speed less than $v_{\max}$. This implies that there exists a Goup 1 motion that arrives at the destination point earlier than motion α.

With Observations 1 and 2 established, it is simple to see that a time-minimal motion from O to G satisfies Property 1. $\Diamond$

Proposition 16. Suppose that a time-minimal motion π passes through an internal point P of an edge e_i. Motion π enters and leaves the boundary segment generated by e_i at equal angles.

Proof: Let $\pi_{i-1} = AP$ and $\pi_i = PB$ be incoming and outgoing motion segments at P, respectively. Let ξ_i denote the boundary segment generated by e_i about A (Fig. 5.14). As a consequence of Proposition 15, if a motion contains a portion that is traversed at a speed less than $v_{\max}$, then the motion is not time-minimal. This implies that motion APB must also be the shortest path from A to B that is constrained to pass through a point on ξ_i.

Let c denote the length of the shortest path APB. Consider the set of points $\{X|\ |AX|+|BX| = c\}$. This defines an ellipsoid whose foci are A and B. This ellipsoid must be tangent to ξ_i at P; for otherwise APB would not be the shortest. Noting that any tangent to an ellipsoid makes equal angles with the lines joining the foci to the point of tangency, AP and BP make equal angles with ξ_i, which proves the proposition. $\Diamond$

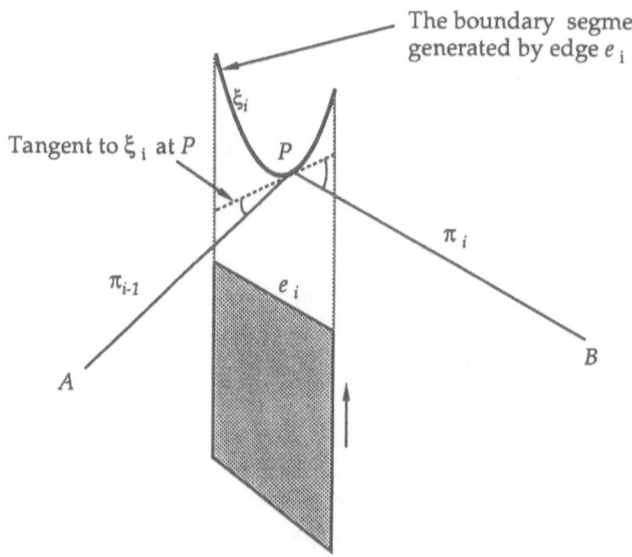

Fig. 5.14. Equal incoming and outgoing angles

Alternately, the shortest path from A to B in the above proof can be found as follows. Let P be the point on ξ_i at which π_{i-1} and π_i subtend the equal incoming and outgoing angles. Let α be the plane containing ξ_i. Consider the plane β that is tangent to ξ_i at P and perpendicular to plane α. By considering the mirror image of B with respect to β, it is simple to show that any other path $AP'B$ is longer than APB.

Proposition 17. If $\pi = (\pi_0, \pi_1, \cdots, \pi_p)$ is a time-minimal motion from X to Y starting X at time t_0 that passes through internal points of a sequence of moving edges $e=(e_1, e_2, \cdots, e_p)$, then π is the unique time-minimal motion from X to Y starting X at time t_0 that is constrained to pass through e in this order.

Proof: Suppose that there exist two time-minimal motions π and π' from X to Y both starting X at the same time. Without loss of generality, we assume that X is the first point that motions π and π' start diverging and that Y is the first point after X at which π and π' converge. We show that there exists a motion ϕ from X to Y passing through the edge sequence e that starts and terminates exactly at the same time as π and π' and that contains a motion segment traversed at a speed strictly less than $v_{\max}$.

Let $\pi = (\vec{u}_0, \vec{u}_1, \cdots, \vec{u}_p)$ and $\pi' = (\vec{v}_0, \vec{v}_1, \cdots, \vec{v}_p)$ be the two time-minimal motions from X to Y that pass through the given sequence of edges e. Here, $\vec{u}_i$ and $\vec{v}_i$ $(i = 0, \cdots, p)$ represent the vector from U_i to U_{i+1} and the vector from V_i and V_{i+1}, respectively, where $U_0 = V_0 = X$ and $U_{p+1} = V_{p+1} = Y$ (See Fig. 5.15). Motion ϕ is constructed in such a way that the point moving along ϕ passes through internal points of each of $U_i V_i$, say W_i, $(i = 1, \cdots, p)$ just as a point on edge e_i passes through W_i. In the following, we let $W_0 = X$ and $W_{p+1} = Y$ for convenience.

We define such a motion ϕ in the following construction. Let a sequence of straight motion segments $(\vec{w}_0, \vec{w}_1, \cdots, \vec{w}_p)$ represent motion ϕ, where vector $\vec{w}_i$ is from W_i to W_{i+1} $(i = 0, \cdots, p)$. Let $T(U_i)$, $T(V_i)$, and $T(W_i)$ be the times at which motions π, π', and ϕ pass through U_i, V_i, and W_i, respectively, for $i = 0, \cdots, p+1$. The location of W_i is defined as

$$\vec{W}_i = m\vec{U}_i + n\vec{V}_i \tag{5.2}$$

and the time at which motion ϕ passes W_i is defined as follows:

$$T(W_i) = m \cdot T(U_i) + n \cdot T(V_i) \tag{5.3}$$

where $m > 0$, $n > 0$, and $m + n = 1$, for $i = 1, \cdots, p$.

Clearly, motion ϕ as defined by (5.2) and (5.3) passes W_i exactly at the same time as a point on edge e_i passes at W_i. Recall that e_i moves at a constant speed. In other words, motion ϕ passes through the sequence of edges e.

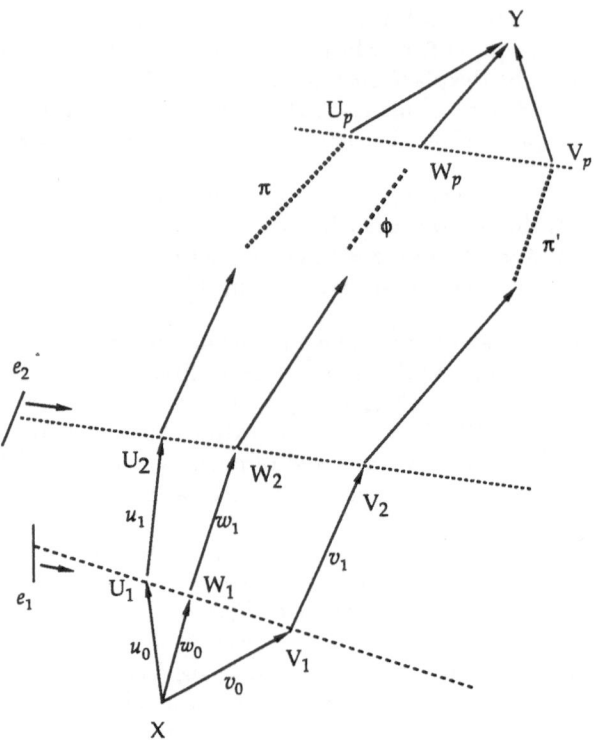

Fig. 5.15. Illustration of Proposition 16

Now we must show that speeds along ϕ are indeed equal or less than $v_{\max}$. Since motions π and π' are traversed at speed $v_{\max}$, the following hold for $i = 0, \cdots, p$.

$$|\vec{u}_i| = v_{\max}(T(U_{i+1}) - T(U_i)) \qquad (5.4)$$

$$|\vec{v}_i| = v_{\max}(T(V_{i+1}) - T(V_i)) \qquad (5.5)$$

From Equation (5.2), we have

$$
\begin{aligned}
\vec{w}_i &= \vec{W_{i+1}} - \vec{W_i} \\
&= (m\vec{U_{i+1}} + n\vec{U_{i+1}}) - (m\vec{U_i} + n\vec{U_i}) \\
&= m\vec{u}_i + n\vec{v}_i \qquad (i = 0, \cdots, p)
\end{aligned}
\qquad (5.6)
$$

Similarly from Equation (5.3), we have

$$T(W_{i+1}) - T(W_i) = m(T(U_{i+1}) - T(U_i)) + n(T(V_{i+1}) - T(V_i)) \qquad (i = 0, \cdots, p) \ (5.7)$$

Using Equations (5.4)-(5.7), the speed along $\vec{w}_i$ is given by

$$
\begin{aligned}
v_{\vec{w}_i} &= \frac{|\vec{w}_i|}{T(W_{i+1}) - T(W_i)} \\
&= \frac{|m\vec{u}_i + n\vec{v}_i|}{T(W_{i+1}) - T(W_i)} \\
&\leq \frac{m|\vec{u}_i| + n|\vec{v}_i|}{T(W_{i+1}) - T(W_i)} \\
&= \frac{m \cdot v_{\max}(T(U_{i+1}) - T(U_i)) + n \cdot v_{\max}(T(V_{i+1}) - T(V_i))}{m(T(U_{i+1}) - T(U_i)) + n(T(V_{i+1}) - T(V_i))} \\
&= v_{\max} \quad (i = 0, \cdots, p)
\end{aligned}
$$

Especially, the first segment of motion ϕ is traversed by a speed strictly less than $v_{\max}$. As a result of Proposition 15, a time-minimal motion does not contain a portion along which the robot moves at a speed less than $v_{\max}$. Thus, motion ϕ is not time-minimal. This implies that neither motion π nor motion π', which arrives at Y at the same time as ϕ, is time-minimal, which is a contradiction. $\Diamond$

Thus, we have established Properties 1, 2, and 3 of time-minimal motions. Making use of the three properties, a time-minimal motion can be determined in the presence of a set of slowly moving polyhedral obstacles. As in the case of stationary obstacles, an exact solution can be obtained as a solution of a system of algebraic equations with n variables with respect to the positions of contact points at edges. Alternately, given an edge sequence that a time-minimal motion passes through, the positions of contact points at the edges can be obtained numerically as follows: We first pick up an arbitrary motion that passes through a given edge sequence. The arrival time is iteratively shortened by choosing one of the contact points, say P_i, that does not satisfy Property 2 with respect to incoming and outgoing angles and replacing it by another point on the same boundary of the collision front where Property 2 holds. As a result, the outgoing motion segment emanating from the new contact point arrives at the contact point on the next edge earlier than before. This effect can be propagated for the rest of the motion, resulting in a motion that arrives at the destination point earlier than the original motion. Since this process strictly shortened the arrival time of the motion, the motion converges to the desired time-minimal motion by repeatedly applying the process.

5.3 Summary

In this chapter, two formulations of dynamic motion planning have been considered. One is motion planning in the plane in the presence of appearing and disappearing obstacles, and the other is motion planning in a three-dimensional space containing moving polyhedra.

Appearing and disappearing obstacles may be used to approximate fast-moving obstacles in the plane. Suppose that a trajectory of a fast-moving obstacle is given. There is a point at which the obstacle is accessible at an earliest time and a point at not accessible at all, we do not have to worry about colliding into the obstacle.) Each collision area can be divided into a series of non-overlapping pieces that are next to each other (Fig. 5.16). Each piece is considered as a transient obstacle; it exists in the scene only for a certain time interval in which the moving obstacle and the piece intersect. If we let the length of each piece be δ, the number of pieces in the scene is $O(\frac{n}{\delta})$. A solution within this resolution is obtained in $O((\frac{n}{\delta})^3 \log n)$ time. In this approach, an important factor is how fine the pieces are. The finer the pieces are, the better the solution is. However, it takes more time to find a better solution.

We have also studied the problem of motion planning among moving polyhedra. The emphasis of the work has been to show the three basic properties of time-minimal motions in three dimensions. Representing moving three-dimensional objects with full generality would require space-time of four dimensions. Our solution based on the idea of three-dimensional collision fronts does not make explicit use of the time dimension. This makes it possible for us to treat the problem as in the case of stationary obstacles. In fact, our solution suggests that the time complexity for motion planning is the same as the stationary case.

We have treated the case that the number of polyhedral obstacles is unbounded. The argument may be made substantially simpler in the case of a single convex obstacle. In this case, the wavefront propagation paradigm can be used to approach the problem. When the robot is on the surface of the obstacle, the speed of the robot relative to the face is determined by the direction of the face movement and the surface normal of the face. This is the case where the cost per unit distance depends on the direction of motion in the framework of the weighted region problem (Rowe and Ross 1990).

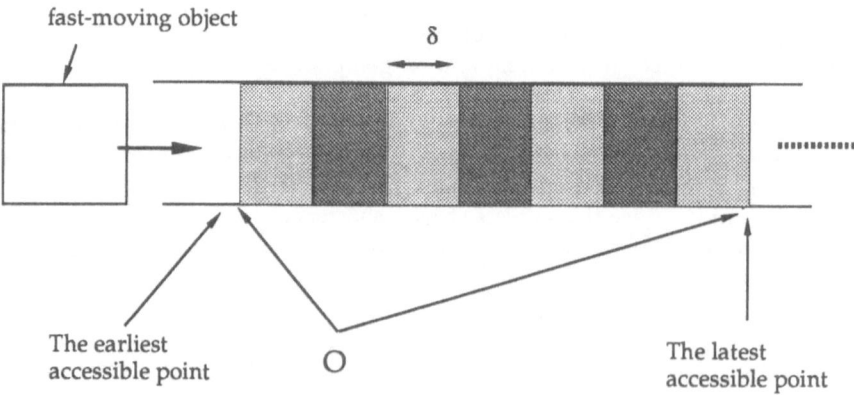

A seires of appearing and disappearing objects can approximate a fast-moving object.

Fig. 5.16. A fast-moving obstacle

Chapter 6
Constrained Motion

So far the only constraint we have imposed on the motion of the robot has been a speed bound. Other factors must be taken into consideration in more realistic situations, because of physical constraints on the robot. For example, a mobile robot cannot accelerate beyond some upper limit. Knowledge about the area in which the robot navigates (e.g., slopes and ground conditions) may also affect the choice of the path.

In this chapter, we consider motions in the plane that satisfy three types of constraints: speed, acceleration, and centrifugal force. In other words, we require that the robot's speed and acceleration remain in given ranges, and that it not negotiate any curve in such a way as to exceed a given upper limit on the allowable centrifugal force. Here we only discuss the case where the robot is considered to be a point. The more general problem in which a robot is a polygon can be transformed into a simpler problem in which a robot is a point as discussed in Section 2.1, but this simpler problem is equivalent to the original problem only when rotation of the robot is not allowed. In case of a car-like robot (i.e., the robot has two front wheels and two rear wheels, and is steered by the two front wheels), the robot is subject to non-holonomic constraints as well as acceleration constraints. The non-holonomic constraint is discussed elsewhere (Tournassoud 1988) and is not considered here. We assume that each obstacle is a polygon which moves at a constant speed without rotation.

6.1 Constraints on the Motion of the Robot

The problem of path planning with an acceleration bound and a speed bound is sometimes called the kinodynamic motion planning in the literature. Donald and Xavier (1989) propose an approximate algorithm to produce a time-minimal path among stationary obstacles, while adhering to speed and acceleration bounds. Fortune and Wilfong (1988) solve a decision problem about the existence of a path subject to curvature constraints. Their algorithm runs in an exponential time. It is not known as of today whether the kinodynamic problem in the presence of stationary obstacles is solvable in polynomial time. In view of this, it is certainly a non-trivial problem to find a motion which satisfies bounds on speed, acceleration, and centrifugal force while avoiding moving obstacles.

In a stationary two-dimensional environment, the problem is usually decomposed into two steps. In the first step, a path (or a homotopic path class) without any timing information is determined. In the second step, the path is refined to satisfy conditions on speed and acceleration. The second step is sometimes called 'trajectory planning'. In a time-varying environment, the path must contain some timing information from the beginning; a path may be collision-free for one speed profile, but not for another. The accessibility method does not seem relevant in this problem since the motion generated by the method will always have a constant speed along the path regardless of its curvature.

We address the problem of finding a path with motion constraints by discretizing the search space. This discretization has two aspects. First, we require that the motion be represented as a sequence of points in space. Second, the acceleration of the robot takes on discretized values. In other words, the trajectory of the robot in space-time is represented as a parabolic curve having specific parameters. This is discussed further in Section 6.4.

Our approach to the problem is to use a three-dimensional space in which time is the third dimension. This space is usually called space-time. An object, say O, moving in a two-dimensional plane can be regarded as a three-dimensional stationary object whose space-time volume is swept by the object as it moves. If (x, y, z) is inside that space-time volume, then the point (x, y) was occupied by object O at time z.

Our task now becomes one of finding a collision-free path in space-time. Given a start position, time, and goal position, the search process generates a (space-time) path for the mobile object that connects the start position to the goal position. Minimizing the z value of the goal position corresponds to the problem of time-minimal path generation. In other cases, the z value is irrelevant as long as it leads the object to the final position without collision. Since our third dimension is time, the search should be carefully designed so as not to choose an unrealistic path – e.g., moving in the negative time direction. Moreover, the path must satisfy the given conditions on speed, acceleration, and curvature.

6.2 Space Representation

In this section, we discuss the type of representation that will fit naturally into our space-time formulation. Both the mobile object and the obstacles are defined in a world with bounded x, y, and t values. A point in the space is represented by (x, y, t), where $x1 < x < x2$, $y1 < y < y2$, and $t1 < t < t2$. x and y are positions while t corresponds to time. Usually, it is convenient to let $x1 = y1 = t1 = 0$ and $x2 = y2$. Note that time is also bounded. In this world, every motion of an object on the two-dimensional plane inside the region defined by $x1 < x < x2$, $y1 < y < y2$ and taking place during the time period between $t1$ and $t2$ is represented as a three-dimensional object. The concept of space-time has been also used in computer vision and computer graphics. Bolles and Baker (1985) has used space-time to construct a three-dimensional solid from an image sequence for motion analysis. Glassner (1988) has applied the idea in computer graphics for animation.

We adopt an octree-type hierarchical data structure (Hunter 1978; Meagher 1982; Jackins and Tanimoto 1980) to represent space-time. This structure has an advantage over other representations such as boundary representations (Requicha and Voelcker

1982; Mäntylä 1987; Hoffmann 1989); using a tree structure as an index to the model world makes it possible to efficiently access a location. For this reason, hierarchical data structures have been often used in robotics, in particular, for the purpose of collision detection and motion planning (Esterling and Van Rosendale 1983; Samet and Tamminen 1985; Kambhampati and Davis 1986; Roach and Boaz 1987; Noborio, Naniwa, and Arimoto 1990).

Recall that we have assumed that the motion of the obstacles does not involve rotation. When a polygon moves at a constant speed without rotation, its trajectory (i.e., the space-time volume swept by the polygon) is a polyhedron in three dimensions. When the polygon rotates, the decomposition rules described below are still valid; however, the trajectory is no longer a polyhedron. For this reason, we restrict the motions of the obstacles to be translations.

Methods of storing polygonal and polyhedral shapes using quadtree-type decompositions have been studied in the context of computer cartography (Samet and Weber 1985) and computer-aided design (Ayala, Brunet, and Navazo 1985; Carlbom, Chakravarty, and Vanderschel 1985). Our representation is built by repeatedly subdividing three-dimensional space-time into eight subspaces of equal size called cells, until every cell satisfies one of the following conditions:

(A) It contains part of the trajectory of a vertex of an obstacle.

(B) It does not contain any part of the trajectory of a vertex, but contains part of the trajectory of an edge of an obstacle.

(C) It does not contain any part of the trajectory.

(D) It is entirely contained in the trajectory.

The cells defined by these criteria are called vertex cells, edge cells, empty cells, and full cells, respectively. (This terminology is not compatible with that used in (Ayala, Brunet, and Navazo 1985; Carlbom, Chakravarty, and Vanderschel 1985). Here, we use terms based on a two-dimensional rather than a three-dimensional viewpoint. For example, a cell that satisfies criterion (B) is called a surface cell in the papers cited above. We call it an edge cell to make it clear that a two-dimensional edge has moved in the cell.)

An octree is built corresponding to the volume swept by the motions of objects along given trajectories. This is done in the following way. Initially, the entire universe is treated as a single cell which is represented by an octree containing one node. If any of conditions (A)-(D) are violated by this cell, then the cell is subdivided and the resulting cells are checked for violation of conditions (A)-(D). This process is applied recursively. For more details, see (Ayala, Brunet, and Navazo 1985; Fujimura and Kunii 1985).

Unlike conventional octrees (Yau and Srihari 1983; Meagher 1982) in which objects are approximated, our tree structure stores polygonal shapes exactly and requires less memory space. Figure 6.1 illustrates the concept described above. Suppose that an object moves in the x direction (Fig. 6.1a). A solid line and a dashed line depict the initial and final position of the object, respectively. Figure 6.1b shows the volume swept by the object in space-time. A tree representation of this three-dimensional image is shown in Fig. 6.1d, where the cell numbering convention of Fig. 6.1c is used.

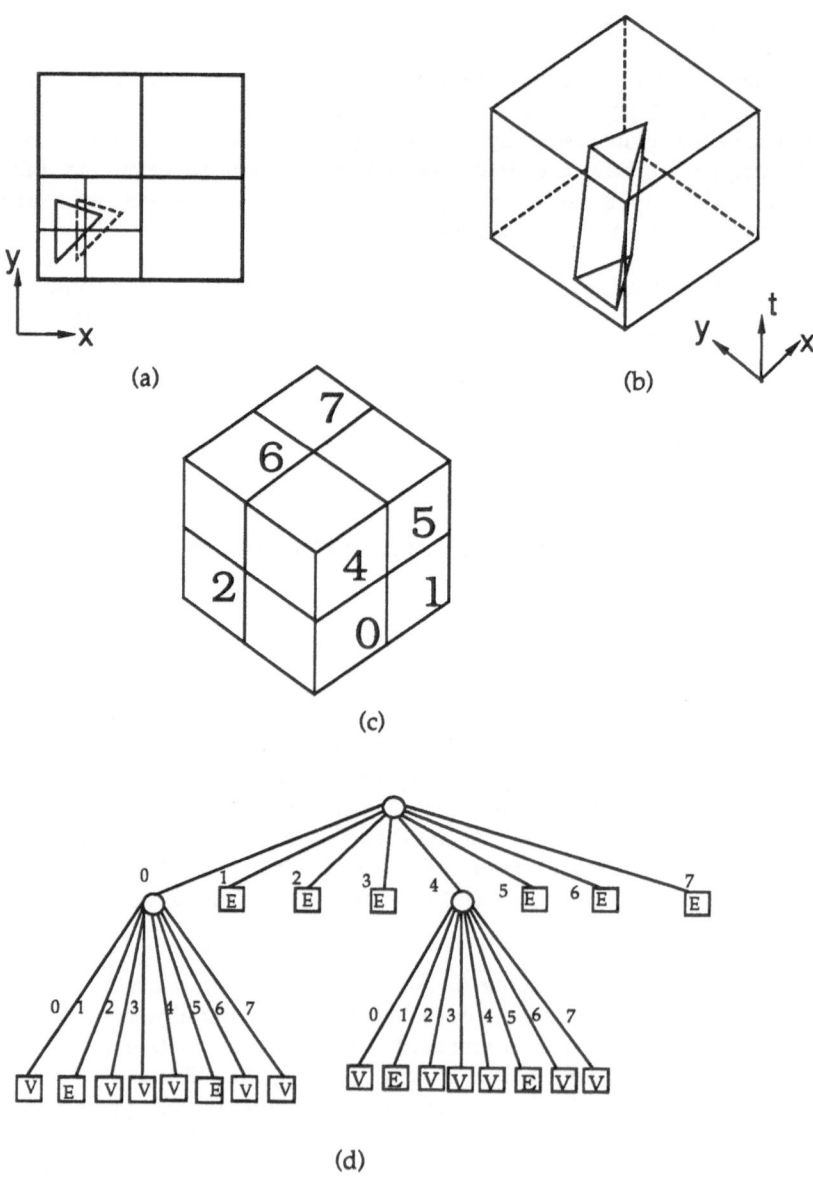

(a)

(b)

(c)

(d)

Fig. 6.1. Octree representation of space-time

6.3 Path Search

This section describes how the search procedure generates a collision-free motion using the representation introduced in Section 6.2.

6.3.1 Control Points

A method frequently used in path planning is to represent a path by a sequence of empty spaces. The free space is divided into possibly overlapping pieces of empty space, and the path is constructed by connecting these empty spaces. Applying this idea in a dynamic environment gives rise to the problem of determining the path inside the free space.

For example, we see from Fig. 6.2 that two possible paths (a) and (b) can be chosen in the same free space. However, the difference in length and curvature between paths (a) and (b) is not negligible. Factors such as speed, acceleration and curvature are highly sensitive to changes in the trajectory. Also, storing timing information with these representations is not trivial.

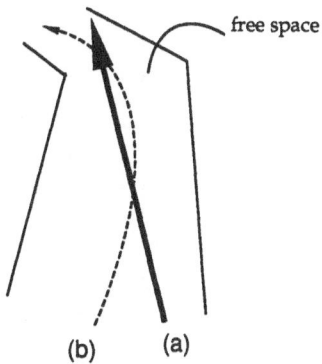

Fig. 6.2. Cylinder representation of a path

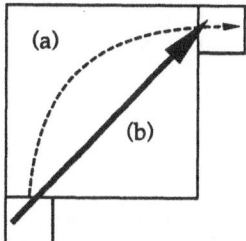

Fig. 6.3. Quadrant representation of free space

These comments also apply to the quadtree approach. Quadrants are not sufficiently specific to pinpoint a particular path. In Fig. 6.3, path (a) requires more time than path (b), which means that the next quadrant chosen by path (a) should be different from that for path (b). This difference in time must be explicitly expressed in the representation.

We define points called *C-points* (control points) in the space. The sequence of these C-points forms a skeleton of the final path. A C-point is an ordered pair consisting of an L-point and a T-point (Fig. 6.4a). The L-point represents the two-dimensional projection (x, y) of the C-point, and the T-point represents the time at which the object passes the L-point. The x and y values of an L-point take on discrete values. The square in Fig. 6.4b denotes the projection of a three-dimensional space-time cell (Fig. 6.4a) onto the $x - y$ plane. We define the L-points so that their x and y coordinates lie only at the nine locations shown in Fig. 6.4b. Figure 6.4c is an example to how L-points are distributed over the plane. The value of a T-point is assigned during the search stage. The search procedure first chooses the next location to go to from the nine points shown above. Next, it determines the appropriate speed. This, in turn, determines the T-point. Thus two identical sequences of L-points with different sets of T-points represent two different motions. The T-point is determined by the T-point component of the previous C-point on the path and by the acceleration chosen at the L-point component of the previous C-point.

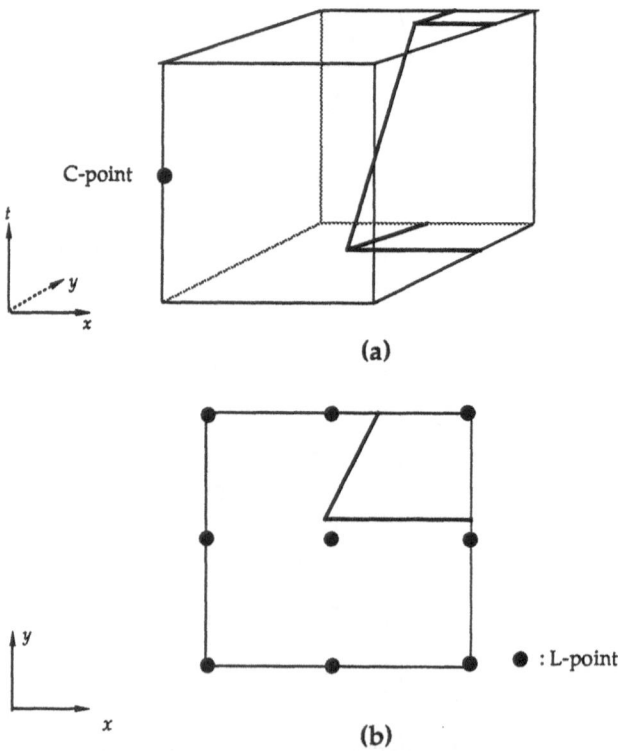

(a)

(b)

Fig. 6.4. C-points and L-points

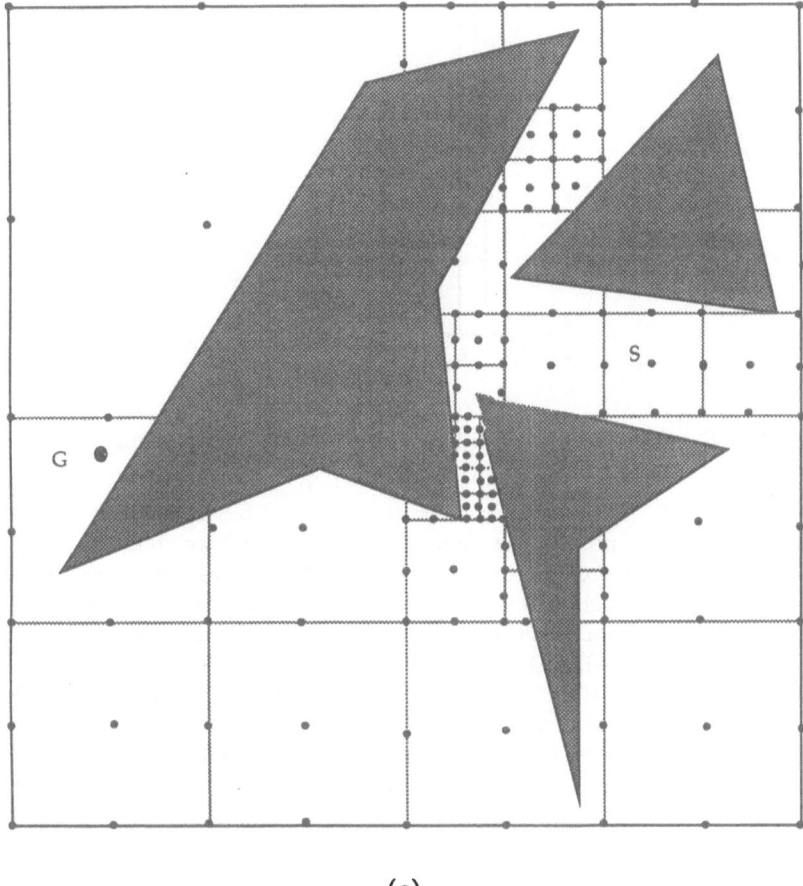

(c)

Fig. 6.4.

In order to make our search feasible, we impose two restrictions on the choice of acceleration. An object can change its acceleration and direction of motion only at L-points; it retains the same acceleration between successive L-points. We also assume that the acceleration takes on discrete values. These restrictions are necessary, since otherwise there would be infinitely many possibilities as to when and where to change acceleration. Since the acceleration can be 0, moving at a constant speed is also allowed. In general, the speed of the mobile object, which is a function of its acceleration, changes continuously throughout the entire path. In our implementation, there is no restriction on the choice of the acceleration value at an L-point as long as it stays between the predetermined upper and lower limits. In reality, a moving object does not pass exactly through an L-point. Instead, it follows a curved path that does not pass through the L-point, in order to avoid a sudden change of movement direction. However, we will assume that the distance traveled can be approximated by the sum of the lengths of the two tangents to the curve that meet at the L-point. For example, in Fig. 6.5, we approximate the path depicted by the dashed line by the two line segments AC and BC.

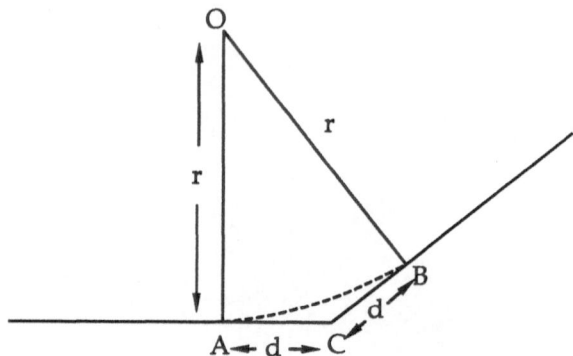

Fig. 6.5. Example path (broken line) that avoids a sudden change in direction

The more L-points we use, the more degrees of control we gain. However, having too large a branching factor can easily lead to a combinatorial explosion; thus a smaller number of L-points is desirable. On the other hand, with too small a number of L-points, frequent changes in direction and speed over a short distance are not realizable; hence, the search process may fail to find a feasible path. Thus, the choice of L-point configuration is an important problem in our approach. Our L-point configuration is adaptable so that areas of importance (in the vicinity of obstacles) have a higher density of points, while areas far from the obstacles have a relatively sparse distribution of points. To embody this principle, a hierarchical representation is appropriate. The space is organized using various sizes of cells. Large cells are used to represent areas having a low density of obstacles while areas with many obstacles are subdivided further into smaller cells.

6.3.2 The search procedure

The main search procedure is as follows. We use a priority queue of C-points where the T-point component of a C-point serves as the point's priority.

1. Push the start point into the queue.

2. While the queue is not empty, recursively perform the following:

   Remove the lowest cost element from the queue. If it is the goal point, then report the path and exit the procedure. Generate all the neighboring L-points (described below) of the L-point component of the removed element, and select an acceleration value. Determine T-points corresponding to the generated L-points. Put the C-points that satisfy the path conditions (described below) into the queue.

3. Report that the procedure has not found the goal.

In the second step of the procedure, we need to inspect all the neighboring candidate L-points (Samet 1982). Neighboring L-points are all the L-points in the cells that share an edge with the cell in which the current L-point is found. See Fig. 6.6. A neighboring L-point can be quite distant, like the ones in cell D of Fig. 6.6c, so that we can move rapidly over an area where there are few obstacles.

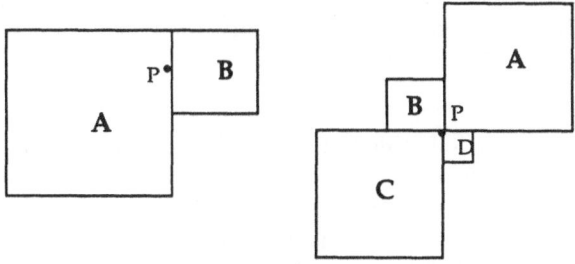

(a) L-point P is on an edge. Its neighboring points are the L-points in the cells A and B.

(b) L-point P is at a corner. Its neighboring points are the L-points in the cells A, B, C, and D.

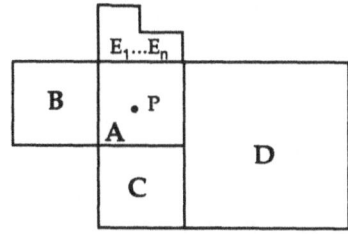

(c) L-point P is at the center of a cell. Its neighboring points are the L-points in the cells A, B, C, D, E_1, E_2, ..., and E_n.

Fig. 6.6. Neighboring L-points

6.3.3 The path conditions

The path conditions to be satisfied in step 2 are defined as follows. Suppose we are at some L-point, say P. The current speed of the robot and the location of the previous L-point are known. We now choose the acceleration and the L-point to which we proceed next. Once an acceleration value has been chosen, we have to maintain it until the next L-point. The choice of L-point must satisfy the following path conditions.

(1) The acceleration is not out of range.

(2) The speed at the next L-point will not be out of range.

(3) The angle at P satisfies the conditions on centrifugal force and speed at P.

(4) The path between P and the next L-point is collision-free.

Checking that conditions (1) and (2) are satisfied is straightforward. We can choose an acceleration within the range, and then compute the speed of the next L-point from the current values of speed and acceleration, and the distance between the current and next L-points.

As for condition (3), the following formulation is used for estimating the centrifugal force. We assume that the robot negotiates a curve having a curvature which depends on the angle formed by the two lines meeting at the L-point (C in Fig. 6.5). Let d be the distance between an L-point and the points where the robot begins to deviate from a trajectory which would have taken it to the L-point (Fig. 6.5). Then the radius r is

$$ r = d \cdot \tan \left(\frac{\alpha}{2} \right), $$

where α is the angle made by the two line segments that meet at the L-point. We assume d to be small in comparison with the distance between the two L-points. Thus requirement (3) can be expressed as

$$ \frac{mv^2}{r} < constant, $$

where v is the current speed and m is the mass of the robot. This means that on each curve we are required to satisfy the inequality

$$ \frac{v^2}{\tan(\frac{\alpha}{2})} < C $$

for some constant C.

As regards condition (4), the cells containing the path segment connecting the current point and the next point are inspected for intersection points. If there is an intersection, the next point is not qualified as a candidate point.

Regarding the cost estimation in step 2 of the search procedure, we can use different criteria depending on which aspects we wish to optimize. Here, we describe an estimation function used in our implementation that optimizes time. We define a function f at the current control point, say CP, by $f(CP) = g(CP) + h(CP)$, where g is the T-point component of CP, i.e., the time elapsed so far, and h is equal to the distance between the L-point component of CP and the goal point, divided by the maximum speed of the robot. The function g is the cost of the path from the start point to CP, and h is the heuristic estimate of the cost of the path from CP to the goal. Since h never overestimates the actual time cost from CP to the goal point, this A* heuristic search process (Nilsson 1980) having f as its estimate is admissible, i.e., the procedure is guaranteed to compute a time-optimal solution in this search space. In the next section, we will present some results obtained by using this heuristic. As alternatives, it is possible to use estimation functions based on distance traveled or energy consumed.

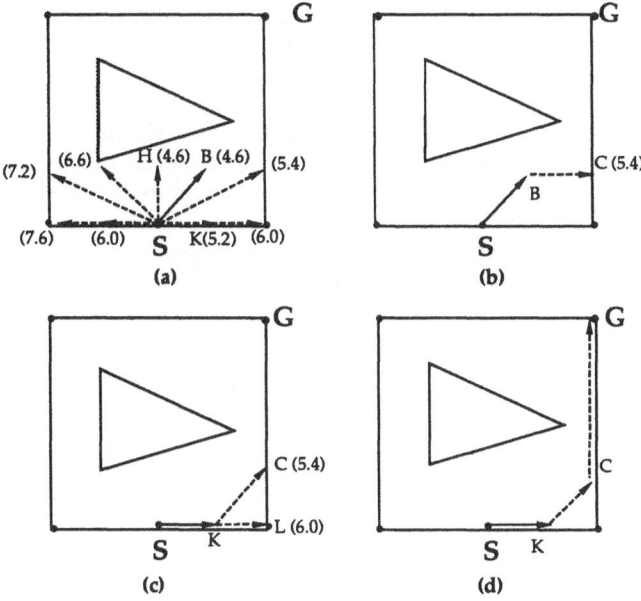

Fig. 6.7. Example path computation using A* algorithm

Figure 6.7 is an example of path computation using the A* algorithm. Let S and G denote the start and goal points, respectively. Assume that the path conditions do not allow the robot to make a turn of less than $90°$. Broken lines are drawn from S to the L-points that are reachable from the current L-point. The numbers within the parentheses correspond to the values of the function f at those L-points. The L-point with the minimum f value is selected as the next L-point to which the robot moves; this path is shown as a thick line in Fig. 6.7. The following is a more detailed explanation. Starting at S, there are nine candidate L-points from which to choose. They are all placed in the queue. f is at a minimum at L-points H and B (see Fig. 6.7a). We reject H since none of the L-points that are reachable from H satisfy the path conditions. Thus we are left with B. Continuing our search from B, we find that C is the only L-point reachable from B (see Fig. 6.7b). However, at this point we find that the minimum value of f is at K (i.e., $f(K)$ is smaller than $f(C)$) and hence K is the next node to be processed in the search process. L-points C and L are reachable from K while also satisfying the path conditions (see Fig. 6.7c). At this point, the goal point G is reachable from C (see Fig. 6.7d) and the path segment CG satisfies the path conditions. In this example, this is the optimal path. Of course, in a more general situation, the search process would continue to check if a lower-cost solution exists.

6.3.4 Search failure

One drawback of our method is that it may not find a solution in the search space. This can be interpreted as indicating either that a feasible solution does not exist at all, or that it does not exist in our search space. In the latter case, some possible reasons are that the arrangement of L-points is too coarse, the discretized acceleration values are not appropriate, etc.

One way to remedy this drawback is to note that when the initial number of L-points is not large enough to compute a solution, we can increase the number of L-points in the search space until a path is found or a predetermined resolution limit is reached. Instead of increasing the set of L-points uniformly, we can selectively refine the L-points. For example, we can have more L-points in areas which have more obstacles than a given threshold. This can be done by deepening the tree by one level at each search failure. This has an effect of dividing a cell into eight smaller cells, resulting in more L-points. Since deepening a tree does not require much work in an octree structure, this method is simple to implement. However, the granular nature of time as well as distance requires us to have a pre-defined resolution limit in our search space.

6.4 Simulation Results

In this section we present some experimental results obtained using the technique described in Sections 6.2 and 6.3.

Suppose that our spatial region is 512 [m] by 512 [m] and that the time dimension varies between 0 [sec] and 512 [sec]. Our first examples are shown in Fig. 6.8. O_1 is an obstacle moving at 0.5 [m/sec] toward the right and O_2 is a stationary object. The start and goal points are denoted by S and G, respectively. The acceleration has possible values 1.0, 0.5, 0.0, -0.5 and -1.0 [m/sec^2]. In addition, we require that the speed at the start and goal points be 0.

(Case 1): If the mobile robot is fast enough, it will proceed to the right of O_1, to the left of O_2, and get to the goal. Figure 6.8a shows the trajectory and its speed transition graph. The maximum allowable speed in this case is 4 [m/sec].

(Case 2): If the mobile robot is not fast enough, it will not be able to proceed to the left side of O_2, and will have to go to the right side of O_2. Figure 6.8b shows the case where the maximum speed of the robot is 3 [m/sec].

(Case 3): If the mobile robot is much slower, it will let A go by first. Figure 6.8c shows the case where the maximum speed of the robot is 2 [m/sec].

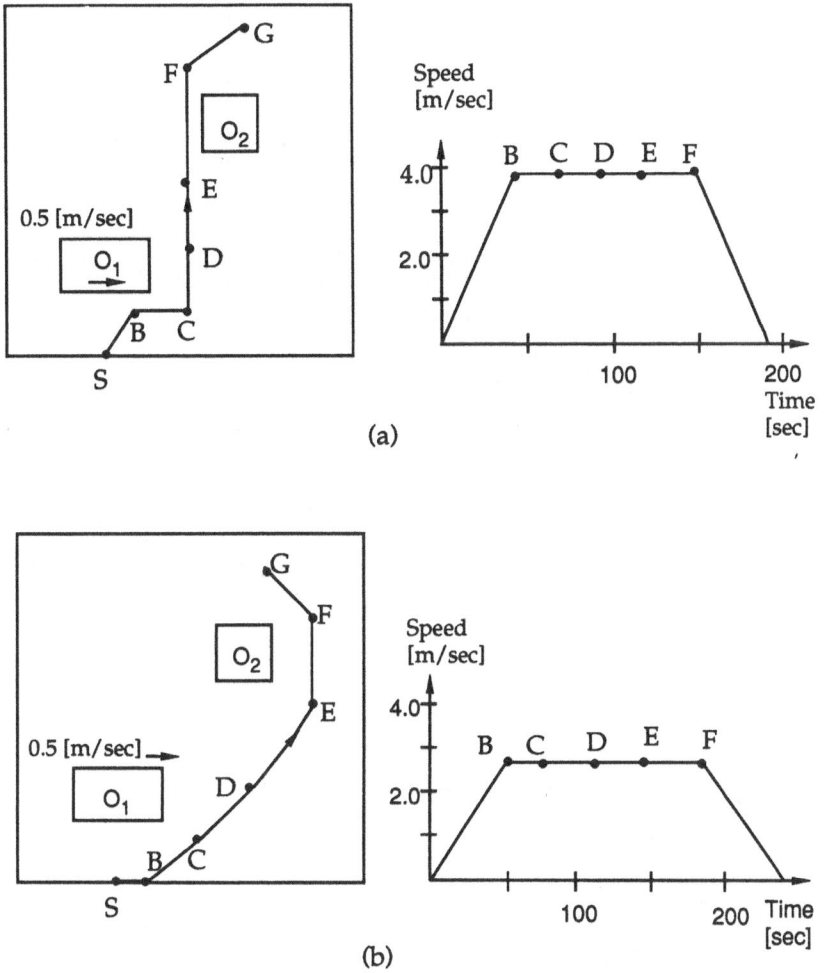

Fig. 6.8. Simulation results (Continued)

Figure 6.9 shows a problem involving three moving obstacles. Obstacle O_1 moves in toward the right at 0.5 [m/sec] as in the previous example. There are two other triangular obstacles, O_2 and O_3, whose speeds are 1.4 [m/sec] and 1.0 [m/sec], respectively. S and I represent the start and goal points, respectively. In this example, the maximum speed of the robot is 4.5 [m/sec]. Note that the robot starts decelerating at D to avoid a collision that would have occurred if it had proceeded at constant speed. This has the effect of letting obstacle O_2 go by first. The broken lines show the position of obstacle O_2 at time F. This technique of avoiding obstacles characterizes path planning among moving obstacles and can only be realized by taking the speed and acceleration of the robot into consideration.

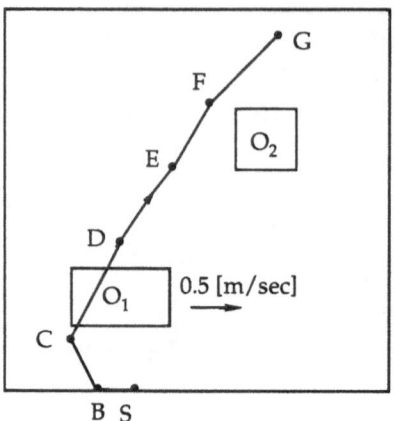

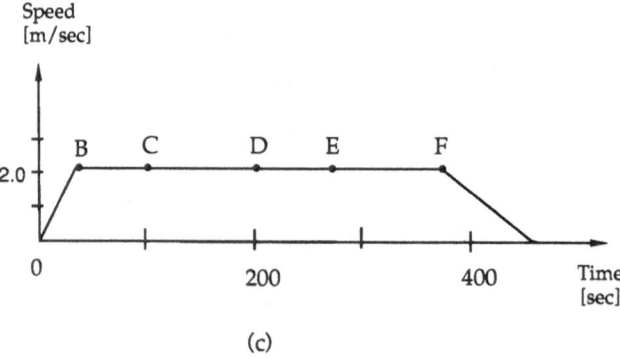

(c)

Fig. 6.8.

6.5 Summary

An approach has been proposed to solve the motion planning problem for a mobile robot within an environment that contains moving obstacles. By adding time as an additional dimension to the world, a simple formulation was obtained. We have discussed representation methods that can make good use of this formulation and have adopted a quadtree-type hierarchical structure to represent space-time. Our representation is based on a cell decomposition scheme in which each cell has a simple geometry, i.e., it contains at most one vertex or one edge of an obstacle.

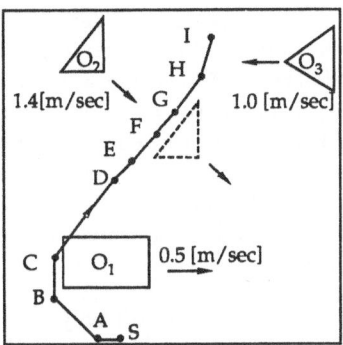

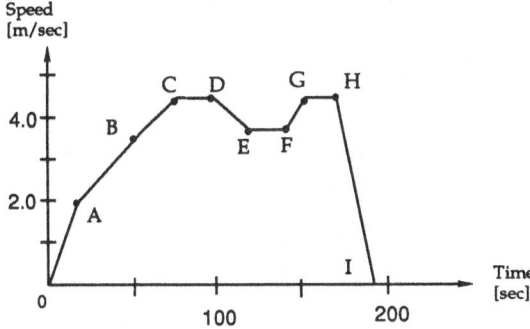

Fig. 6.9. Example with three moving obstacles

In this chapter, we have restricted our attention to three fundamental factors in navigation: speed, acceleration, and centrifugal force. These factors are essential in any real path planning application. They also form the basis for further considerations, such as optimization of the path with respect to energy consumption, etc. To model these factors, we introduced conditions that are imposed on the path during the search procedure. We have shown that a time-minimal motion is obtained using this formulation.

An important goal in path planning is to avoid being concerned with details that do not affect the choice of the path. In this respect, hierarchical structures are very useful. As pointed out by (Fujimura and Samet 1989), since the search space in a time-varying environment tends to become greater than that for stationary path planning, this comment is even more applicable to our problem. For this reason, we used a hierarchical decomposition in the time dimension as well. The cells are large in areas where there is not much motion within some time period or within some distance. Hence the planner is not affected by the motions of distant obstacles, thus facilitating the planning procedure. If we simply stack two-dimensional planes as in (Erdmann and Lozano-Pérez 1987), the path planner will lack this advantage since it has to consider every motion of the obstacles, even though some of them are relatively remote from the robot and would not have affected its path.

In spite of this, our approach still involves a large search space; the set of possible L-points tends to grow rapidly as the number of obstacles increases. For example, suppose that the world consists of $2^l \cdot 2^l \cdot 2^l$ octants of the same size. Then the number of L-points can be as large as $O(2^{3l})$. At each L-point, the next location and the next acceleration are selected using the path conditions. Since this choice must be made at every L-point in the worst case, the worst case execution time of our algorithm is exponential in the number of nodes in the input octree. The closer two objects are, the deeper the level of subdivision becomes, resulting in more nodes in the tree. For this reason, our algorithm is faster in an uncluttered environment.

In the preceding chapters, the robot was subject only to a speed bound. A globally time-minimal motion was obtained in polynomial time. Factors such as acceleration were not incorporated in the formulation. As a result, the robot always made turns at its maximum speed. The method discussed in this chapter incorporates bounds on acceleration and centrifugal force. However, it takes exponential time to determine a motion. This is because the number of control points generated by our representation can be exponential. It may be possible to use information obtained by our earlier approach, using the accessibility graph, to reduce the search space of the method discussed in this chapter. For example, the accessibility graph can be used to specify a homotopic path class— in other words, it determines the order in which the obstacles are encountered by the robot. If this information is used, the search space of the octree representation may be significantly reduced. Given a path class, the method of this chapter can then produce a motion that satisfies other constraints along the path, such as an acceleration bound. This direction deserve further investigation.

Our discussions shows how we can incorporate other time-varying factors into the path planning process. Navigation is affected by road or field conditions. More advanced and intelligent path planning must be combined with the ability to understand the motion of objects in the real world, and to utilize world knowledge obtained from spatial information systems.

Chapter 7
Multiple Mobile Agents

In this chapter we study the case where more than one robot is involved in the same environment. The approach taken is distributed, i.e., each mobile robots independently plans its own action based on its map information. The environment contains mobile robots of different capacities regarding knowledge about the environment, planning algorithms, etc. A model for such reactive mobile robots is described and simulation results are presented to show their behavior patterns.

As we have surveyed in Chap. 2, there has been much research on motion planning for a single mobile robot in known environments containing stationary obstacles as well as moving obstacles. There is also research on sensor-based planning systems for a robot in uncertain environments (Moravec 1983; Crowley 1985; Borenstein and Koren 1988; Elfes 1989; Weisbin *et al* 1989; Arkin 1990; Thorp *et al* 1988). Consider a situation where multiple autonomous robots must carry out their tasks concurrently in the same environment. In such a case, we would like the autonomous robots to work cooperatively without interfering with each other. In such a multi-robot environment, one of the requirements for each agent (i.e., mobile robot) is to coordinate its motion with those of others. This requires an agent to have a higher level of ability than simply planning a motion in the presence of obstacles that move along known trajectories, since the motions of other agents are, by nature, not known ahead of time. In this chapter we introduce a model of such dynamic reactions for multiple mobile agents in dynamic domains.

7.1 Distributed Approaches

The few previous authors dealing with multiple mobile robots (Tournassoud 1986; Freund and Hoyer 1988; Saito and Tsumura 1989; Lee and Bien 1990; Kajitani, Fukuo, and Masuda 1990; Caloud *et al* 1990; Premvuti and Yuta 1990; Sugihara and Suzuki 1990) consider a set of *homogeneous* robots, i.e., all robots are identical in the sense that they are operated under an identical set of simple rules. Realistically, however, the workspace may contain robots of different capacities. For example, sensor data processing abilities as well as mobility may vary for all robots.

Motivated in this manner, we consider *heterogeneous* multiple robots, i.e., a set of agents with different capabilities with respect to their sensors, planning algorithms, etc. We would like the mobile agents to be completely autonomous, determine their actions on their own, and react properly to the actions of other agents. Humans are capable of handling such a situation fairly well. For example, in a shopping center, people with shopping carts manage to reach their destinations, while avoiding each other in a cooperative manner without any explicit conflict resolving mechanism.

We observe that humans are involved in various mental processes in doing so. They see each other, guess where other people are heading, plan their own actions, execute their actions while confirming that their actions do not interfere with those of others, revise their plans if necessary, etc. At times, it may become necessary to build a mental model of other people, infer what their actions would be, based on that mental model, possibly revise the mental model in the course of action, and learn behavior patterns from experience. As can be seen, a seemingly simple human behavior certainly involves a fair amount of high level intelligence. It is desirable to build such an autonomous mobile agent that is capable of acting intelligently with other mobile agents. This chapter reports a first step toward such a goal.

When several mobile agents with various degrees of intelligence interact, the resulting scenario can be quite complex. To cope with this situation, we have built a simulation system that enables us to observe various behaviors of heterogeneous mobile agents of a set of different capacities at various settings. We consider three factors to model the mobile agent: planning algorithms, knowledge about the environment, and action intervals. Our study is distinguishable from other approaches for multi-robot coordination in that our aim is to observe how planning, knowledge about the environment, and processing speed affect the overall performance of coordination of the agents, rather than designing a set of robots that simply follow predetermined rules of action. In this study, we report some experimental results obtained through simulation of such autonomous mobile agents. Our simulation results reveal some counter-intuitive facts about the roles of planning and knowledge for a reactive system in dynamic domains — agents with more knowledge about the environment do not necessarily plan a better path.

A survey of previous work on coordination of multiple robots shows that the motion planning problem for multiple robots is usually stated as follows. Given a set of objects B, a set of obstacles, initial and goal positions for the objects of B, plan motions for the objects of B from their initial positions to their goal positions such that they do not collide with the obstacles or with each other. There have been two formulations of this problem: centralized approaches and distributed approahces.

In centralized approaches, all computation is performed at a single site (called *central planner* or *arbitrator*) that has all information about the shapes of the robots and geometry of the environment (Freund and Hoyer 1988). Motions for all robots are completely determined by the central planner at one time. After the solution is found, each robot follows the motion determined by the central planner. The planner determines exactly whether or not there exists a solution for a given set of robots, and plans such motion if it exists. The planning process usually terminates before execution of the motions.

For central approaches, efficient solutions are possible when the environment contains a few robots (Yap 1984; Sharir and Sifrony 1988; Parsons and Canny 1990).

However, for an environment that contains more than a few robots, a solution requires computation time that is exponential in the number of robots in the environment (Hopcroft, Schwartz, and Sharir 1984). This means that the problem becomes intractable when the number of objects to be moved increases or geometry of the environment is very complex. However, in most practical situations where several robots are sparsely populated in a large environment, a solution is possible (Liu *et al* 1989).

One heuristic to solve the multiple mobile robot problem is to assign priorities to all mobile robots. Erdmann and Lozano-Pérez (1987) assign priorities globally over the robots; first the motion for the robot with the highest priority is planned. Then, the motion for the robot with the second highest priority is determined regarding the first robot as the sole moving obstacle in the environment, and so on. In this approach, the problem of moving obstacle avoidance is a prerequisite to the solution. Warren (1990) also adopts the global priority approach, but he uses a different obstacle avoidance algorithm. Buckley (1989) uses a local priority scheme, i.e., priorities are assigned to two robots only when their trajectories potentially intersect. MacNish and Fallside (1990) also use local priority. They use modal temporal logic to detect possible collisions between two mobile robots.

Approaches making use of a central planner are feasible when it is possible to move each mobile robot along a specified path exactly. Also, in these approaches, the central planner is assumed to have complete knowledge about all the mobile robots. It also requires a dependable communication means between the robots. Realistically, however, it may not be possible to satisfy all these requirements. This motivates us to consider distributed approaches.

Distributed approaches do not assume a central planner. Instead, each robot acts as an independent agent and determines its motion based on a limited amount of information about each agent. The agent needs to revise its plan as new information arrives. Usually, each agent makes use of local information (typically obtained through its sensors) to plan its motion to the goal location. Our approach in this chapter fits in this category. As opposed to the centralized approach where global information about the environment is completely known, only partial information of other agents is known to each agent. Planning is reactive in the sense that a plan will have to be revised as new information invalidates the old plan. In a distributed approach, a general strategy for resolving conflicts when two robots get near is to move away from each other so as to avoid collision. Saito and Tsumura (1989) use velocity vector modification together with risk evaluation functions. Lee and Bien (1990) use neural networks to handle multiple mobile robots. A drawback of distributed approaches is that solutions are usually not globally optimal. Also, it is possible for robots to be trapped in a deadlock situation (Wang 1989).

Some researchers propose use of a hybrid of these two approaches. A central planner determines global routes for the robots, while local conflicts are resolved by independent robots (Yeung and Bekey 1987; Pape 1990). In such a system, the central planner is evoked when an event occurs that cannot be resolved between the agents (e.g. deadlock). Cammarata *et al* (1983) consider several schemes to achieve coordination by means of centralization among distributed aircraft.

7.2 Mobile Agents

This section describes the model of mobile agents that is used for our simulation. An agent is modeled by the combination of three factors: a planning algorithm, knowledge about the environment, and an action interval. These factors respectively represent how well the agent can navigate to the destination point based on knowledge about the environment, how much the agent knows about the current status of the environment, and how quickly the agent can react to changes in the environment. In our current simulation system, the agent model is limited in the sense that the agents only take into consideration a set of relatively simple factors for determining their actions. There are many factors that are not considered in this model. For example, the agents are not able to infer other agents' planning processes.

In our system, each robot is assumed to have a local map through which knowledge about its surroundings is obtained. The map is assumed to be constantly updated as the agent moves. Each map has a scope such that objects that are inside the scope of the map are precisely known to the agent, while objects outside the scope are not. This models a situation where each agent is equipped with a sensor with a limited scope that enables the agent to acquire information around itself. (A priori knowledge about the environment may also be contained in the scope.) Given a destination point to be reached, each agent plans its future action based on the map information surrounding the agent and generates a plan so as to minimize its own motion (e.g., with respect to time, distance) to the destination point. The agents are completely independent and do not communicate with each other (other than seeing each other). In this chapter, we restrict ourselves to the interaction of two robots that meet on their way to destination points. This type of interaction happens in multiple-robot domains frequently. Now we describe the three factors that define the agent model.

Planning algorithms: The agents use either visibility or accessibility for planning algorithms. As discussed in Section 2.1, the visibility graph is often used for path planning among stationary obstacles together with configuration spaces in which the robot is treated as a point. Note that in a dynamic environment, the graph must be constantly updated.

Tournassoud (1986) uses a similar concept of separating-lines. If two objects both move in the direction that is parallel to their tangent, they will not collide. The tangent line constantly changes as they move. This way, the direction of the motion corresponds to an edge of the visibility graph generated at the current position of the agent. This method is effective when two robots choose the same separating line between them, which may not be always the case in distributed domains.

Another algorithm we have adopted for our simulated agent is based on the concept of accessibility. Each agent moves in the direction in which a future collision can be avoided. Suppose that the robot moves at a constant speed. All directions around the start point can be decomposed into subsets of directions in which the robot will meet or not meet an obstacle. The robot is moved to a direction in which it does not meet any of the obstacles. As we have seen in Chap. 3, a time-minimal motion is obtained as a sequence of edges in the accessibility graph.

Both algorithms are known to run quite fast (i.e., a low degree of polynomial time). Therefore, it does not pose any computational problem even if an agent must compute the whole motion to the goal frequently. The two planning algorithms are contrasted by the fact that both try to optimize the motion using different quantities (time or distance). We presume that the one based on accessibility is "smarter" than the one based on visibility since accessibility takes the motions of other objects into consideration, while visibility does not. As a result of this choice, each agent avoids collision by changing the direction of motion, while moving at a constant speed. Alternately, we could have adopted other planning algorithms among moving obstacles such as the ones described in (Kant and Zucker 1986; Warren 1990).

The map: Each robot needs to plan its motion based on its map information. The map represents the current information available to each agent. Each map has a limited amount of information around the agent. The shapes and locations of objects that lie within a given scope are assumed to be correct. However, an agent may not have any information about objects outside the scope, or even if it does, the information about the objects outside the scope of the map may not correctly reflect the status of the environment. For example, objects that were previously inside the scope and not in the current scope may or may not be in the same location. In the future when communication is possible between agents, an agent may have information local to other agents as well.

The scope of the map is a variable that can be changed in our model. The larger the scope is, the more information is available to the agent. The speeds and moving directions of other agents can be computed from their locations in two consecutive maps (assuming that map updates are frequent enough).

Action interval: Each robot repeats the process of planning, acting, and updating its map. The duration of this cycle is called the action interval. This quantity (which is a relative quantity) represents how quickly the agent reacts to changes in the outside world and can be varied in our model. Of course, the agent whose interval is shorter can react more sensitively. However, whether the agent with a shorter interval always performs better or not is an issue to be investigated.

All agents compute an optimal solution with respect to either distance (based on visibility) or time (based on accessibility) for their motions toward their goals based on their maps at each instant of time. When planning a motion, an agent assumes that objects that are not currently in its map (i.e., unknown obstacles) do not exist and that the current status of the world will hold in the future (until told otherwise). However, the world will change because (i) a new object enters its map, (ii) the course of motion of the other agent changes, and (iii) an optimal solution at an instant of time may not be optimal at another instant. In these cases, the plan must be revised. As a result of the revision, other agents may also be affected and may need to revise their plans.

Even with this simple model of a mobile agent, when two robots interact, the resulting motion can be complex. We have built a simulation system that simulates behaviors of independent mobile agents with different capabilities. Our results show that there may arise a counter-intuitive scenario when agents interact. This suggests that we need to be careful before any algorithm is implemented for multiple independent mobile agents working in the same environment.

Our simulation system assumes the following for each mobile agent. Each agent needs to plan its motion based on its local map information. The map contains exact information about the shapes and locations of objects that lie within a certain distance from the agent (called scope of the map). It plans its motion, moves, and acquires information from the outside world iteratively. Each robot avoids collision by changing the direction of motion, while moving at a constant speed (alternately, it could slow down, etc).

7.3 Simulation Results

This section presents some of our simulation results. As we have shown in the previous section, there are three parameters that define a mobile agent. We can change each of them (or two or three of them at a time) to see the effect on the performance of the agents. We first show that deadlock is possible with two identical mobile agents. Next, we show two agents that are identical except for their planning algorithms. Then, we compare two identical agents except for the scopes of their maps. Then, we illustrate somewhat counter-intuitive scenario for two robots that are different both in their planning algorithms and scopes of the map. Finally, we show two agents with different action intervals.

Agents are of finite-size and denoted by the symbols 'o' and '◇.' At each action interval, the following steps are executed:

1. The map of each agent is updated based on its scope. The environment within the scope is represented using a configuration space. (In our simulation, objects are expanded with some additional safety margin.)

2. Each agent plans a motion based on their map information.

3. Each agent is moved to a new location based on the plan generated in Step 2. (The safety margin in Step 1 is chosen such that agents do not collide in this step.) If the new location is not the desired goal, go to Step 1.

Deadlocks: Figure 7.1 contains an example where two robots with identical capabilities run into a deadlock. Mobile agent 1 starts from S1 towards its goal G1, while mobile agent 2 starts from S2 and tries to move to G2. Both agents use visibility. A deadlock occurs since when Agent 1 moves toward the right to avoid Agent 2, Agent 2 moves towards the left, and vice versa. Generally, this type of deadlock is possible when two identical agents are placed in a symmetrical situation.

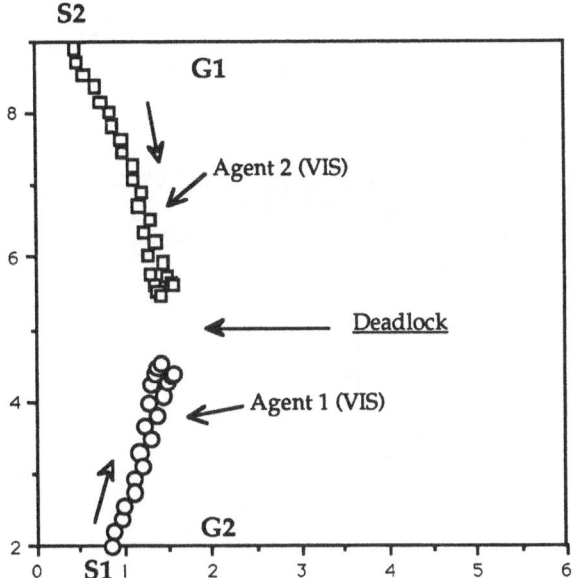

Fig. 7.1. A deadlock

Agents with different planners: Figure 7.2a contains a result of two mobile agents with different planning algorithms. Agent 1 uses accessibility, while agent 2 uses visibility to plan their motions. As a result, two agents move to their respective goals smoothly. Agent 2 (with visibility) starts moving straight toward its destination point, as its destination point is visible from its start point. For Agent 1 (with accessibility), the destination point is not accessible from the start point, as Agent 2 will be in its way. Thus, Agent 1 has a choice as to whether it moves toward the right or the left to avoid Agent 2. Agent 1 chooses to go toward the right, since it turns out to be faster. As a result, for Agent 2 (with visibility), the destination point remains visible throughout its motion, and it ends up having a straight line motion. Agent 1 changes its direction of motion when the destination point becomes accessible. In this example, none of the agents needed to change the plans that they created in the beginning.

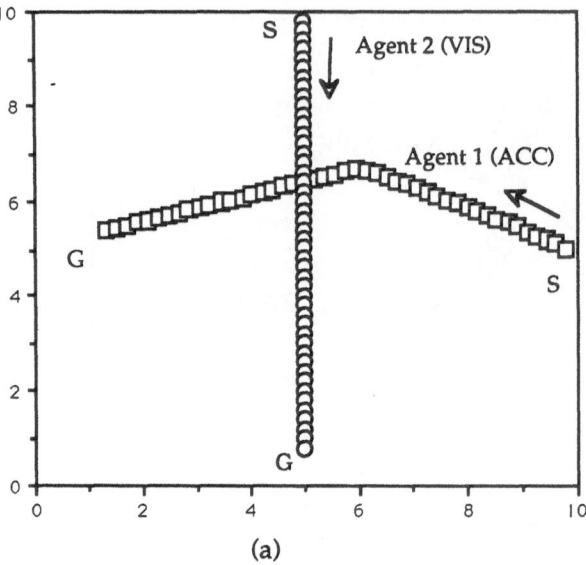

(a)

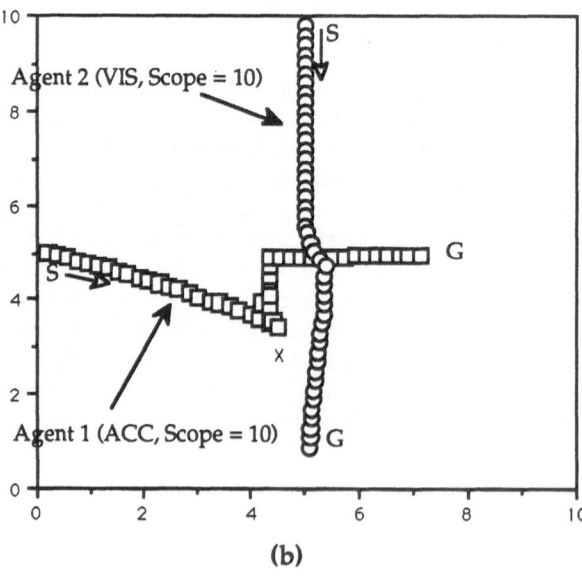

(b)

Fig. 7.2. Agents with different planners (Continued)

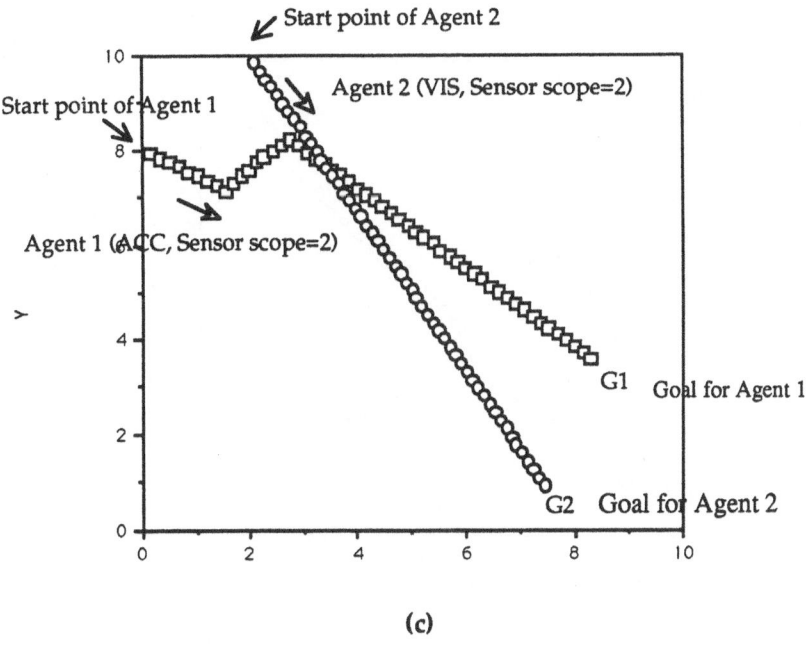

(c)

Fig. 7.2.

Figure 7.2b contains a similar set-up of the environment with the difference being that the start point of Agent 1 is in the left hand side instead of the right hand side. The resulting motions, however, differ qualitatively from that of Fig. 7.2a. Here is our explanation. Agent 2 starts moving straight toward its destination point as before, while Agent 1 starts heading toward the right, trying to avoid Agent 2, soon after it leaves the start point. Agent 2 does not react to Agent 1 until Agent 1 comes near location X, where the destination point of Agent 2 becomes no longer visible due to Agent 1(i.e., Agent 1 is in its way). This requires Agent 2 to revise the current plan. Agent 2 chooses to move toward the left, since it turns out to be shorter, assuming the current motion of Agent 1. This action of Agent 2 affects Agent 1. It requires Agent 1 to reconsider its course of action when it comes to point X. At X, going around Agent 2 from the right becomes no longer time-minimal for Agent 1. As a result, Agent 1 revises its action and determines to move toward the left to avoid Agent 2.

Figure 7.2c contains a similar situation where two agents try to pass each other. Agent 1 uses accessibility, while Agent 2 uses visibility. Both agents will not notice each other until the distance between them becomes 2 due to the map scope. When both agents detect each other, Agent 1(with accessibility) moves behind Agent 2 to avoid a possible conflict and both agents end in their respective destination points.

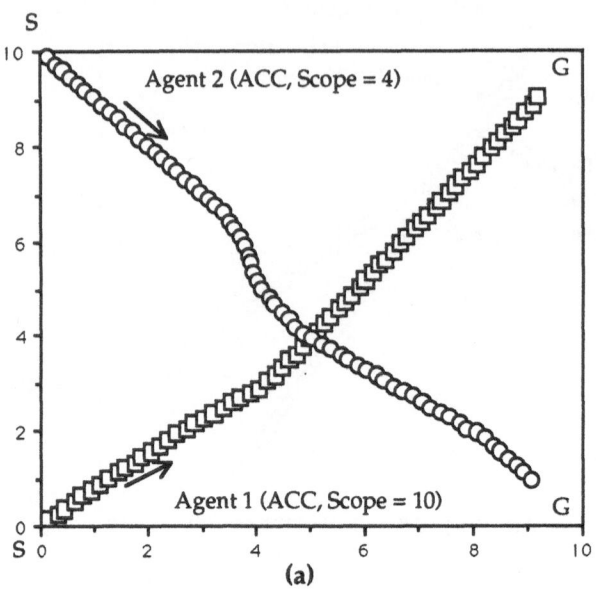

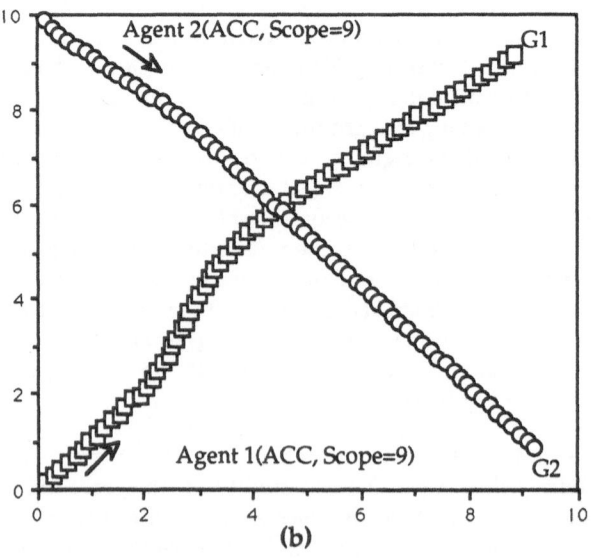

Fig. 7.3. Agents with different planners

Agents with different scopes of map: Figure 7.3a contains a result of two robots that use accessibility, but with different scopes of the maps. The scope of the map of Agent 1 is 10, while that of Agent 2 is 4. (These figures are comparative and do not represent any actual measurements. Note that the environment is 10 by 10.) Here, the result is consistent with our intuition. Agent 2 does not start reacting to the motion of Agent 1 until Agent 1 comes into its field of view, while Agent 1 starts reacting much earlier. See Fig. 7.3b where both agents' scopes of the map is 9.

Agents with different scopes of the map as well as different planners: So far, we have changed only one variable of the agent model. We have seen that the one that uses accessibility (or a larger scope of the map) is the key agent, since it takes action toward resolving a potential conflict between the two agents. An interesting question is: what happens if the agent with a better planner has a narrower scope of the map? Figures 7.4a-c show a set of motions generated by the two agents, one of which has a better planner and the other has a larger scope of the map.

Agent 1 uses accessibility while Agent 2 uses visibility. The scope of the map for Agent 1 is varied from 3 to 10, while that of Agent 2 is fixed to 10. In other words, Agent 2 always has more information about the environment than Agent 1. As we vary the scope of the map of Agent 1 from 3 to 10, we expect that the performance of Agent 1 will continually improve. However, the results do not show this.

We observe from Fig. 7.4a and Fig. 7.4b that the performance of Agent 1 certainly improves as its scope of the map gets wider. However, when we move to Fig. 7.4c where the scope of the map is even wider, the motion of Agent 1 is qualitatively different from those of Figs 7.4a and 7.4b and its performance degrades. It exhibits a behavior pattern shown in the previous examples (Fig. 7.2). This phenomenon follows from the fact that Agent 1 with the scope of the map 5 was too far away from Agent 2 when it perceived Agent 2 and concluded going around Agent 2 in the right would still work.

One explanation is that Agent 1 had a greater amount of information only about what the environment is now, but it did not have any information about (or did not use the current information effectively to predict) what the environment was going to be in the future. In other words, it was not able to infer the future from the available information at present. This results in a poorer performance (with respect to the final arrival time at the destination point) despite the fact that the amount of available information was greater.

A similar result was obtained by Lumelsky and Skewis (1990).   They have investigated how vision affects the efficiency of maze search in comparison with a robot with a tactile sensor. Our intuition is that the robot with a visual sensor will outperform the robot with only a tactile sensor. They have shown that for some environments, however, the performance of the robot with vision is poorer than the robot with tactile sensor.

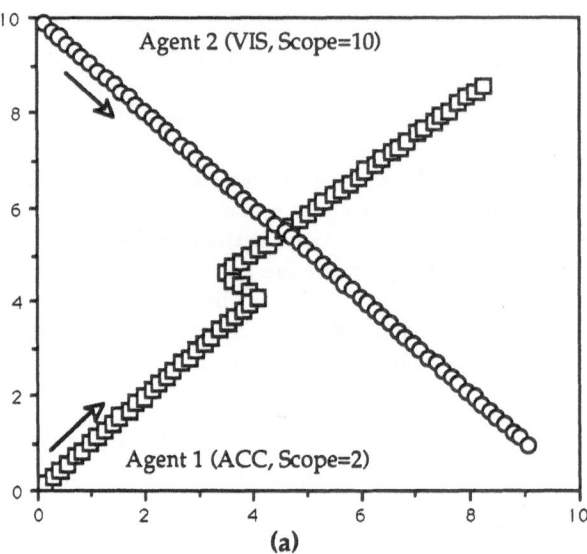

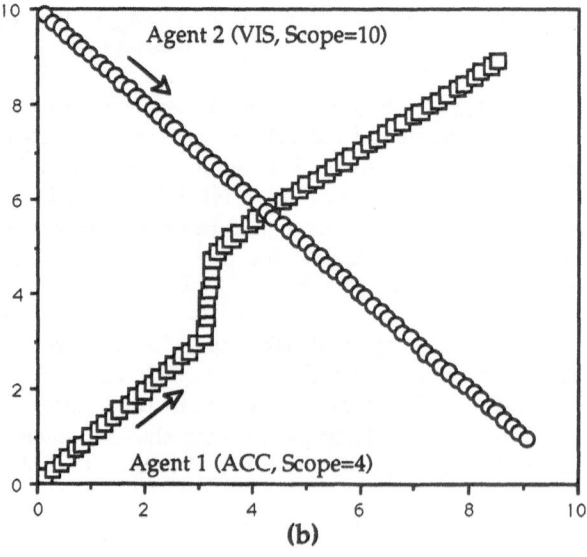

Fig. 7.4. Agents with different planners as well as different scopes

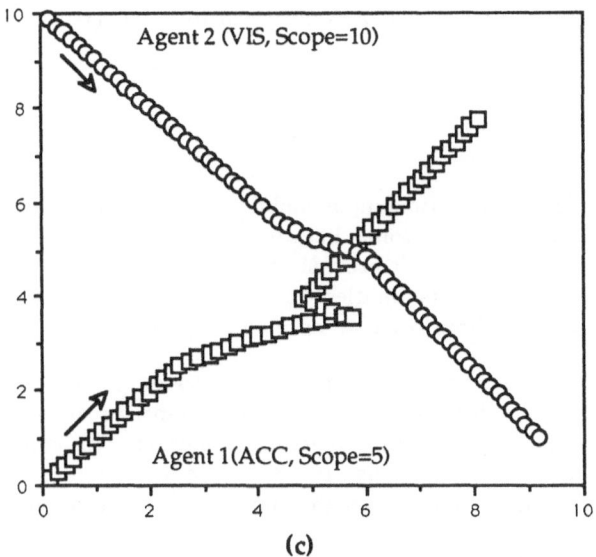

Fig. 7.4.

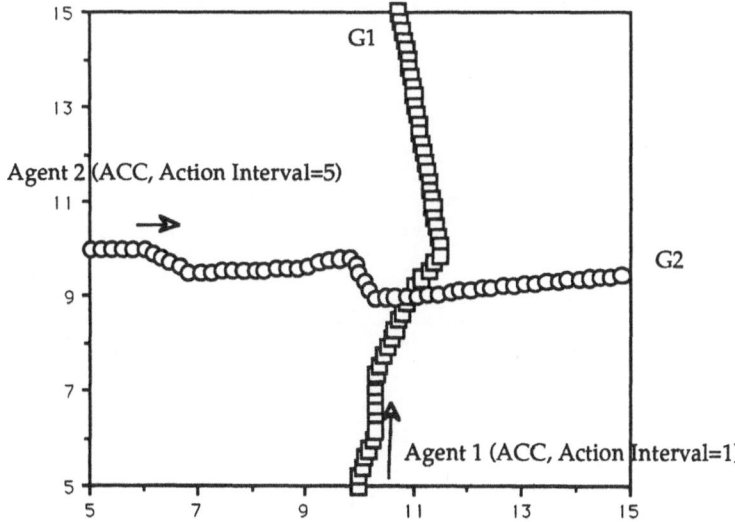

Fig. 7.5. Agents with different action intervals

Agents with different action intervals: Figure 7.5 shows an example of two agents with different action intervals. Agent 1 can perform the plan-and-act process five times as often as Agent 2 does. As a result, Agent 2 makes sharper turns at times compared with those made by Agent 1. Agent 1 does not seem to be affected by the motion of Agent 2 very much.

7.4 Summary

We have considered a model of autonomous mobile agents in dynamic domains. The agents differ in their planning algorithms, knowledge about the environment, etc. We have built a simulation system which provides a testbed for conducting experiments using mobile agents with various capabilities. In some cases, the behavior of the agents is shown to be quite different from what we normally expect.

Our model for the mobile agents can be extended so as to achieve more versatile agents. The following are a few directions in which extensions are possible. In our model, we have used two algorithms for planning a motion. We can adopt various planning algorithms in dynamic domains. It remains of interest to see how an agent that makes use of other motion planning algorithms copes with those in our model.

The map of the agent can get complex if we allow communication between agents. Also, we expect that the agents capable of inferring other agents' behavior and of learning behavior patterns from experience will perform much better in a complex dynamic domain. For example, in Fig. 7.4c, Agent 1 exhibits a back-up motion. This motion could have been avoided if Agent 1 knew the planning algorithm employed by Agent 2. Agent 1 could have planned a better motion that would not interfere the motion of Agent 2 from the beginning. We leave these extensions as our future work.

Chapter 8
Conclusions

8.1 Summary

The ability to handle dynamic obstacles is expected to become increasingly important for intelligent mobile robots in the future. For motion planning among stationary obstacles, minimizing the total path length is frequently a major concern. The visibility graph and space decomposition are often used to generate shortest or reasonably short paths in the plane. Time-minimality is one of the critical considerations; the robot may be crushed between obstacles unless it takes a time-minimal motion from a start point to a destination point. For this reason, our primary concern in this monograph has been to generate time-minimal motions. We have studied motion planning in a variety of dynamic domains. Here is a brief summary of results of our work.

1. The concept of *accessibility* was proposed and used to define the accessibility graph for two-dimensional moving objects. We proved that a time-minimal motion for a point robot subject only to a speed bound in the plane is obtained as a sequence of edges in the accessibility graph, when the robot can move faster than the obstacles.

2. We demonstrated the use of accessibility by solving a number of dynamic motion planning problems. When the robot can move faster than the obstacles, many formulations of the problem with a speed bound were solved in polynomial time using the accessibility graph and its extensions. These involve piecewise linear motion of the obstacles, fast-moving destination point, etc.

3. We solved the motion planning problem amidst transient obstacles— obstacles that exist in the environment for certain periods of time. We have shown that the concept of accessibility is a key to obtain a time-minimal motion in such an environment. A series of transient obstacles may be used to approximate obstacles that move very fast.

4. Motion planning in the presence of slowly moving polyhedral obstacles in three dimensions was investigated. A time-minimal motion was shown to have three properties that are generalization of those exhibited by a shortest path in three-dimensions cluttered with stationary polyhedral obstacles.

5. We extended a space decomposition method to a time-varying environment. We made use of an octree to represent space-time in which time corresponds to one of the dimensions of the world model. In this case, the robot is subject to additional constraints on its motion, e.g., bounds on acceleration and centrifugal force as well as

a speed bound. A heuristic was used to search for a time-minimal motion in space-time. Experimental results show that this heuristic can handle an environment containing a few moving obstacles.

6. A reactive model for multiple mobile agents was proposed. We considered three elements (planning algorithm, knowledge about the environment, and sampling frequency) for a mobile agent and showed how these elements affect their behavior patterns by simulation.

The following table summarizes some of our complexity results.

Obstacle Motion	Obstacle Shape	Lower Bound	Section Discussed
linear	convex polygon	NP-hard	2.2
slow and linear	arbitrary polygon	$O(n^2 \log n)$	3.1-4, 4.1
slowly growing and shrinking; slowly deforming		$O(n^2 \log n)$	3.5
slow and linear	convex polygon	$O(nk \log k)$	4.2
slow and piecewise linear	arbitrary polygon	$O(n^2 \log (mn))$	4.4
transient	arbitrary polygon	$O(n^3 \log n)$	5.1
fast and linear	rectangular polygon	$O((n/d)^3 \log n)$	5.3
slow; splitting and merging	convex polygon	$O((n+p)^2 \log (n+p))$	4.6

n: number of vertices
k: number of polygons
m: number of turns
p: number of splits and merges
d: resolution for approximation

Table 8.1. Summary

8.2 Open Problems

Our work suggests a number of problems for future investigation:

1. Refinement of the algorithm. We have shown a time complexity of $O(n^2 \log n)$ for motion planning for a point robot subject to a speed bound in the presence of moving obstacles. This bound may be improved. Suppose that we wish to find time-minimal motions from k different sets of start and destination points, or from the same start point but starting at k different times in the presence of the same set of moving obstacles. Currently, we must run the algorithm k times. It may be possible to store a time-varying environment in a data structure from which such a query can be answered in time less than $O(n^2 \log n)$.

2. Heuristics for searching for a path in a Euclidean graph in a time-varying environment. The density of the obstacles may be used to determine the choice of a path.

3. Motion planning with rotation in the presence of moving obstacles. In this case, it may be appropriate to impose a bound on the angular speed of the robot. One approach would be to use a configuration space of a higher dimension.

4. In our simulation, it took on the order of seconds to generate a motion in an environment containing about 20 moving obstacles using the accessibility graph. It took on the order of minutes to generate a motion among a few moving obstacles by the approach using the octree representation. It seems impractical to use this method in an environment that contains more than a few moving obstacles. To put this in other words, the accessibility approach is a fast method of generating a first order approximation of a desired path (or path class). The method using the octree representation generates a motion with additional constraints on the path, but it takes more time. This suggests that if information obtained by the first method could be effectively used in the second approach, the overall computation time might be reduced.

5. Planning safe motions in the presence of moving obstacles. In time-varying environment, a motion may have to be time-minimal to be safe. However, the environment may not be so critical to the robot. In such a situation, the robot may want to trade time for safety along the motion, as a time-minimal motion is not very safe in general in the sense that it brings the robot close to the obstacles. Minimum safety may be guaranteed by adding some safety margin around all obstacles. However, safety has also to do with speeds of the obstacles. It would be useful to generate safer motions without sacrificing too much time.

6. Planning a shortest length path among moving obstacles. For a person who carries heavy suitcases, a shortest length path may be more important than a time-minimal path.

7. Planning amidst programmed obstacles. In a multiple-robot environment, other mobile robots in the environment can be considered as programmed automata —

they are programmed to follow a certain set of rules, for example, to go around obstacles when they are detected on their way. Such obstacles are "intelligent" moving obstacles in the environment. They are different from ordinary moving obstacles in the sense that their motions cannot be predetermined. This class of obstacles is relevant to multiple mobile robot coordination discussed in Chap. 7, and poses a new issue in motion planning to be investigated.

References

Abelson H, DiSerra A (1982) *Turtle geometry: The computer as a medium for exploring mathematics*. MIT Press, Cambridge (Mass.)

Aho AV, Hopcroft JE, Ullman JD (1974) *The design and analysis of computer algorithms*. Addison-Wesley, Reading (Mass.)

Akman V (1987) *Unobstructed shortest paths in polyhedral environments*. In: Goos G, Hartmanis J (ed) Lecture Note in Computer Science 251, Springer-Verlag, Berlin (Germany)

Arkin RC (1990) Integrating behavioral, perceptual, and world knowledge in reactive navigation. *Robotics and Autonomous Systems 6*: 105–122

Asano T, Asano T, Guibas L, Hershberger J, Imai H (1986) Visibility of disjoint polygons. *Algorithmica 1*: 49–63

Asano T, Asano T, Imai H (1987) Shortest path between two simple polygons. *Information Processing Letters 24*: 285–288

Ayala D, Brunet P, Navazo I (1985) Object representation by means of nonminimal division quadtrees and octrees. *ACM Transactions on Graphics 4*: 41–59

Bajaj C, Kim MS (1990) Generation of configuration space obstacles: The case of moving algebraic surfaces. *International Journal of Robotics Research 9*: 92–112

Ballard DM, Brown CM (1982) *Computer vision*. Prentice-Hall, Englewood Cliffs (N.J.)

Baltson A, Sharir M (1988) On the shortest paths between two convex polyhedra. *Journal of the ACM 35*: 267–287

Barraquand J, Latombe JC (1990) A Monte-Carlo algorithm for path planning with many degrees of freedom. *Proceedings of the IEEE International Conference on Robotics and Automation*, Cincinnati (Ohio) 1712–1717

Basu A (1990) Model-based navigation. PhD Thesis, Department of Computer Science, University of Maryland, College Park (Md.)

Bhattacharya BK, Zorbas J (1988) Solving the two-dimensional findpath problem using a line-triangle representation of the robot. *Journal of Algorithms 9*: 449-469

Bolles RC, Baker HH (1985) Epipolar-plane image analysis: A technique for analyzing motion sequences. *Proceedings of the Third Workshop on Computer Vision: Representation and Control*, Bellaire (Mich.) 168–178

Borenstein J, Koren Y (1988) Obstacle avoidance with ultrasonic sensors. *IEEE Journal of Robotics and Automation 4*: 213–218

Brady M, Hollerbach JM, Johnson TL, Lozano-Pérez T, Mason MT (ed) (1984) *Robot motion: planning and control.* MIT Press, Cambridge (Mass.)

Brooks RA (1983) Solving the find-path problem by good representation of free space. *IEEE Transactions on Systems, Man, and Cybernetics 13*: 190–197

Brooks RA, Lozano-Pérez T (1985) A subdivision algorithm in configuration space for findpath with rotation. *IEEE Transactions on Systems, Man, and Cybernetics 15*: 224–233

Buckley SJ (1989) Fast motion planning for multiple moving robots. *Proceedings of the IEEE International Conference on Robotics and Automation*, Scottsdale (Ariz.) 322–326

Caloud P, Choi W, Latombe J, Pape CL, Yim, M (1990) Indoor automation with many mobile robots, *Proceedings of the IEEE International Workshop on Intelligent Robots and Systems*, Tsukuba (Japan) 67–72

Cameron SA (1985) A study of the clash detection problem in robotics. *Proceedings of the IEEE International Conference on Robotics and Automation*, St. Louis (Mo.) 488–493

Cameron SA (1990) Collision detection by four-dimensional intersection testing. *IEEE Transactions on Robotics and Automation 6*: 291–302

Cammarata S, McArthur D, Steeb, R (1983) Strategies of cooperation in distributed problem solving, *Proceedings of International Joint Conference on Artificial Intelligence*, Karlsruhe (Germany) 767–770

Canny J (1986) Collision detection for moving polyhedra. *IEEE Transactions on Pattern Analysis and Machine Intelligence 8*: 200–209

Canny J (1988a) *The theory of robot motion planning.* MIT Press, Cambridge (Mass.)

Canny J (1988b) Some algebraic and geometric computations in PSPACE. *Proceedings of the 20th Annual ACM Symposium on Theory of Computing*, Chicago (Ill.) 460–467

Canny J, Reif J (1987) New lower bound techniques for robot motion planning problems. *Proceedings of the 27th Annual IEEE Symposium on the Foundations of Computer Science*, Los Angeles (Calif.) 49–60

Carlbom I, Chakravarty I, Vanderschel D (1985) A hierarchical data structure for representing the spatial decomposition of 3-D objects. *IEEE Computer Graphics and Applications 5*: 24–31

Chattergy R (1985) Some heuristics for the navigation of a robot. *International Journal of Robotics Research 4*: 59–66

Chazelle B, Guibas LJ, Lee DT (1985) The power of geometric duality. *BIT 25*: 76–90

Collins GE(1975) Quantifier elimination for real closed fields by cylindrical algebraic decomposition. Lecture Notes in Computer Science, No. 33, Springer-Verlag, New York, 135–183

Crowley JL (1985) Navigation for an intelligent mobile robot. *IEEE Journal of Robotics and Automation 1*: 31–41

Donald B (1987) A search algorithm for motion planning with six degrees of freedom. *Artificial Intelligence 31*: 295–353

Donald B (1988) A geometric approach to error detection and recovery for robot motion planning with uncertainty. *Artificial Intelligence 37*: 223–271

Donald B, Xavier P (1989) A provably good approximation algorithm for optimal-time trajectory planning. *Proceedings of the IEEE International Conference on Robotics and Automation*, Scottsdale (Ariz.) 958–963

Elfes A (1989) Using occupancy grids for mobile robot perception and navigation. *Computer 22*: 46–57

Erdmann M, Lozano-Pérez T (1987) On multiple moving objects. *Algorithmica 2*: 477–522

Esterling DM, Van Rosendale J (1983) An intersection algorithm for moving parts. *Proceedings of the NASA Symposium on Computer Aided Geometry Modeling*, Hampton (Va.) 119–123

Faverjon B (1984) Obstacle avoidance using an octree in the configuration space of a manipulator. *Proceedings of the IEEE International Conference on Robotics and Automation*, Atlanta (Ga.) 504–507

Fortune S, Wilfong G (1988) Planning constrained motion. *Proceedings of the 20th Annual ACM Symposium on Theory of Computing*, Chicago (Ill.) 445–459

Freund E, Hoyer H (1988) Real-time pathfinding in multirobot systems including obstacle avoidance. *International Journal of Robotics Research 7*: 42–70

Fryxell RC (1987) Navigation planning using quadtrees. Oak Ridge National Laboratory TM-10481, Oak Ridge (Tenn.)

Fu KS, Gonzalez RC, Lee CSG (1987) *Robotics: control, sensing, vision and intelligence.* McGraw-Hill, New York (N.Y.)

Fujimura K, Kunii TL (1985) A hierarchical space indexing method. In: T.L. Kunii (ed) *Computer graphics: Visual technology and art*, Springer-Verlag, Tokyo (Japan) 21–31.

Fujimura K, Samet H (1988) Accessibility: A new approach to path planning among moving obstacles. *Proceedings of the IEEE Conference on Computer Vision and Pattern Recognition 88*, Ann Arbor (Mich.) 803–807 (Revised version is to appear in *Algorithmica*)

Fujimura K, Samet H (1989) A hierarchical strategy for path planning among moving obstacles, *IEEE Transactions on Robotics and Automation 5*: 61–69

Garey MR, Johnson DS (1979) *Computers and intractability: A guide to the theory of NP-completeness*. Freeman, San Francisco (Calif.)

Georgeff M, Lansky A, Schoppers M (1987) Reasoning and planning in dynamic domains: An experiment with a mobile robot. SRI International, Technical Note 380, Menlo Park (Calif.)

Gewali LP, Ntafos S, Tollis IG, (1990) Path planning in the presence of vertical obstacles. *IEEE Transactions on Robotics and Automation 6*: 331–341

Ghosh SK, Mount DM (1987) An output-sensitive algorithm for computing visibility graphs. *Proceedings of the 28th Annual IEEE Symposium on the Foundations of Computer Science*, Los Angeles (Calif.) 11–19 (To appear in *SIAM Journal on Computing*)

Gilbert EG, Hong SM (1989) A new algorithm for detecting the collision of moving objects. *Proceedings of the IEEE International Conference on Robotics and Automation*, Scottsdale (Ariz.) 8–14

Glassner AS (1988) Spacetime ray tracing for animation. *IEEE Computer Graphics and Applications 8*: 60–70

Griswold NC, Eem J (1990) Control for mobile robots in the presence of moving objects. *IEEE Transactions on Robotics and Automation 6*: 263–268

Guibas L, Hershberger J, Leven D, Sharir M, Tarjan RE (1987) Linear-time algorithms for visibility and shortest path problems inside triangulated simple polygons. *Algorithmica 2*: 209–233

Guibas L, Sharir M, Sifrony S (1989) On the general motion-planning problem with two degrees of freedom. *Discrete and Computational Geometry 4*: 491–521

Hague T, Brady M, Cameron S (1990) Using moments to plan paths for the Oxford AGV. *Proceedings of the IEEE International Conference on Robotics and Automation*, Cicinnati (Ohio) 210–215

Herman M (1986) Fast, three-dimensional, collision-free motion planning. *Proceedings of the IEEE International Conference on Robotics and Automation*, San Francisco, (Calif.) 1056–1063

Hoffmann CM (1989) *Geometric and solid modeling: An introduction.* Morgan Kaufmann, San Mateo (Calif.)

Hopcroft JE, Schwartz JT, Sharir M (1984) On the complexity of motion planning for multiple independent objects: PSPACE hardness of the 'warehouseman's problem'. *International Journal of Robotics Research 3*: 76–88

Hunter GM (1978) Efficient computation and data structures for graphics. PhD thesis, Department of Electrical Engineering and Computer Science, Princeton University, Princeton (N.J.)

Ilari J and Torras C (1990) 2D path planning: A configuration space heuristic approach, *International Journal of Robotics Research 9*: 75–91

Jackins CL, Tanimoto SL (1980) Oct-trees and their use in representing three-dimensional objects. *Computer Graphics and Image Processing 14*: 249–270

Kajitani M, Fukuo K, Masuda T (1990) Basic study of cooperative motion of mobile robots. *Journal of Robotics and Mechatronics 2*: 46–49

Kambhampati S, Davis LS (1986) Multiresolution path planning for mobile robots. *IEEE Journal of Robotics and Automation 2*, 135–145

Kanayama Y, DeHaan GR (1988) A mathematical theory of safe path planning. TRCS88-16, Department of Computer Science, University of California, Santa Barbara (Calif.)

Kanayama Y (1989) A mathematical theory of object centered path planning. TRCS89-07, Department of Computer Science, University of California, Santa Barbara (Calif.)

Kant K, Zucker SW (1986) Toward efficient planning: the path-velocity decomposition. *International Journal of Robotics Research 5*: 72–89

Kapoor S, Maheshwari SN (1988) Efficient algorithms for Euclidean shortest path and visibility problem with polygonal obstacles. *Proceedings of the Fourth ACM Symposium on Computational Geometry*, Urbana-Champaign (Ill.) 172–182

Kedem K, Sharir M (1985) An efficient algorithm for planning collision-free translational motion of a convex polygonal object in 2-dimensional space amidst polygonal obstacles. *Proceedings of the First ACM Symposium on Computational Geometry*, Baltimore (Md.) 75–80

Kehtarnavaz N, Li S (1988) A collision-free navigation scheme in the presence of moving obstacles. *Proceedings of the IEEE Conference on Computer Vision and Pattern Recognition*, Ann Arbor (Mich.) 808–813

Kehtarnavaz N, Griswold N (1990) Establishing collision zones for obstacles moving with uncertainty. *Computer Vision, Graphics, and Image Processing 49*: 95–103

Khatib O (1986) Real-time obstacle avoidance for manipulators and mobile robots. *International Journal on Robotics Research 5*: 90–98

Killough SM, Pin FG (1990) Design and control of a fully omnidirectional and holonomic wheeled platform for robotic vehicles, Internal Report, CESAR-90/36, Oak Ridge National Laboratory, Oak Ridge (Tenn.)

Koditschek DE (1989) Robot planning and control via potential functions. In: Khatib O, Craig JJ, Lozano-Pérez T (ed) *The robotics review 1*, MIT Press, Cambridge (Mass.) 349–367

Koren Y, Borenstein J (1991) Potential field method and their inherent limitations for mobile robot navigation. *Proceedings of the IEEE International Conference on Robotics and Automation*, Sacramento (Calif.) 1398–1404

Kuc R, Viard VB (1991) A physically based navigation strategy for sonar-guided vehicles. *International Journal of Robotics Research 10*: 75–87

Koyama H, Maeda Y, Fukami S, Takagi T (1991) Study of obstacle avoidance problem for mobile robot using fuzzy production system. *Journal of the Robotics Society of Japan 9*: 76–78.

Kuk R, Viard VB (1991) A physically based navigation strategy for sonar-guided vehicle. *International Journal of Robotics Research 10*: 75–87

Kyriakopoulos KJ and Saridis GN (1991) Collision avoidance of mobile robots in non-stationary environments. *Proceedings of the IEEE International Conference on Robotics and Automation*, Sacramento (Calif.) 904–909

Lamadrid JG (1986) Avoidance system for moving obstacles. *Proceedings of the SPIE Symposium on Mobile Robots*, Cambridge (Mass.) 304–311

Latombe JC (1991) *Robot motion planning*. Kluwer Academic Publishers, Norwell (Mass.)

Lee DT, Preparata FP (1984) Euclidean shortest paths in the presence of rectilinear barriers. *Networks 1*: 393–410

Lee BH, Lee CSG (1987) Collision-free motion planning of two robots. *IEEE Transactions on Systems, Man, and Cybernetics 17*: 21–32

Lee J, Bien Z (1990) Collision-free trajectory control for multiple robots based on neural optimization network. *Robotica 8*: 185–194

Lin MC, Canny JF (1991) A fast algorithm for incremental distance calculation. *Proceedings of the IEEE International Conference on Robotics and Automation*, Sacramento (Calif.) 1008–1014

Liu Y, Kuroda S, Naniwa T, Noborio H, Arimoto S (1989a) A practical algorithm for planning collision-free coordinated motion of multiple mobile robots. *Proceedings of the IEEE International Conference on Robotics and Automation*, Scottsdale (Ariz.) 1427–1432

Liu Y, Noborio H, Arimoto S (1989b) A new solid model HSM for checking on interference between moving robots. *Journal of the Robotics Society of Japan* 7: 26–34

Lozano-Pérez T, Wesley MA (1979) An algorithm for planning collision-free paths among polyhedral obstacles. *Communications of the ACM 22*: 560–570

Lozano-Pérez T (1983) The configuration space approach, *IEEE Transactions on Computers 32*: 108–120

Lumelsky V, Stepanov A (1987) Path planning strategies for a point mobile automaton moving amidst unknown obstacles of arbitrary shape, *Algorithmica 2*: 403–430

Lumelsky V, Skewis T (1990) Incorporating range sensing in the robot navigation function. *IEEE Transactions on Systems, Man, and Cybernetics 20*: 1058–1069

MacNish C, Fallside F (1990) Temporal reasoning: A solution for multiple agent collision avoidance, *Proceedings of the IEEE International Conference on Robotics and Automation*, Cincinnati (Ohio) 494–499

Maeda Y, Takegaki M (1988) Collision avoidance control among moving obstacles for a mobile robot on the fuzzy reasoning. *Journal of the Robotics Society of Japan 6*: 50–54

Mäntylä M (1987) *An introduction to solid modeling.* Computer Science Press, Rockville (Md.)

McDermott DV, Davis E (1984) Planning routes through uncertain territory. *Artificial Intelligence 22*: 107–156

Meagher D (1982) Geometric modeling using octree encoding. *Computer Graphics and Image Processing 19*: 129–147

Mitchell JSB, Mount DM, Papadimitriou CH (1987) The discrete geodesic problem. *SIAM Journal on Computing 16*: 647–668

Mitchell JSB (1988) An algorithmic approach to some problems in terrain navigation. *Artificial Intelligence 37*: 171–202

Mitchell JSB (1990a) A new algorithm for shortest paths among obstacles in the plane. TR-832, School of Operations Research and Industrial Engineering, Cornell University, Ithaca, N.Y. January 1990

Mitchell JSB (1990b) Shortest paths among obstacles in the plane. Manuscript, Cornell University, Ithaca (N.Y.)

Mitchell JSB, Papadimitriou CH (1990) The weighted region problem: Finding shortest paths through a weighted planar subdivision. TR-885, School of Operations Research and Industrial Engineering, Cornell University, Ithaca, N.Y. January 1990 (To appear in *Journal of ACM*)

Mobasseri B (1990) Path planning under uncertainty from a decision analytic perspective, *Proceedings of the IEEE International Symposium on Intelligent Control*, Albany (N.Y.) 556–560

Moravec HP (1983) The Stanford cart and the CMU rover. *Proceedings of the IEEE 71*: 872–884

Mount DM (1985) On finding shortest paths on convex polyhedra. CS-TR-1495, Department of Computer Science, University of Maryland, College Park (Md.)

Nilsson NJ (1969) A mobile automaton: An application of artificial intelligence techniques. *Proceedings of the First International Joint Conference on Artificial Intelligence*, Washington DC, 509–520.

Nilsson NJ (1980) *Principles of artificial intelligence.* Tioga Press, Palo Alto (Calif.)

Noborio H, Naniwa T, Arimoto S (1990) A quadtree-based path-planning algorithm for a mobile robot. *Journal of Robotics Systems 7*: 555–574

Ó'Dúnlaing C, Yap C (1985) A retraction method for planning the motion of a disc. *Journal of Algorithms 6*: 104–111

Ó'Dúnlaing C (1987) Motion planning with inertial constraints. *Algorithmica 2*: 431–476

Oommen BJ, Iyengar SS, Rao NSV, Kashyap RL (1987) Robot navigation in unknown terrains using learned visibility graphs. Part I: the disjoint convex obstacle case. *IEEE Journal of Robotics and Automation 3*: 672–680

Orda A, Rom R (1990) Shortest-path and minimum-delay algorithms in networks with time-dependent edge-length. *Journal of ACM 37*: 607–625

O'Rourke J (1987) *Art gallery theorems and algorithms.* Oxford University Press, Oxford (UK)

Ottman T, Wood D (1984) Dynamic sets of points. *Computer Vision, Graphics, and Image Processing 27*: 157–166

Pan T, Luo RC (1990), Motion planning for mobile robots in a dynamic environment with moving obstacles. *Proceedings of the IEEE International Conference on Robotics and Automation*, Cincinnati (Ohio) 578–583

Papadakis NA, Perakis AN (1990) Deterministic minimal time vessel routing. *Operations Research 38*: 426–438.

Papadimitriou, CH (1985) An algorithm for shortest-path motion in three dimensions. *Information Processing Letters 20*: 259–263.

Pape CL (1990) A combination of centralized and distributed methods for multi-agent planning and scheduling. *Proceedings of the IEEE International Conference on Robotics and Automation*, Cincinnati (Ohio) 488–493

Parker LE (1988) A robot navigation algorithm for moving obstacles. MS thesis, University of Tennessee, Knoxville (Tenn.)

Parsons D, Canny J (1990) A motion planner for multiple mobile robots. *Proceedings of the IEEE International Conference on Robotics and Automation*, Cincinnati (Ohio) 8–13

Pavlidis T (1982) *Algorithms for graphics and image processing.* Computer Science Press, Rockville (Md.)

Perakis AN, Papadakis NA (1989) Minimal time vessel routing in a time-dependent environment. *Transportation Science 23*: 266–276

Premvuti S, Yuta S (1990) Consideration on the cooperation of multiple autonomous mobile robots. *Proceedings of the IEEE International Workshop on Intelligent Robots and Systems*, Tsuchiura (Japan) 59–63

Preparata FP, Shamos MI (1985) *Computational geometry: An introduction.* Springer-Verlag, New York (N.Y.)

Reif J (1979) Complexity of the mover's problem and generalizations. *Proceedings of the 20th Annual IEEE Symposium on the Foundations of Computer Science*, New York (N.Y.) 241–247

Reif J, Sharir M (1985) Motion planning in the presence of moving obstacles. *Proceedings of the 26th Annual IEEE Symposium on the Foundations of Computer Science*, Portland (Oreg.) 144–154

Reif JH, Storer JA (1985) Shortest paths in Euclidean space with polyhedral obstacles. Technical Report CS-85-121, Computer Science Department, Brandeis University, Waltham (Mass.)

Reister DB (1991) A new wheel control system for the omnidirectional HERMIES-III robot. *Proceedings of the IEEE International Conference on Robotics and Automation*, Sacramento (Calif.) 2322–2327

Requicha AAG, Voelcker HB (1982) Solid modeling and contemporary assessment. *IEEE Computer Graphics and Applications 2*: 9–24

Roach JW, Boaz MN (1987) Coordinating the motions of robot arms in a common workspace, *IEEE Journal of Robotics and Automation 3*: 437–444

Rohnert H (1986) Shortest paths in the plane with convex polygonal obstacles. *Information Processing Letters 23*: 71–76

Rosenfeld A (ed) (1983) *Multiresolution image processing and analysis.* Springer-Verlag, Berlin (Germany)

Rowe NC, Richbourg RF (1990) An efficient Snell's law method for optimal-path planning across multiple two-dimensional, irregular, homogeneous-cost regions. *International Journal of Robotics Research 9*: 48–66

Rowe NC, Ross RS (1990) Optimal grid-free path planning across arbitrarily contoured terrain with anisotropic friction and gravity effects, *Transactions on Robotics and Automation 6*: 540–553

Rueb KD, Wong AKC (1987) Structuring free space as a hypergraph for robing robot path planning and navigation. *IEEE Transactions on Pattern Analysis and Machine Intelligence 9*: 263–273.

Saito M, Tsumura T (1989) Collision avoidance between mobile robots. *Proceedings of IEEE/RSJ International Workshop on Intelligent Robots and Systems.* Tsukuba (Japan) 473–478

Samet H (1982) Neighbor finding techniques for images represented by quadtrees. *Computer Graphics and Image Processing 18*: 37–57

Samet H (1990a) *The Design and Analysis of Spatial Data Structures.* Addison-Wesley, Reading (Mass.)

Samet H (1990b) *Applications of Spatial Data Structures.* Addison-Wesley, Reading (Mass.)

Samet H, Tamminen M (1985) Bintrees, CSG trees, and time. *Proceedings of the SIGGRAPH '85 Conference,* San Francisco (Calif.) 121–130

Samet H, Webber RE (1985) Storing a collection of polygons using quadtrees. *ACM Transactions on Graphics 2*: 182–222

Sanborn JC, Hendler JA (1988) A model of reaction for planning in dynamic environments. *Artificial Intelligence in Engineering 3*: 95–102

Schoppers M (1987) Universal plans for reactive robots in unpredictable domains. *Proceedings of the 10th International Joint Conference on Artificial Intelligence,* Milan (Italy) 1039–1046

Schwartz JT, Yap C (ed) (1987) *Advances in robotics Vol. 1.* Lawrence Erlbaum, Hillsdale (N.J.)

Schwartz JT, Hopcroft J, Sharir M (ed) (1987) *Planning, geometry, and complexity of robot motion.* Ablex Publishing, Norwood (N.J.)

Schwartz JT, Sharir M (1986) A survey of motion planning and related geometric algorithms. *Artificial Intelligence 37*: 157–170

Sedgewick R, Vitter JS (1985) Shortest paths in Euclidean graphs. *Algorithmica 1*: 32–48

Shaffer CA, Samet H (1987) Optimal quadtree construction algorithms. *Computer Vision, Graphics, and Image Processing 37*: 402–419

Sharir M, Schorr A (1986) On shortest paths in polyhedral spaces. *SIAM Journal on Computing 15*: 193–215

Sharir M (1987) On shortest paths amidst convex polyhedra. *SIAM Journal on Computing 16*: 561–572

Sharir M, Sifrony S (1988) Coordinated motion planning for two independent robots. *Proceedings of the Fourth ACM Symposium on Computational Geometry*, Urbana-Champaign (Ill.) 319–328

Sharir M (1989) Algorithmic motion planning in robotics. *IEEE Computer 22*: 9–19

Shih C, Lee T, Gruver WA (1990) A unified approach for robot motion planning with moving polyhedral obstacles. *IEEE Transactions on Systems, Man, and Cybernetics 20*: 903–915

Slack M, Miller D (1987) Planning through time and space in dynamic domains. *Proceedings of the 10th International Joint Conference on Artificial Intelligence*, Milan (Italy) 1067–1070

Spirakis P, Yap C (1984) Strong NP-hardness of moving many discs. *Information Processing Letters 19*: 55–59

Sugihara K, Suzuki I (1990) Distributed motion coordination of multiple mobile robots. *Proceedings of the 5th IEEE International Symposium on Intelligent Control*, Philadelphia (Penn.) 138–143

Suh SH, Shin KG (1988) A variational dynamic programming approach to robot-path planning with a distance-safety criterion. *IEEE Transactions on Robotics and Automation 4*, 334–349

Sutner K, Maass W (1988) Motion planning among time dependent obstacles. *Acta Informatica 26*: 93–122

Suzuki H, Arimoto A (1990) A recursive method of trajectory planning for a point-like mobile robot in transient environment utilizing paint procedure. *Journal of the Robotics Society of Japan 8*: 9–19

Takahashi O, Shilling RJ (1989) Motion planning in a plane using generalized Voronoi diagrams. *IEEE Transactions on Robotics and Automation 5*: 143–150

Takeuchi T and Nagai Y (1988) Fuzzy control of a mobile robot for obstacle avoidance. *Information Science 45*: 231–248

Thorp CE, Herbert M, Kanade T, Shaffer SA (1988) Vision and navigation for the Carnegie-Mellon Navlab. *IEEE Transactions on Machine Intelligence and Pattern Analysis 10*: 362—373

Tilove RB (1990) Local obstacle avoidance for mobile robots based on the method of artificial potentials. *Proceedings of the IEEE International Conference on Robotics and Automation*, Cicinnati (Ohio) 566–571

Tournassoud P (1986) A strategy for obstacle avoidance and its application to multi-robot systems. *Proceedings of the IEEE International Conference on Robotics and Automation*, San Francisco (Calif.) 1224–1229

Tournassoud P (1988) Planification de trajectoires en robotique: complexité et approche pratique. PhD Thesis, Université de Paris-sud, Paris (France)

Udupa S (1977) Collision detection and avoidance in computer controlled manipulators. *Proceedings of the 5th International Joint Conference on Artificial Intelligence*, Cambridge (Mass.) 737–748

Vere S (1983) Planning in time: Windows and durations for activities and goals. *IEEE Transactions on Pattern Analysis and Machine Intelligence 5*: 246–267

Wang PKC (1989) Interaction dynamics of multiple mobile robots with simple navigation strategies. *Journal of Robotics Systems 6*, 77–101

Warren CW (1990) Multiple robot path coordination using artificial potential fields. *Proceedings of the IEEE International Conference on Robotics and Automation*, Cincinnati (Ohio) 500–505

Weisbin CR, de Saussure G, Einstein JR, Pin FG, Heer E (1989) Autonomous mobile robot navigation and learning. *Computer 22*: 29–35

Welzl E (1985) Constructing the visibility graph for n line segments in $O(n^2)$ time. *Information Processing Letters 20*: 167–171

Whitesides SH (1985) Computational geometry and motion planning. In: G. T. Toussaint (ed) *Computational geometry*, North-Holland, Amsterdam (The Netherlands) 377–427

Wilfong G (1988) Motion planning in the presence of movable obstacles. *Proceedings of the fourth ACM Symposium on Computational Geometry*, Urbana-Champaign (Ill.) 279–288

Wong EK, Fu KS (1986) A hierarchical orthogonal space approach to three-dimensional path planning. *IEEE Journal of Robotics and Automation 2*: 42–52

Yagi Y, Kawato S, Tsuji S (1991) Collision avoidance using omnidirectional image sensor (COPIS). *Proceedings of the IEEE International Conference on Robotics and Automation*, Sacramento (Calif.) 910–915

Yap C (1984) Coordinating the motion of several discs. TR-105, Courant Institute of Mathematical Sciences, New York University, New York (N.Y.)

Yap C (1987) Algorithmic motion planning. In: Schwartz JT, Yap C (ed) *Advances in robotics Vol. 1*, Lawrence Erlbaum, Hillsdale, (N.J.) Chapter 3, 95–143

Yau M, Srihari SN (1983) A hierarchical data structure for multidimensional digital images. *Communications of the ACM 26*: 504–515

Yeung T, Bekey GA (1987) A centralized approach to the motion planning problem for multiple robots. *Proceedings of the IEEE International Conference on Robotics and Automation*, Raleigh (Ga.) 1779–1784

Zhu D, Latombe J (1991) New heuristic algorithms for efficient hierarchical path planning. *IEEE Transactions on Robotics and Automation* 7: 9–20

Index